Contextually Competent Applied Practice Across Sport, Exercise, and Performance Domains

This edited collection offers global perspectives on contextually competent applied service delivery within the field of sport, exercise, and performance psychology (SEPP).

Professionals from around the globe join together to share their perspectives and experiences in SEPP, with each chapter offering insight across three different areas within a specific sport, exercise, or performance domain. This book begins with physical activity domains, sharing perspectives on working with athletes—including those with hidden and physical disabilities—in youth sport, with coaches, and with exercisers, including elderly exercisers. It then goes on to look at other performance domains, providing insights into working in esport, with military and tactical professionals, within business contexts, with performing artists, and in the healthcare sector. Brought together, the authors offer a diverse perspective on what it means to provide competent service delivery across a range of settings that a SEPP practitioner might work within.

Global in scope and offering a comprehensive overview of service delivery within SEPP, this is a valuable resource for graduate students seeking to understand the areas within which they could work, early career professionals starting out, and practitioners at any career stage looking to continue their professional development.

Andrew P. Friesen is an Associate Professor in the Department of Kinesiology at Penn State Berks, USA, and Fellow of the Association for Applied Sport Psychology (AASP). His research focuses on emotion regulation in sport and the professional development of practitioners. In addition to his academic role, Andrew runs a private practice providing mental performance services to athletes and performers. He has authored and edited numerous publications in applied sport psychology and actively mentors emerging professionals pursuing certification and careers in the field.

Sebastian Brueckner is a Mental Performance Consultant and Leadership Coach based in Germany whose work bridges applied practice, teaching, and international collaboration. He has served as a consultant to athletes, coaches, and organizations across levels of performance, with an emphasis on evidence-based approaches to mental skills training and professional development. His scholarship and service reflect a global commitment to advancing the profession, with particular interest in practitioner identity and the integration of research into applied practice.

Lauren S. Tashman is the Senior Research Scientist for Mursion, Inc. and a Mental Performance Consultant and Leadership Coach based in New York City, USA. As a Certified Mental Performance Consultant (CMPC), she has worked with athletes, coaches, healthcare professionals, business leaders, and performing artists to help individuals and teams consistently perform at their best. She has extensive experience in higher education and professional training, and she is passionate about helping emerging professionals build sustainable, values-driven careers. Her contributions to the field include applied practice, supervision, applying the science of high performance in the business world, and international professional service.

Global Perspectives on Sport, Exercise, and Performance Psychology

This series brings together global perspectives on sport, exercise, and performance psychology (SEPP). Books cover becoming a SEPP professional, navigating the field of SEPP, and applied practice within sport, exercise and performance domains.

Titles in the series:

Becoming a Sport, Exercise, and Performance Psychology Professional
A Global Perspective
Edited By J. Gualberto Cremades and Lauren S. Tashman

Navigating the Globally Evolving Field of Sport, Exercise, and Performance Psychology
Edited by Andrew P. Friesen, Sebastian Brueckner, and Lauren S. Tashman

Contextually Competent Applied Practice Across Sport, Exercise, and Performance Domains
Edited by Andrew P. Friesen, Sebastian Brueckner, and Lauren S. Tashman

For more information about this series, please visit: https://www.routledge.com/Global-Perspectives-on-Sport-Exercise-and-Performance-Psychology/book-series/GPSEPP

Contextually Competent Applied Practice Across Sport, Exercise, and Performance Domains

Edited by
Andrew P. Friesen, Sebastian Brueckner, and Lauren S. Tashman

Routledge
Taylor & Francis Group
NEW YORK AND LONDON

Designed cover image: Getty Images

First published 2027
by Routledge
605 Third Avenue, New York, NY 10158

and by Routledge
4 Park Square, Milton Park, Abingdon, Oxon, OX14 4RN

Routledge is an imprint of the Taylor & Francis Group, an informa business

ISBN: 9781041319542 (hbk)
ISBN: 9781041319535 (pbk)
ISBN: 9781003781486 (ebk)

DOI: 10.4324/9781003781486

Typeset in Galliard
by codeMantra

Contents

About the Editors

Dr. Andrew P. Friesen (Canada)

Dr. Andrew P. Friesen is Associate Professor in the Department of Kinesiology at Penn State Berks, where he teaches sport, exercise, and performance psychology to the next generation of professionals. His research focuses on emotional intelligence and the applied practice of sport psychology. He has served on numerous integrated sport science teams supporting national sport programs across Canada, Great Britain, Australia, and the United States. His experience spans a wide range of sports, including hockey, baseball, softball, taekwondo, basketball, volleyball, synchronized swimming, swimming, lacrosse, golf, archery, racquetball, tennis, badminton, snowboarding, and figure skating. He is a Certified Mental Performance Consultant (CMPC) and a Fellow of the Association for Applied Sport Psychology (AASP). Originally from Manitoba, Canada, He completed his undergraduate studies under the tutelage of Drs. Cal Botterill and Tom Patrick at the University of Winnipeg. He then went on to earn a Master's degree from the University of Ottawa under the supervision of Dr. Terry Orlick. Benefitting from a network of "global citizen" sport psychology professionals (e.g., Dr. Paul Davis), he was then awarded a PhD studentship with the Emotion Regulation of Others and Self (EROS) research group funded by a £2.1m grant from the Economic and Social Research Council in England. Joining a network of British researchers studying emotion, he completed a PhD on Interpersonal Emotion Regulation in Sport under the guidance of Prof. Andy Lane at the University of Wolverhampton. He is an active member of AASP, having served as AASP Newsletter Editor and Chair of the Newsletter Committee, and served on the Dorothy V. Harris Memorial Award Review Committee and the Graduate Program Accreditation Committee. He held academic positions in Canada, the UK, and Miami, FL prior to relocating to Pennsylvania, where he currently resides.

Dr. Sebastian Brueckner (Germany)

Dr. Sebastian Brueckner is an internationally recognized expert in Applied Sport Psychology. Besides working in private practice in Münster, Germany, as a mental performance consultant and a leadership coach, he provides consultancy to ongoing projects funded by the German Federal Institute of Sport Science (BISp) and the European Union, and acts as a reviewer for (inter)national sport psychology journals. His international career journey has included serving the Association for Applied Sport Psychology (AASP) as chair of the International Relations as well as the Nominations and Leadership Development Committees, as AASP Newsletter Editor, member of the inaugural Advocacy Committee, and co-editor of the 13th edition of AASP's Graduate Program Directory. He is an AASP Fellow and certified as an expert in Sport Psychology Services by the German Association of Sport Psychology (asp). His applied work, specifically with the German National Badminton Team, has led to the facilitation of elite coaches' education and leadership training programs for German Gymnastics. He has established projects with colleagues at Muenster University, Boston University, and Kingston University London, where he was appointed as Honorary Research Fellow. After transitioning from a 13-year career as a competitive swimmer that led him to participate in Olympic trials to studying sport science with a focus on Motor Behavior at Saarland University (Germany) and Texas A&M University, he earned his PhD at the University of Tennessee with a specialization in Applied Sport Psychology. For 10 years, he worked at Saarbruecken Olympic Training Center, supporting (junior) national team and Olympic-caliber athletes on mental training and dual-career transitions from a holistic, humanistic performance-enhancement perspective. He has served as Executive Manager and Head of Applied/Certification Services for the German asp and shifting into private practice strategically broadened his clientele and service contexts. He now serves not only high-performers in sport and business contexts across the globe but also educators and coaches working with athletes with disabilities and exercisers.

Dr. Lauren S. Tashman (USA)
Dr. Lauren S. Tashman is the Senior Research Scientist at Mursion Inc., leading the Learning Strategy and Content team who develop immersive simulations and coaching solutions for workforce skill development. She is a Certified Mental Performance Consultant (CMPC) and a Fellow of the Association for Applied Sport Psychology. Residing in New York City, she also owns a part-time consulting business supporting athletes, performing artists, leaders, and teams in developing high-performance mindsets and cultures. Growing up in New Jersey, a 13-year professional equestrian showjumping career led her to study psychology. She completed her Bachelor of Arts degree at The College of New Jersey and then earned both her Master's and PhD in Educational Psychology with a major in Sport Psychology from The Florida State University. While completing her PhD she also received certificates in Research Methods and Program Evaluation, and studied expert performance as a graduate assistant in The Human Performance Lab led by Dr. K. Anders Ericsson. After finishing her graduate studies she was an Associate Professor and the Coordinator of Sport Psychology Services at Barry University, began her consulting business working with a wide variety of performers across performance levels and domains including spending six years consulting with the Canadian Women's National Softball team, mentored many diverse young professionals pursuing the CMPC credential, and then pursued coaching for the corporate and healthcare contexts as well as product research and development when she moved to New York, leading her to where she currently finds herself on her winding career journey.

Contributors

Our list of global contributors for volumes II and III is presented here by nation of current affiliation. Their country of origin appears in parentheses if different from their country of current affiliation. Contributors listed with an asterisk have contributed to *Contextually Competent Applied Practice Across Sport, Exercise, and Performance Domains.*

Australia

Eugene Aidman (Russia)
Renee N. Appaneal (USA)
Jeffrey Bond
John Crampton
Kim Encel
Gerry Fogarty
Sandy Gordon* (UK)
Stephanie J. Hanrahan (USA)
Christopher Mesagno (USA)
Donna O'Connor* (UK)
Remco Polman* (The Netherlands)
Véronique Richard (Canada)
Michael Spittle

Austria

Ulla Geifes

Belgium

Paul Wylleman

Botswana

Kapule David Mabuta

Brazil

Claudio Godoi*

Canada

Veronica Allan*
Sommer Christie*
Diane M. Culver
Natalie Durand-Bush
Roger Friesen
Stefanie Gazmin
Cole E. Giffin
Sydney Graper
Aman Hussain*
Chantale Lussier*
Ashley-Raye Miles
Ashwin J. Patel
Siobhan Rourke
Robert J. Schinke
Elizabeth A. Steadman
Penny Werthner*
Michael Whitehead*

Croatia

Sanja Vrančić

Denmark

Kristoffer Henriksen*
Louise Kamuk Storm*
Nikos Ntoumanis (Greece)
Jacob Vinholt*

Finland

Niilo Konttinen
Aku Nikander
Hannaleena Ronkainen
Montse C. Ruiz (Spain)
Tatiana V. Ryba

Germany

Eric Biener* (USA)
Sebastian Brueckner
Caren D.P. Diehl
Anne-Marie Elbe
Barbara Halberschmidt
Lena Henning
Oliver Höner*
Hannah Hüttemann
Sascha Leisterer-Härtig
Mathias Liebing
Monika Liesenfeld
Nicki Marquardt*
Lisa Musculus*
Ismael Pedraza-Ramirez* (Colombia)
Nick Powell* (USA)
Bernadette Ramaker* (The Netherlands)
Maximilian Richert
Helena Schmitz
Oliver Stoll
Maike Tietjens
Svenja Wachsmuth*
Christian Zepp

Greece

Vassilis Barkoukis
Anna Kavoura

Hong Kong, China

Karen Lo

Hungary

Lekgobo Masake (Botswana)

India

Nimrod Mon Brokman* (Israel)
Varadayini Gorhe
Shruti Nair*
Keerthana Swaminathan

Indonesia

Rebecca Wong (Malaysia)

Ireland

Shannon Burke
Cathal Sheridan

Italy

Maurizio Bertollo

Malaysia

Young-Eun Noh (South Korea)

Mexico

Jimena González Menendez

New Zealand

Craig Barretto
Aramis Dennan
Paula Dennan
Daryl Gibson*
Ken Hodge
Ian Lambie
Antoinette Minniti* (USA)

Norway

Stiliani "Ani" Chroni (Greece)

Poland

Natalia Pawelska
Małgorzata Sławińska
Grzegorz M. Więcław

Singapore

Hansen Bay*
Harry Lim

Slovakia

Michala Bednáriková

South Africa

Heinrich Grobbelaar
Deborah Skinstad

Sweden

Paul Davis (Canada)
Göran Kenttä
Sanna M. Nordin-Bates*
Nicole Robertson* (USA)

Switzerland

R. Zsanett Bondár (Romania)
Violetta Oblinger-Peters (Germany)
Roland Seiler

Uganda

Edgar Kazibwe

United Kingdom

Dawn-Marie Armstrong (Barbados)
Lee Baldock
Joanne Butt
Isabella Cacciatore*
Helen R Church*
Brendan Cropley
Jennifer Cumming* (Canada)
Tracey J. Devonport
Martin Eubank
Sahen Gupta* (India)
Sheldon Hanton
Chris Harwood
Karen Howells
Heather Hunter
Emma Huntley*
Carrie Taylor Johnson*
Anastasiya Khomutova (Ukraine)
Aleksandra "Ola" Krukowska-Burke (Poland)
Moira E. Lafferty
Andrew M. Lane
Daniel R. F. Martin
Kyle F. Paradis (Canada)
David Price*
John Sandars*
Lee-Ann Sharp
Matt Slater
Katy Steel
Clara Swedlund* (France)
Richard Thelwell*
James Tomlinson*
Nick Wadsworth
Christopher R. D. Wagstaff

United States of America

Shelby Anderson
Nicholas E. Anton*
Paul Ashbrook*
Alex Auerbach
Timothy Baghurst* (UK)
Jessica Bartley
Eric Bean*
William Bean
Matthew P. Bejar
Robbi Beyer*
Matthew D. Bird (UK)
Lindsey C. Blom*
Robyn Braun-Trocchio*
Angela Breitmeyer
Kristin Brooks
Charles H. Brown, Jr
Angel Brutus
Chelsea Butters Wooding*
Carla Carter
Greg Cartin*
Elmer A. Castillo
Sarah L. Castillo
Hillary Cauthen
Greg Chertok
Dolores Christensen
Tsz Lun (Alan) Chu (Hong Kong, China)
Damien Clement (Trinidad and Tobago)
Stephany C. Coakley (The Bahamas)
Bruce Cohen

Kaitlin Cohen-Maher
Ashley Coker-Cranney
John E. Coumbe-Lilley (UK)
Frances Dallas
Nicole DeFerrari
Mitchell DeSimone*
Jerry DeVore
Alex Diaz (Argentina)
Kristen Dieffenbach*
Urska Dobersek* (Slovenia)
Brad Donohue
David W. Eccles (UK)
Frank O. Ely
Anna Farello
Adrian Ferrera
Désarée Festa
Cristina Fink (Mexico)
Leslee A. Fisher
Margaret M. Flores*
Janaina Fogaça (Brazil)
Joanna Foss
Megan Fox
Andrew P. Friesen* (Canada)
Charlie Frost*
Mary D. Fry
Alexander Gamble
Lori A. Gano-Overway
Rich Gordin
Thomas W. Gretton (UK)
Marta Guivernau (Spain)
Kensa K. Gunter
Peter Haberl (Austria)
Colleen M. Hacker*
Lindsey Hamilton
Jon Hammermeister
Tracy Heller
Tim Herzog
Jerry Holt*
Takehiro Iwatsuki (Japan)
Riley Jensen
Jackson Jin*
Meighan Julbert
Cindra Kamphoff
Abby Keenan
Mi-Sook Kim (South Korea)
Grayson Kimball*
E. Earlynn Lauer
Larry Lauer*
Saemi Lee (South Korea)
Eric LeNorgant*
Bart Lerner
Jack J. Lesyk
Hannah Levy
Marc Lochbaum
Leilani Madrigal
Charles A. Maher
Phoebe Manalang-Monnier
Jeffrey Martin (Canada)
Sydney Masters
Michelle M. McAlarnen
Gily Meir (Israel)
Tyler Miles
Thomas O. Minkler
Taryn K. Morgan
Irene Muir (Canada)
Adam Naylor
Maria Newton
Carl Ohlson
Robert E. Owens*
David Pargman*
Amanda M. Perkins-Ball
Artur Poczwardowski (Poland)
Melanie Poudevigne (France)
Alessandro Quartiroli* (Italy)
Johannes Raabe (Germany)
Selen Razon*
Nina Rios-Doria
Seth Rose
Michael L. Sachs*
Christine Sanchez
Jen Schumacher
Kimberly Shaffer
Vanessa R. Shannon
Sari Shepphird
Amber M. Shipherd
Elizabeth L. Shoenfelt
Duncan Simpson (Tanzania)
Leigh Skvarla*
Christian Smith (UK)
David J. C. Smith
Christopher Stanley*
Lauren S. Tashman
Melissa Thompson*
Tshepang Tshube (Botswana)
Tiffanye M. Vargas*
Amanda J. Visek*

Justine Vosloo (South Africa)
Lennie Waite (UK)
Jack C. Watson II
Craig A. Wrisberg
Danielle Wong Vickland
Greg Young (UK)
Shameema Yousuf (Zimbabwe)
Leonard Zaichkowsky (Canada)
Rebecca A. Zakrajsek*
Derek M. Zike*

Preface

This third volume of *Becoming a Sport, Exercise, and Performance Professional: A Global Perspective* is entitled *Contextually Competent Applied Practice Across Sport, Exercise, and Performance Psychology Domains.* It continues our mission to provide a global perspective of sport, exercise, and performance psychology (SEPP). Whereas Volume II, *Navigating the Globally Evolving Field of Sport, Exercise, and Performance Psychology*, explored many relevant topics when navigating careers in SEPP, namely the SEPP profession, career development, practitioner development, and the SEPP practitioner, researcher, teacher, and mentor, this third volume turns our attention outward—toward the people and performance domains we serve.

SEPP professionals work with individuals and groups whose needs, identities, and performance environments vary widely—not only between contexts but also across the globe. Effective service delivery, therefore, requires not only a solid grounding in theory and evidence but also an appreciation for the unique circumstances, challenges, and opportunities that characterize each population. This volume brings together leading scholars and experienced practitioners from around the globe to offer insights rooted in research, informed by lived professional experience, and shaped by the evolving realities of performance across global contexts.

Similar yet different from the first book in this series, *Becoming a Sport, Exercise, and Performance Psychology Professional: A Global Perspective*, we aimed to provide global perspectives; however, this time, we wanted to incorporate more voices. To do so, you'll notice that each chapter is made up of several contributions from different authors or author groups. While our contributors had the challenging task of distilling their wisdom and experiences into a short amount of pages, our hope is that this multi-lens approach provides readers with even more diverse perspectives on each topic. We open each chapter with a brief introduction written by one of us editors to provide insight into why we included the topic in this book and frame the discussion on it provided by the various contributors. Then, following the individual contributions, we close out the discussion with some editor takeaways aimed to provoke further reflection. Each chapter culminates with a set of recommended exercises for readers to further engage with what they read and apply it to their unique contexts and situations—essentially making this volume a practical workbook to apply learnings and prepare for or enhance one's service delivery with clients across the various performance domains.

Across these chapters, readers will find guidance on working with traditional sport performers, including athletes and coaches, as well as those whose performance domains are less visible yet equally demanding—youth sport participants, athletes with hidden or physical disabilities, exercisers, esports competitors, and performers navigating corporate, military, tactical, artistic, and healthcare settings. By spanning these diverse populations, this volume underscores a central truth of our profession: performance psychology is not confined to stadiums or studios. It lives wherever individuals pursue excellence.

The global contributors in this volume highlight the importance of cultural competence, contextual awareness, and flexibility in applied practice. Our chapters not only describe the unique features of each population but also offer exercises to develop practical tools, strategies, and considerations to support effective and ethical service delivery. Collectively, they invite readers to broaden their understanding of where and how performance occurs, and to reflect deeply on the responsibilities we hold as practitioners committed to supporting people in complex, ever-changing environments. We hope that this third volume of the *Global Perspectives on Sport, Exercise and Performance Psychology* series serves as a valuable resource for students, scholars, and practitioners alike, and that it inspires continued learning, collaboration, and innovation in service of the many populations we have the privilege to support.

Acknowledgments

First, we would like to acknowledge Gualberto Cremades. Without his vision of promoting a global perspective in SEPP, we would not have had the opportunity to honor his legacy and continue the cause.

Second, we would like to acknowledge and thank Adél Stankovics who offered her time, helping us to do the many, many tasks involved in making an edited book like this come together. Her tireless work in structuring, compiling, and aligning the huge amount of information in the two volumes was invaluable in bringing this project over the finish line. As a current graduate student and "global citizen student" herself, we hope the deep dive into the global perspective of SEPP has also inspired her to broaden her global perspective and professional career journey.

1 Working with Athletes

Working in sport often represents the first, and subsequently primary, specialization within the broader client base served by sport, exercise, and performance psychology professionals. For many practitioners, sport is the initial performance context through which they enter the field, shaping their foundational skills and perspectives. Athletes, coaches, and teams operate in high-pressure environments with deeply embedded norms around toughness, identity, and performance, which influence how they engage with mental training and support services. Recognizing sport as a special population allows consultants to tailor their approaches to the specific demands and subcultures of athletic contexts while maintaining ethical and evidence-based practice. Collectively, our authors in this chapter share some strategies and new perspectives that might help you, as the reader, rediscover nuances and opportunities in this seemingly familiar performance space.

EMBRACING THE PERIPHERAL IN SPORT PSYCHOLOGY

Andrew P. Friesen

When students first enter the field of sport psychology, their aspirations often reflect the sports and athletes they grew up idolizing. As a Canadian, I was no different—my early vision of becoming a Mental Performance Consultant included standing behind the bench of a professional hockey team, clipboard in hand, contributing to Stanley Cup glory. It wasn't until I began working in the field that I realized how narrow that vision was, and how many meaningful, impactful, and unexpected opportunities lie outside the mainstream. In this reflection, I'll share lessons I've learned from embracing the "peripheral" in sport psychology service delivery—whether it's working in lesser-known sports, supporting overlooked members of the performance environment, or even setting aside personal fandom in service of professional growth.

Realize the "Peripheral" Sports

Being a Canadian, my first visualizations of "Andrew Friesen, Mental Performance Consultant" unsurprisingly had me working in ice hockey. My undergraduate student cohort of fellow Canadians at the Universities of Winnipeg and Manitoba had similar aspirations for hockey with additional consideration for curling—not exactly stretching the Canadian stereotype. And now 15 years into my career, I talk with students who have similar regionally

DOI: 10.4324/9781003781486-1

influenced aspirations; when I worked in Miami, a graduate student shared that she specifically entered the sport psychology field because she wanted to work with Dwayne Wade and the Miami Heat basketball club. Now in Pennsylvania, my students emphatically proclaim their preference to work with either the Philadelphia Eagles or Pittsburgh Steelers American football clubs once they graduate (I now keep a pitcher of ice-cold water under my desk ready to douse their dreams).

To help point them toward a broader (and more realistic) aspirational pathway, I often share with students that one of the best lessons I learned as a neophyte consultant was to consider seeking out the "peripheral" sports—sports that typically do not receive much regional attention but nevertheless offer athletes that are just as intensely focused on competitive glory. I learned this lesson shortly after completing my Master's degree and was contracted to work with our provincial artistic (then known as synchronized) swim team. I remember sitting poolside at my first observation and marveling at the raw athleticism, the precisely timed movement patterns, and the full range of team dynamics that were on display; suddenly, I didn't perceive hockey to be my end-all/be-all career aspiration. That moment taught me that "performance is performance," whether you are putting a puck in a net, expressing yourself through movement, engaging in combat against an opponent, or any other athletic objective and pursuit of performance excellence. The thrill of competition is found in the actual competition itself, not in the nuanced movement of the sport. And so, I encourage sport psychology students and young professionals to expand their interests especially to those sports that might be off their radar, and I am confident they will find awesome opportunities for professional development in those "peripheral" sports.

"Peripheral" Performers in the Support Network

While athletes and coaches often receive the most attention from sport, exercise, and performance psychology professionals (SEPPPs), a key opportunity is found in offering mental training services to "peripheral" members of the support network. This allows us to manage the psychological effects from the athlete's social environment and move closer to providing a more holistic service delivery (Friesen & Orlick, 2010). Parents are often regarded as the primary influences on athletes; as such, there is an opportunity to manage the psychological effects experienced by athletes by working directly with parents. For example, Vincent and Christensen (2015) offered a series of workshops designed to promote collaborative conversations with parents in youth sport. There is also a growing opportunity to manage the psychological effects of coaches and athletes at a systemic level by providing applied services to organizations. In doing so, SEPPPs can have positive, and arguably longer lasting, effects on the training environment and competition policies. For example, Friesen and Patrick (2024) detailed how a SEPPP embedded in the Australian Institute of Sport as a senior high-performance leader managed the psychological effects from COVID-19 disruptions to optimize coach and athlete training enroute to the 2020 (2021) Tokyo Olympics. Lastly, working with referees can also be a fruitful applied opportunity. Part of my Ph.D. program included a study with lacrosse referees at a U19 world championship (Friesen et al., 2017). This collaboration was a great opportunity for me to see the mental skills that referees use in every competition, particularly as it pertains to emotion regulation (both their own and the emotions of athletes and coaches). Many leagues, federations, and associations seek to provide professional development opportunities for their referees and SEPPPs certainly have a service to offer in that regard.

Your Fandom Stays on the Peripheral

When I give my lecture on goal-setting in my undergraduate sport psychology class, I present the students with some "key questions" that should be involved in the goal-setting discussion. One of those questions is, "What are you willing to sacrifice for your goals?" because anything worth having usually comes with a sacrifice of something else. What I learned while becoming a SEPPP is that one of the more seldom mentioned sacrifices that we professionals endure is to our sport fandom. This is of course an ironic twist because the very fandom that often fuels the motivation for many of us to enter this field is that which we must sacrifice as we establish ourselves professionally and diversify our client portfolio. For example, as a Canadian, I have proudly plastered the "maple leaf" on every piece of luggage I've ever owned. My most formative consulting experiences have come with athletes embedded in the national Canadian Sport Institute system. To borrow the tagline from Molson Canadian beer, "I. Am. Canadian!" However, now as a scholar-practitioner in Pennsylvania, USA, I work with athletes who wear the "red, white, and blue" of one of Canada's fiercest sport rivals, and I have assisted athletes in finding victory against my compatriots from "the True North, strong and free." I learned that our devotion to our athletes and their endeavours (note the defiant inclusion of the letter u) supersedes our own loyalties and fandoms.

Ultimately, success in the sport psychology field often means redefining what we consider to be the "main stage." The deeper I've gone into my career, the more I've realized that the most rewarding moments often happen in the periphery—on the margins of the mainstream, but at the center of someone's competitive world. Whether it's helping a referee regulate their emotions, collaborating with a parent to support a youth athlete, or working in a sport you once knew nothing about (perhaps didn't even know existed), the common thread is the pursuit of excellence. As sport psychology professionals (SPPs), we grow when we look beyond the obvious and invest in the broader ecosystem of sport. So, keep your eyes open, your aspirations flexible, and your ice water pitcher ready; opportunities working with athletes often show up where you least expect it, on the peripheral.

"LOOKING UNDER THE CARPET": SERVICE DELIVERY ACROSS DIVERSE (BUT NEGLECTED) SPORTS

Sahen Gupta, David Price, & Richard Thelwell

The sporting landscape is inherently diverse, and SPPs might find themselves operating across a plethora of sports. While different sports have their own unique features, most sports have commonalities in psychological challenges. This requires SPPs to actively focus on developing competencies to ensure ethical and effective service delivery. Due to the concentration of focus on the so-called dominant sports (ranked either by regional cultural significance, participation, or financial success), sometimes SPPs are left to troubleshoot applied practice considerations in specific sports which might not have a strong evidence-base to inform their service delivery. When faced with such challenges, it is important for SPPs to reflect on how to contextualize the evidence-base which might not be grounded in the context they are working in. The T-R-E-E-S model (Gupta, 2022), is one such reflection-to-act model which can guide us. The T-R-E-E-S allow us to (a) isolate a theoretical element; (b) isolate the research around it; (c) ethically review whether a direct, unchanged transfer is valid; and (d) integrate context-specific experience to apply any changes as relevant. In the T-R-E-E-S model, Theory (T) consists of the literature and theoretical understandings about a specific topic (e.g., self-talk in sport). Research (R) includes the current evidence on the Theory, and isolation of the context from which evidence was produced to check validity (e.g., most self-talk literature comes from English-speaking countries, and might not be automatically applicable to other languages). Ethics (E) includes an application of ethics for practice, including knowledge and decision-making around the question "is it ethical to directly transfer this theory-evidence without change?" (e.g., this brings with it the questions on colonial impositions of perspectives that are alien to the context). Experience (E) includes the SPP's prior experience that may be secondary or lived (or lack of experience) in working in the context at hand (e.g., it may be the first time of having to apply self-talk after taking a job in a majority non-English-speaking country). Specificity (S) is the unique element in the current context to make a reflection-on-context to determine if any adaptations are required (e.g., if the athlete has a different mother-tongue with English being their third language, self-talk in English might not be relevant). In this chapter, we link the T-R-E-E-S model (Gupta, 2022) to explorations of niche sports that were not in the practitioner's dominant cultural consciousness. In doing so, we hope to blend professional experiences and best practice literature to showcase how looking under the carpet to support athletes in neglected sports might be achieved.

From Cricket...

Cricket is a blend of individual skill (batting/bowling/fielding), combined with team tactical play. The competitive structure of cricket is unique given that it is "superior" nations with advanced development in the sport which are afforded "Test" status (India, Australia, UK, South Africa, West Indies, Pakistan, Bangladesh, Sri Lanka, New Zealand, Zimbabwe, Ireland & Afghanistan), with other nations called "Associate" status, who only compete in One-Day International (ODI) and Twenty-20 Over Game (T20s). I (Sahen) was born and brought up in India and played age-grade performance cricket. During the latter stages of my training, I joined one of the Associate nations in international men's cricket as the SPP. My lived experience and sport-specific knowledge were supportive aspects of my eventual service delivery process (Woolway & Harwood, 2020). This contextual intelligence from familiarity with the sport and prior experience as an athlete in the sport allowed quicker rapport building, comprehensive needs analysis, and sport-specific intervention.

Yet the challenge was in cultural intelligence. Prior knowledge always has some form of bias, and it is important to be aware of that. Cricket started as a colonial sport and then became a means for post-colonial expression (Mondal & Rampersad, 2020). As a result, each country has a unique subculture to cricket, which has shaped the game's development structure, perception, social capital, and behaviors. Thus, Indian cricket and my knowledge of how it works did not automatically translate into my new job role. I distinctly remember writing in my professional practice logbook, "Ctrl+X and Ctrl+V is not working... but it makes sense, we are three continents away." This helped, but the value of cultural understanding of the people and cricket-in-context became extremely relevant.

I reflected on this aspect of my professional development using the T-R-E-E-S model (Gupta, 2022). Theory (T) consisted of handpicking the effective psychological skills training (PST) in cricket, and understanding its potential applications for the level of cricketers I was working with. Research (R) included using assessment methods and other informal qualitative methods like interviews and focus groups with coaches to understand the cultural uniqueness of cricket in the context. This allowed me to understand key differences from my lived experience. Ethics (E) included an application of ethics for practice, including knowledge and decision-making. Experience (E) included reflecting on how I could transfer my cricket knowledge and understanding without imposing. Specificity (S) was the unique elements of the team and the sport which I had to be aware of and act in accordance with. This process involved looking under the carpet of my own experience, but also of the sport in the context and culture of operation. There was an asymmetry in my lived experience and the professional context in terms of values, "meaning of cricket," and opportunities for evidence-informed practice (Gupta & Divekar, 2022). As early career SPPs, we will often be in these niche areas where our prior experience could be very valuable, yet careful adaptation to the context at hand which has its own unique people, identity, and sociocultural elements, is critical to effective service delivery.

... To Snowboarding

As three UK-based SPPs, we have worked in a range of diverse sports including some that would be considered "neglected" from a UK perspective. One such sport that I (David) have practiced in is snowboarding, which is considered an extreme winter sport, with unique psychological, physical, technical, and tactical demands imposed on the athletes. Within the UK, snowboarding is not a common sport not least because of the necessary outdoor conditions (e.g., weather) but because of a lack of funding, resources, and training facilities. For context, prior to working in snowboarding, I had no previous knowledge or experience and therefore, several opportunities and challenges were presented. Unsurprisingly, I perceived my lack of snowboarding-specific knowledge as a challenge given the evidence that suggests that sport-specific knowledge is an important characteristic for effective service delivery (Woolway & Harwood, 2020). For example, not being able to speak the language of snowboarding may prevent the SPPs from understanding the contextual nuances of the sport.

Nevertheless, not having any prior knowledge of a sport such as snowboarding may provide an opportunity to be curious and learn about its technical aspects. Curiosity is a core value I hold and through being inquisitive I can demonstrate a willingness to learn about the athlete and their sport, which can help foster a strong working alliance. Moreover, not having any prior experience or knowledge of a sport will remove any biases or preconceived ideas that may influence professional judgment during the service delivery process. As such, one opportunity of working in neglected sports where the SPP has no prior knowledge is the alternative perspectives they can share that challenge the current status quo of the sport.

When reflecting on my experiences working in snowboarding, I draw on the T-R-E-E-S model (Gupta, 2022) and will demonstrate it by referring to an applied case study (see Price et al., 2022) that involves working with a youth snowboarder regarding a fear of injury. As alluded to above, theory is the first principle of the T-R-E-E-S model, and in this case, I explored theory related to developmental psychology, youth sport consulting models, and Acceptance and Commitment Therapy (ACT; Hayes et al., 2012). With regards to the research principle, I drew on ACT-based interventions for youth athletes with a specific focus on injury anxiety. When working with the youth snowboarder, there were several noteworthy ethical principles to be cognizant of; for example, obtaining parental consent given the athlete's age, working remotely due to being geographically dispersed, and managing professional boundaries when working online. As noted above, I had no prior experience working in snowboarding, yet I could draw on my experiences of working in youth sport and contextualize this to snowboarding. Lastly, there were a number of specifics related to the case, not least the unique sport of snowboarding, the level of the athlete, and the triad between athlete, coach, and parent which all needed to be considered carefully.

Applied Practice Recommendations

When reflecting on our experiences in practice, we offer several applied practice recommendations for SPPs of all experiences and supervisors. First, it is imperative that trainees move beyond working in sports they are familiar with and develop their competencies by challenging themselves to work in sports that are unfamiliar and often "neglected." Nevertheless, this road should not be ventured down alone, and supervisors are encouraged to balance appropriate amounts of support and challenge when trainees step into the unknown. Throughout this process, practitioners and supervisors should continually engage in reflective practice; the T-R-E-E-S model can be an appropriate starting point to aid reflection when working in diverse sports. Lastly, experienced career SPPs should share their reflections with early career SPPs on working in diverse sports to support early career SPPs when developing their service delivery.

INTEGRATING THE ART AND SCIENCE OF TEACHING MENTAL SKILLS TO ATHLETES

Colleen M. Hacker

To perform at their best, athletes need to address each of these four pillars in every — performance domain: technical, tactical, physiological, and psychological. Technical aspects of —performance include the fundamental skills of the sport, positional knowledge, and technique. Performers train tactically when they learn team strategies, offensive and defensive principles, and race or event plans. The physical pillar refers to any training designed to improve speed, strength, power, flexibility, sleep, and nutrition. The fourth pillar refers to the mental or psychological skills (PST) required for peak performance. PST typically includes improving relaxation and activation-control, imagery, focus, concentration and distraction control, self-confidence, pressure training, injury management, pre-and post-practice (and competition preparation), productive self-talk, goal-setting, responding to errors, emotional control, and team building, to name a few. While each of the four pillars of sport is essential to competitive excellence, there are still some participants who focus almost exclusively on the first three pillars. If athletes are not systematically, appropriately, and consistently training in all four pillars, they are leaving part of their potential on the table. Some athletes and coaches have embraced PST for years, while others are early in their adoption and development. Working with a receptive coaching and support staff and an invested sport organization that welcomes and embraces PST is essential for sport psychology consultants (SPCs) to have an optimal impact.

A preponderance of evidence underscores the efficacy of PST programs (Weinberg & Gould, 2024) and, as such, SPCs should be able to both convey the impact and value of training mental skills as well as measure and evaluate their own PST programs. Effectively integrating a range of elements into a comprehensive evidence-based PST program is challenging. Not only must an SPC carefully consider which psychological skills to target (e.g., anxiety management, concentration, confidence, goal-setting, mindfulness, performance routines, and self-talk, among others), they must also identify the order, sequence, and timing of presenting each strategy. These decisions should be considered alongside other salient situational constraints (e.g., time availability, tele-consulting services, referral needs), cultural context (e.g., age, gender, ethnicity, religion across performers or with consultants), and personal variables (e.g., consultant experience level, presentation style, ethical boundaries related to educational training). Psychological skills mirror physical training parameters in that they are developed and refined with consistent, individualized, and systematic training.

At the heart of PST are two cornerstone principles that anchor the work, namely self-awareness and self-regulation (Hacker & Mann, 2023). *Self-awareness*, to know oneself and one's needs at any given moment, is essential. For a performer to notice the difference between current and preferred performance states is the first step to being able to control one's own internal environment. If proper mental training and preparation have not occurred leading up to that event, then performers might be unaware of what they need in the pressure-packed moments of competition. Developing self-awareness of the essential elements, behaviors, and routines needed to bring about the best performance under any condition creates a sense of control and allows an athlete to assume responsibility for their personal execution. Once they become aware of their own needs, habits, and tendencies and start to develop the ability to recognize when they are not in that preferred performance state, learning to gain control over oneself and one's performance is the next critical key in mental skills training. *Self-regulation* refers to the ability to control one's thoughts, emotions, and behaviors toward optimum performance. What good is recognizing when you are not in your preferred state or when you are directing your focus inappropriately if you do not follow that knowledge with the ability to redirect and correct yourself? Ultimately, it is the athlete's commitment to becoming self-aware and to developing their ability to self-regulate that determines how well they will implement these skills into performance (Hacker & Mann, 2023).

Athletes can be expected to progress through four stages of PST development (Burch, 1970): (1) "Unconscious and Unskilled" where the athlete is either unaware of or uninterested in PST and is therefore obviously unskilled, (2) "Conscious and Unskilled" when the athlete becomes aware of a new strategy or technique but is not yet skilled. It is often forgotten or neglected in competition and may feel awkward or unnatural, (3) "Conscious and Skilled" where the athlete becomes more skilled and comfortable with the new behavior or technique and more consistently utilizes it in practice and competition, and (4) "Unconscious and Skilled" occurs when the athlete does not have to think about the skills anymore and the behavior is implemented seemingly as an unconscious habit.

A Soccer-Specific Application of the Four Stages of Development

Stage One: "Unconscious and Unskilled"

A defender may be frustrated that they play more attacking soccer in one game but play a more timid, defensively safe style in the very next game. They don't know why that's the case, and they don't know what to do about it. Frequently, athletes then begin to re-invest in their performance. They think. They analyze. They worry, either about past or future concerns.

Stage Two: "Conscious and Unskilled"

The next step is to accurately establish baseline behaviors and patterns of behavior and thought in different situations. For example, using a form of confidence profiling, I might ask an athlete, "When you are confident and playing well, how would I notice that"? They might say, "When I'm confident I get forward on attack, and I'm comfortable holding the ball under pressure." Both of those "confidence indicators" are also associated with observable, common, effective soccer performance behaviors. It's at that point that athletes may begin to understand that their style of play is demonstratively different when they are confident versus when they are worried about making mistakes or focused on past poor performances. At this point, they now "know" what happens and why but do not yet have the skill to actively change their confidence and mindset mid-game.

Stage Three: "Conscious and Skilled"

At this point, they're aware that performance fluctuates not because of deficits in skill or superiority of opponents but rather due to their perceived low level of confidence along with an ineffective focus (e.g., fear of errors). The next task is to learn and practice their individual confidence-enhancing techniques in practice first, then in games. For example, they might immediately shift from a worry focus to a strengths and capabilities focus, such as their fitness, their past successes, or remembering past attacking highlights. Or, they might use performance cues such as "explode" "get forward," or "attack."

Stage Four: "Unconscious and Skilled"

By consistently and effectively practicing their individualized confidence-enhancing techniques in practice and games, they begin to automate those skills. They exhibit confidence in their skills under a variety of competitive challenges and rarely "think about performance," worry about mistakes, or ruminate on potential problems. They play freely and are fully engaged in the present moment and when they become aware of confidence lapses, they automatically engage in well-honed confidence restoration.

Summary

Evidence-based programs are keystones of psychological research and intervention, yet research alone is rarely enough to ensure successful adoption by athletes. SPCs can't simply know, cite and present facts, scholarly literature, and theory to clients. Generally, athletes and coaches are not concerned with what "the literature shows" regarding a particular intervention as much as they are with having meaningful, verifiable, and direct evidence of performance benefits. The point of emphasis is on what athletes *do* (not simply what they *know*), and the proof is in action (performance). The goals are self-awareness, mastery, and personal agency.

No matter the SPC's approach, whether it's grounded in Cognitive Behavioral Therapy, mindfulness, positive psychology, Rational Emotive Behavior Therapy, etc. I recommend utilizing a strength-based approach (Ludlam et al., 2016) to the consulting process. First, athletes need to observe, analyze, and evaluate themselves on factors over which they have control and that are characteristic of their best performance. They need to accurately know what their individual strengths are and to display those skills in practice and games. If gaps in capabilities or performance concerns have arisen in the past, athletes need to identify and consistently practice the requisite intervention skills individually and in performance settings. In time, they will be able to apply those skills, strategies, and protocols in practice and in competition, ultimately doing so automatically.

It is challenging and rewarding work to partner with athletes and teams in the active construction of go-to mental toughness plans for diverse and recurrent competitive demands. The solutions are individually tailored and athlete-specific based on sport, position, team, coach, situation, and event particulars. However, it is possible (with collaborative work, commitment, and creativity) to design PST programs that provide observable, quantifiable, and controllable evidence of value and merit.

EDITORS' TAKEAWAYS

I (Sebastian) appreciate Andrew's rich personal account, which he shares with readers. Intentionally leaning into "new," "non-mainstream" sports certainly is a very rewarding endeavor, as I can attest from my own experience. I already started engaging with athletes from a wide variety of sports before I started my SEPP journey—while still working as a sports writer. Being curious about new sports and each athlete's personal lived experience was as much a foundation of my work back then, as it is now as a SEPPP. Gupta, Price, and Thelwell also highlight the value of curiosity. I do like how they point out that making sure you stay curious can even serve you well when you think you know all there is to know about a given sport. Yet, gaps and biases regarding cultural awareness might negatively affect how you engage with your athletes. Their TREES model certainly provides an actionable approach to navigating challenges to optimal service provision. Importantly, in her contribution Hacker then shifts the focus to the athletes themselves—and how they engage and progress through PST. With a background in motor learning, to me her four-stage model of PST development makes perfect sense. In the same way athletes learn new movements and techniques until they have them internalized, that is, automatized, we can also encourage them to embrace this very approach to the development and implementation of mental skills in everyday practice and competition. Again, a very actionable strategy that helps create athlete-centered PST programs.

RECOMMENDED EXERCISES

1 Consider your home country. Choose one sport that is popular in your country but with which you have minimal exposure and experience.
   a What does contextual intelligence mean in that sport?
   b What two or three words would you use to describe it?
   c Using Fogaça's four-stage model, where would you place yourself in terms of familiarity and competency?
   d Based on that stage, identify three development needs you want to work on over the next 12 months.

2 Choose a sport outside your usual interest or expertise. Spend 30–60 minutes learning its rules, competitive structure, and mental demands (watch a competition if possible).
   a What psychological challenges surprised you?
   b How could a mental performance consultant support athletes or coaches in this environment?
   c Use the T-R-E-E-S framework to outline what Theory, Research, Ethics considerations, personal experience, and sport-specific knowledge you would need before consulting in this sport.

3 Reflect on what first drew you to sport psychology.

   a How has your fandom shaped your professional direction?
   b What biases or blind spots might stem from personal loyalties?
   c How might loosening those attachments support your growth as a practitioner?

4 Reflect on your own interpersonal and professional strengths.

   a What qualities (e.g., confidence, sport knowledge, patience, curiosity) do you bring to work with athletes?
   b What areas do you find, or anticipate finding, challenging (e.g., delivering critical feedback, working with resistant clients, managing boundaries, teaching mental skills)?
   c Pick a population of athletes you are interested in working with. How will your qualities and blind spots impact your work with them?

5 Create a sociogram of a sport environment you know—include athletes, coaches, officials, parents, administrators, and support staff.

   a Who are the less visible stakeholders who might benefit from mental performance support?
   b How could supporting them indirectly enhance athlete well-being and performance?

6 Imagine you are about to meet a new athlete for the first time.

   a How do you want the athlete to feel during and after the first session?
   b What will you say or do to establish trust and clarity?
   c What behaviors or habits might get in the way?
   d How will you prepare yourself prior to the session (i.e., pre-performance routine)?

7 Consider an athlete you are working with.

   a How do you currently balance art (relationship, intuition) and science (evidence-based methods)?
   b Outline how you could help them progress from Unconscious & Unskilled → Conscious & Skilled → Unconscious & Skilled.

8 Picture a "difficult" athlete (e.g., resistant, withdrawn, overly eager for quick results, doesn't do the work between sessions).

   a Which athlete behavior(s) feel most challenging for you personally?
   b What feelings arise when athletes exhibit this behavior?
   c How will you navigate work with "difficult" athletes to remain effective and compassionate?

REFERENCES

Burch, N. (1970). *Four stages of competency.* Gordon Training International.

Friesen, A., & Orlick, T. (2010). A qualitative analysis of holistic sport psychology consultants' professional philosophies. *The Sport Psychologist, 24*(2), 227–244. https://doi.org/10.1123/tsp.24.2.227

Friesen, A. P., Devonport, T. J., & Lane, A. M. (2017). Beyond the technical: The role of emotion regulation in lacrosse officiating. *Journal of Sports Sciences, 35*(6), 579–586. https://doi.org/10.1080/02640414.2016.1180419

Friesen, A. P., & Patrick, T. (2024). A case study of a senior high-performance leader managing psychological effects during the COVID-19 pandemic. *Case Studies in Sport and Exercise Psychology, 8*(1), 1–7. https://doi.org/10.1123/cssep.2023-0008

Gupta, S. (2022). Reflect in and speak out: An autoethnographic study on race and the embedded sport psychology practitioner. *Case Studies in Sport and Exercise Psychology, 6*(S1), S1–S10. https://doi.org/10.1123/cssep.2022-0020
Gupta, S., & Divekar, S. (2022). A symmetry or asymmetry: Reflecting upon realities of cultural practice in sport psychology. *Sport and Exercise Psychology Review, 17*(1), 60–72.
Hacker, C. M., & Mann, M. E. (2023). *Achieving excellence: Mastering mindset for peak performance in sport and life*. Human Kinetics.
Hayes, S. C., Strosahl, K. D., & Wilson, K. G. (2012). *Acceptance and commitment therapy: The process and practice of mindful change* (2nd ed.). Guilford Press.
Ludlam, K. E., Butt, J., Bawden, M., Lindsay, P., & Maynard, I. W. (2016). A strength-based consulting approach in elite sport: Exploring super strengths. *Journal of Applied Sport Psychology, 28*(2), 153–171. https://doi.org/10.1080/10413200.2015.1105881
Mondal, S., & Rampersad, A. (2020). Cricket. In *Routledge handbook of global sport* (pp. 197–205). Routledge.
Price, D., Wagstaff, C. R., & Thelwell, R. C. (2022). "What if I get injured?": An acceptance and commitment therapy approach for fear of injury with a semielite youth snowboarder. *Case Studies in Sport and Exercise Psychology, 6*(1), 12–20. https://doi.org/10.1123/cssep.2021-0020
Vincent, A. P., & Christensen, D. A. (2015). Conversations with parents: A collaborative sport psychology program for parents in youth sport. *Journal of Sport Psychology in Action, 6*(2), 73–85. https://doi.org/10.1080/21520704.2015.1054535
Weinberg, R. S., & Gould, D. (2024). *Foundations of sport and exercise psychology* (8th ed.). Human Kinetics.
Woolway, T., & Harwood, C. G. (2020). Consultant characteristics in sport psychology service provision: A critical review and future research directions. *International Journal of Sport and Exercise Psychology, 18*(1), 46–63. https://doi.org/10.1080/1612197X.2018.1462230

2 Working with Athletes with Hidden Disabilities

Sport, from youth to Olympic level, has made huge advancements to provide opportunities for learning, growth, fun, and enjoyment for diverse groups and individuals—the growth in Paralympic sports and competition, maybe, being the most noticeable change. Diversity within sport, exercise, and performance, however, does not only pertain to apparent physical impairments or disabilities. A considerable number of performers, sometimes without being aware of it themselves or having been formally diagnosed, actually fall under the umbrella of hidden disabilities or conditions. Attention-deficit/hyperactivity disorder and autism are but two of those differences in sensory and cognitive functioning, and those "hidden disabilities" have received growing attention outside of sport, exercise, and performance settings. Within the field of sport, exercise, and performance psychology (SEPP), these diverse individuals and their specific needs haven't received much attention so far. Addressing this gap, three diverse author groups dive deeper into this timely and relevant topic, sharing insights and frameworks relevant for any SEPP professional.

WORKING WITH NEURODIVERGENT ATHLETES: ENHANCING PARTICIPATION, PERFORMANCE, AND ENJOYMENT

Christopher Stanley, Timothy Baghurst, & Nicole Robertson

Disability and Neurodivergence in Sport

According to the World Report on Disability, approximately 15% of the global population experiences some form of disability (Wylie et al., 2013). Disabilities can be congenital or acquired and range from hidden to visible. The United Nations defines *disability* as long-term physical, mental, intellectual, or sensory impairments that, when combined with various barriers, may hinder full societal participation (United Nations, Convention on the Rights of Persons with Disabilities, 2006). This definition also notes the challenging environments and discrimination that people with disabilities might face, aligning with the social model of disability, which views *disability* as a social construct (Oliver, 2013).

Humans display an array of physical and mental features. The term *neurodivergence* suggests that a diversity of minds and brains exists between individuals and how they process and interpret environmental stimuli (Dwyer, 2022). Neurodivergence does not imply a disability, but rather, *neurodiversity theory* suggests that differences in cognitive functioning are natural functional variations (Chapman & Botha, 2023). Nonetheless, some differences in sensory and cognitive variations (e.g., autism, ADHD, and dyslexia) may be referred to as a "hidden disability."

DOI: 10.4324/9781003781486-2

Sport can be a platform for promoting inclusion for divergent people, with approaches emphasizing a continuum whereby, at one extreme, inclusion is "forced," lacking true accessibility and inclusivity. Further along the continuum, partial inclusion exists, but full accessibility is still absent. The ideal scenario is complete inclusion across all sports, where spaces are accessible to everyone, reflecting a truly inclusive society (Forber-Pratt & Lyew, 2020). Sport, exercise, and performance psychology professionals (SEPPPs) should consider neurodivergence and hidden disabilities and conditions (HDCs) when working to enhance performance, wellness, and inclusion in sport contexts.

Hidden Disabilities and Conditions

The term "hidden" applies to some disabilities and conditions that are not immediately visible or obvious to others yet impact various aspects of life, including daily routines, social interactions, and performance. HDCs include specific learning disabilities (SLDs), such as dyslexia, Autism Spectrum Disorder (ASD), and attention-deficit/hyperactivity disorder (ADHD). Additional HDCs include sensory and communication challenges, visual and auditory impairments, and language disorders. Physical and mental conditions such as relative energy deficiency in sport (RED-S), fibromyalgia, bone and joint diseases, motor disorders, diabetes, allergies, sleep disorders, and mental health issues related to trauma may also be considered (Stanley & Baghurst, 2023). HDCs can be easily overlooked, leading to misunderstandings or a lack of awareness. Next, we offer an overview of the considerations and implications of working with neurodivergent athletes (for more, see Stanley & Baghurst, 2023).

Specific Learning Disabilities

SLDs involve challenges in acquiring specific academic skills, such as reading, math, and writing, without necessarily affecting other areas (e.g., dyslexia, dyscalculia, and dysgraphia). Approximately 10–15% of people globally experience an SLD (Grigorenko et al., 2020). Dyslexia, the most common SLD, can be identified as early as preschool and continues into adulthood. In early education, dyslexia is evident through sound-symbol correspondence, spelling, and reading challenges. As students progress, difficulties with reading comprehension and learning from written text become more pronounced, particularly as tasks requiring these skills increase (Sanfilippo et al., 2020). In sports, fundamental tasks like reading playbooks, writing on whiteboards, or managing game clocks can highlight challenges. Athletes with SLDs might struggle with tasks requiring recall, following directions, or maintaining spatial awareness. Researchers have provided valuable insights for working with athletes who have SLDs, ASD, and ADHD (Braun & Braun, 2015). Athletes with SLDs may require special considerations, such as direct instruction and breaking down tasks and movements into clear, manageable steps (Braun & Braun, 2015). Additionally, modeling skills and behaviors, whether by coaches, teammates, or through video modeling, can be beneficial. Video modeling, including self-modeling, video prompting, and point-of-view modeling, helps athletes by visually breaking down skills and motor movements (Judge & Morgan, 2020).

Attention-Deficit Hyperactivity Disorder

ADHD is characterized by persistent inattention and/or hyperactivity, affecting daily functioning and development in learning and social settings. It stems from neurological factors, with brain regions related to executive functioning developing more slowly or less efficiently. Severity varies from mild to severe, and about 10% of children aged 4–17 have been diagnosed, with boys more commonly affected. ADHD behaviors often include difficulty focusing, restlessness, and impulsivity. It can cause motor difficulties but does not limit physical capabilities, and with proper support, individuals with ADHD can thrive athletically.

Athletes with ADHD might struggle with focus during instructional sets and drills, and hyperactive or impulsive behaviors can disrupt structured practices. SEPPPs can help coaches understand that these symptoms are not signs of disrespect, lack of motivation, or laziness. Direct instruction, where information is condensed and "chunked" for easier recall, can be particularly beneficial. Visual aids and cues are also helpful for complex tasks (Braun & Braun, 2015). The universal design for learning (UDL) framework customizes learning environments, including athletics, for diverse learners. This approach emphasizes behavioral expectations, management, practice environment considerations, clear directions, and family involvement (Vargas et al., 2018).

Autism Spectrum Disorder

ASD involves a range of social and behavioral symptoms that impact perception, interaction, and communication. Symptoms include repetitive movements, strict routines, specific fixations, and unique sensory responses (Lelong et al., 2021). While ASD does not inherently affect athletic abilities, social and motor challenges can impact sports participation. Approximately 3% of children have ASD, with boys more frequently affected. Symptoms of ASD include persistent challenges in social interaction, communication, and behavior, such as difficulty with social cues, repetitive behaviors, and intense interests. These traits typically emerge early in development and significantly affect daily functioning. A professional evaluation by specialists such as developmental pediatricians or school psychologists is crucial for diagnosis and early intervention.

Social difficulties and strict routines may hinder skill acquisition and relationships in sports, although some ASD traits, such as an intense focus, can be beneficial. Therefore, structured practices can be advantageous. For athletes with ASD, strategies that consider sensory overstimulation, use appropriate language, and foster social skills and special interests are particularly effective (Braun & Braun, 2015). Additionally, identifying "safe spaces" with reduced stimulation can promote arousal regulation during warm-ups, practices, and competitions.

Additional Considerations

Individuals with HDCs are at increased risk for poor mental health outcomes. For instance, those with dyslexia often experience higher rates of generalized anxiety disorder and depression (Mammarella et al., 2016), while ASD individuals also commonly face co-occurring mental health issues, with about 12% having an anxiety disorder (Lai et al., 2019). Mental health symptoms can be subtle and not always visible, making it crucial for SEPPPs to recognize basic signs and be equipped to respond appropriately in mental and physical health emergencies.

Emergency Action Plans

SEPPPs can develop and manage emergency action plans (EAPs) for HDC-specific issues such as ASD, allergic reactions, and seizures. These plans outline steps to handle severe symptoms effectively in various environments, including classrooms, practice settings, and during travel. For example, the *American Academy of Asthma, Allergies, and Immunology* provides a detailed

Anaphylaxis EAP, including critical signs and epinephrine administration steps. Autism Speaks offers safety plans for individuals with ASD, and the Epilepsy Foundation provides guidelines for managing seizures. Incorporating these HDC-specific elements into EAPs ensures they are clear, concise, and understood by key personnel like coaches and educators.

PROVIDING MENTAL PERFORMANCE CONSULTING FOR ATHLETES WITH HIDDEN DISABILITIES: UNDERSTANDING SLD, ADHD, AND ASD

Robyn Braun-Trocchio

HDCs such as ADHD, SLDs, and ASD, impact how athletes learn, communicate, and navigate the demands of training and competition (Braun & Braun, 2015). Mental performance consultants (MPCs) play a pivotal role in facilitating psychological skills training for athletes with hidden disabilities but may encounter challenges in recognizing the needs of these athletes and adapting their instruction (Braun-Trocchio et al., 2024). Before implementing specific strategies, MPCs should be attentive to behavioral cues that may indicate a hidden disability. Although, formal diagnosis may be outside the scope of practice, MPCs may notice patterns such as struggles with sustaining attention, impulsivity, challenges following multistep instructions, trouble remembering newly learned information, difficulties with time management or organization, heightened sensitivity to sensory input, or frequent misunderstandings in communication. Athletes may not always disclose a diagnosis, whether due to being undiagnosed or choosing not to share.

Strategies and Techniques

Although each athlete with HDCs has their own unique characteristics, MPCs can employ a range of strategies to effectively implement psychological skills training, which can be beneficial for all athletes regardless of diagnosis, to foster understanding, retention, and application of psychological skills training (see Table 2.1 for a summary of strategies). MPCs should work closely with coaches, providing them with various instructional strategies to implement during practice and competition. For both athletes with ADHD and SLD, direct instruction is beneficial when introducing psychological skills by focusing attention, providing sequential steps that are easy to follow, time for trial and error, chunking information, and promoting persistence (Martinussen & Major, 2011). Breaking down tasks into smaller, manageable steps helps the athlete stay focused, understand expectations, and learn skills like goal-setting or relaxation. Modeling can also be used to demonstrate a skill, accompanied by specific cues. For example, when teaching relaxation techniques, MPCs might clearly explain the purpose of diaphragmatic breathing by breaking the process into simple steps (e.g., sit comfortably, place hands on the chest and stomach, and focus on breathing deeply into the stomach rather than the chest) and then model the technique first before the athlete tries it at their own pace, with room for trial and error as well as repetition to reinforce learning.

For athletes with ADHD, use external supports, such as tools like visual cues, timers, or apps (e.g., Forest, RoutineFlow, TickTick, or Todoist) to help the athlete stay organized and track their progress (Braun & Braun, 2015). For instance, a visual checklist of goals or a timer for practicing mindfulness exercises can keep the athlete on task. Providing written or graphic instructions for skills gives the athlete a tangible resource to refer to when needed. To promote independence, self-regulatory skills can be implemented, such as goal-setting strategies, self-monitoring, and self-talk (Martinussen & Major, 2011). For instance, athletes

Table 2.1 Strategies and Techniques for Athletes with Hidden Disabilities

Disability	*Strategies*	*Techniques*
ADHD	Direct Instruction	Break tasks into smaller, clear steps
	External Supports	Use timers, visual aids, checklists, and apps
	Self-Regulatory Instruction	Teach self-monitoring (e.g., journals) and self-talk
SLD	Direct Instruction	Sequencing, step-by-step directions, modeling, and repetition
	Metacognitive Strategies	Encourage reflection on learning processes and self-awareness of strengths
ASD	Handling Sensory Overload	Modify environment (e.g., noise-canceling headphones, dim lights)
	Facilitation of Language and Social Skills	Use role-playing and provide feedback for social scenarios

can utilize a journal to track their focus, effort, and use of psychological strategies such as relaxation techniques or imagery, during practice and competition. This not only enhances self-awareness but also helps the athlete and MPC recognize patterns in performance and identify areas for growth. Self-talk is a useful strategy for managing impulsivity and maintaining attention. MPCs might teach the athlete to use short, positive, task-focused statements that can be rehearsed before and during the activity and role-play their use in training scenarios (e.g., "breathe and reset," "one play at a time," or "eyes up, stay with it").

For athletes with SLD, provide structured, accessible, and flexible instruction tailored to their learning needs. Teach athletes to reflect on their learning process (i.e., develop their metacognition), such as identifying which mental techniques work best for them and why (Braun & Braun, 2015). For instance, after practicing imagery, encourage the athlete to discuss or journal how it felt, what specific images or sensations stood out, and whether it helped them feel prepared or focused. Over time, this reflection can help athletes refine their use of strategies and take greater ownership of their mental training. Provide instructions in multiple formats (e.g., verbal explanations, written guides, and visual demonstrations), to accommodate diverse learning preferences, reinforce comprehension, and empower athletes to choose the best format for them. For example, the MPC might record an audio version of an imagery script for the athletes to practice independently, paired with a printed version that includes key cues and reminders, or integrate the script with physical movements to support kinesthetic learning.

For athletes with ASD, create a structured, predictable learning environment and adapt strategies to their social and sensory needs. Establishing routines provides athletes with structure and predictability (Vargas et al., 2012). Routines during psychological skills training sessions can help athletes feel more secure, reduce cognitive load, and improve engagement. A predictable structure such as starting with a check-in, previewing goals, practicing a skill, and closing with a reflection, provides clarity and helps athletes with ASD know what to expect. Handling sensory overload is also a crucial technique and strategy (Braun & Braun, 2015). To address this, create an environment that is calm and free from overstimulating distractions. Incorporating sensory accommodations, such as noise-canceling headphones or dimmed lighting, can help the athlete focus on the task. Proactively prepare athletes for potentially overstimulating environments by discussing the setting, identifying potential triggers and early signs of sensory overload (e.g., irritability, withdrawal, difficulty processing instructions), and co-creating coping strategies that align with the athlete's preferences and needs (e.g., practicing calming techniques like deep breathing, mindfulness, or having a plan of escape to a safe haven when overstimulated).

Facilitation of appropriate language and social skills must also be part of the plan when working with athletes with ASD (Braun & Braun, 2015). These athletes might misinterpret the comments of others (often taken too literally), as they do not pick up on the subtle social cues of body language or the nuances of pragmatic language. Use role-playing to model how to apply psychological skills in social scenarios and provide direct feedback, such as taking on the role of a teammate to practice resolving conflicts or the role of an opponent to practice staying calm under pressure. The athlete can practice responding to various social interactions, focusing on clear, direct communication and appropriate emotional regulation. Additionally, it is essential to avoid abstract language or idiomatic expressions and instead focus on literal, concrete explanations to enhance clarity and skill acquisition (e.g., "see yourself succeeding" while teaching imagery can be vague and confusing, instead use literal and sensory-based language such as imagining the feel of their shoes on the ground, the sounds of the environment, and physical sensations of movements).

Special Qualities

Coaches, parents, and even athletes themselves often concentrate on the aspects of a disability that hinder athletic performance, overlooking the individual's unique strengths and potential. It is important for the MPC to further develop these advantages. These attributes, when supported through appropriate structure and individualized strategies, can be powerful assets in sport. MPCs can assist in helping athletes identify and build upon these qualities.

Athletes with ADHD often display heightened awareness of the environment, the ability to do well in chaos and pressure, quick speed/reaction time, creative approaches to problem-solving, lack of concern about losing in the moment, and spontaneity, which can be leveraged in sport settings with appropriate support and structure (Braun & Braun, 2015). MPCs can use reflections to highlight moments when their strengths enhanced their performance, promote a growth mindset to help athletes view mistakes as opportunities to learn, and reinforce their resilience and adaptability. The profiles of athletes with SLD will vary considerably from one individual to another. MPCs should work collaboratively with the athlete to identify their unique strengths and utilize them effectively. For instance, an athlete with strong verbal reasoning might respond well to self-talk strategies, while athletes with strong visual-spatial skills may benefit from creating imagery routines for each phase of a performance. Athletes with ASD have strengths like attention to detail, strong memory, and exceptional focus on tasks. An athlete's capability to notice small changes in technique or performance mechanics might contribute to rapid skill refinement. Also, they may show reduced emotional reactivity, potentially allowing them to stay calm during stressful situations (Braun & Braun, 2015). Tailored support and understanding can help athletes with hidden disabilities thrive in both individual and team sports.

Conclusion

Many individuals with HDCs struggle with confidence, problem-solving, and executive functioning skills, requiring explicit instruction and extensive practice to learn and adopt these habits. MPCs can play an integral role in developing psychological skills training programs for athletes with HDCs to use in practice and competition. It is important to individualize the strategies and techniques to address the unique strengths and challenges of each athlete with HDCs, tailoring the approach to meet their specific needs. Teaching these self-regulatory skills not only supports performance but fosters autonomy, confidence, and a sense of control.

HELPING COACHES WORK WITH ATHLETES WITH HIDDEN DISABILITIES

Tiffanye M. Vargas, Robbi Beyer, & Margaret M. Flores

Sport psychology consultants (SPCs) will discover that in working with athletes, it is imperative to recognize the importance of understanding how to work with, and communicate with, the coach. Sometimes, it is the intervention with the coach that can make the biggest difference for an athlete. This is particularly true when working with athletes with hidden disabilities. As the name "hidden" implies, an individual with a learning disability, ADHD, or ASD would not appear to be any different from their peers during casual interactions. However, in circumstances that involve learning and practice they would exhibit behaviors that would be different from peers without disabilities. Individuals with HDCs may be unknown or misinterpreted by coaches as obstinate, disrespectful, or insolent (Vargas et al., 2018). Thus, it is important that we understand the interventions that might be needed with athletes and with coaches, based on the level of competition.

At the youth level, coaches are most likely to be volunteers, and to have little or no training (Vargas et al., 2022). At this level, athletes with HDCs might not yet have developed skills to monitor their own behavior, nor have the communicative maturity to tell coaches what they need. As a result, coaches might mistakenly label these participants as "troublesome." The SPC can make an immediate impact by helping the coach understand the need to work with the parents or guardians. One easy way to do this is to help the coach develop a form that collects information about what the parent or guardian thinks are good ways to redirect, motivate, or teach their child without singling anyone out (Flores et al., 2017). This type of form will benefit all participants, as everyone has a different learning style, and the information from parents or guardians helps the coach understand individual needs. Coaches also report feeling overwhelmed and not prepared to handle youth exhibiting behaviors such as attention problems or an inability to follow instructions (Wiersma & Sherman, 2005); because there is little formal training about HDCs, the SPC can assist coaches with locating resources around UDL (Sherlock-Shangraw, 2013). UDL is a framework for designing instruction in a proactive manner such that barriers to learning are reduced. Coaching plans that follow UDL could include more than one way to show or communicate concepts/skills, more than one way in which athletes might demonstrate their understanding of skills, and more than one strategy for capturing athletes' interest to stay engaged in practicing skills (Sherlock-Shangraw, 2013). The following strategies can also be taught to the coach:

- Use methods for increasing focus and impulse control by reducing distractions or access to unnecessary equipment (e.g., providing short, varied blocks of information with clear visual anchors during instructions thus reducing distraction and prompting athletes to attend to particular words, directions, or concepts). For example, Coach Mia recognizes that some of her athletes become distracted by extra balls and cones on the sideline during her basketball practice. As a solution she now sets up only the equipment needed for each drill and keeps the rest stored out of sight.

- Provide a structured and predictable routine or environment and consistent pregame/practice routine. For example, Coach James works with a soccer team that includes athletes with autism and ADHD. He starts every practice with the same warm-up routine, then moves into drills with a consistent order. His athletes now know what to expect, which helps them stay calm and focused during practice.
- Provide a short yet clear visual schedule of verbal instructions. For example, Coach Mary's flag football team includes several neurodivergent players. She uses a whiteboard to sketch out the practice schedule with icons (e.g., cones for drills, whistle for scrimmage). She also verbally walks the team through it.
- Reduce the length of the activity and vary activities with appropriate breaks. For example, Coach Gonzales noticed her younger gymnasts are losing focus during their 15-minute skill blocks. She shortened each station to 5 minutes, added 2-minute water breaks, and rotated stations between strength, balance, and tumbling.
- Provide exploration activities and lead up games. For example, to teach throwing mechanics, Coach Marcus introduces a variety of mini-games using bean bags and targets before moving into overhand throw drills that require immediate accuracy for success. Athletes are engaged, build confidence through play, and are more eager to practice the skill later to become more accurate in their throwing outcomes.
- Assign a role as a helper to the coach to help enhance focus. For example, Coach James has a student who tends to "wander" off during activities. He makes this athlete responsible for shouting the name and counting out each exercise for the team, helping the athlete keep focused and engaged during the activity. He could also use a "job board" with rotating roles like line leader, cone collector, or rule helper, and include "wanders" in those roles to help them stay focused.
- Use strategies to allow for processing time, shortening verbal instructions, and including visual cues. For example, Coach Sam always keeps his soccer directions brief, pairing them with simple gestures and visuals such as cone=dribble, hand up=stop, point to net=shoot. He often uses a laminated visual schedule with symbols that an athlete could follow along with, such as *color-coded instructions on a whiteboard for a relay drill (green = go, red = stop, yellow = wait).*
- Provide step-by-step demonstrations and whole-part-whole instruction, and allow time to watch drills before performing. For example, Coach Oliva shows the tennis backhand, breaks it down into three isolated steps, and then chains it back together. She uses the same short cues and models each step slowly two times before asking the students to mirror her movements and start the drill.
- Provide extra time or peer support. For example, Coach Monica asks a peer to go through the drill as athletes watch side-by-side and allows a highly active player to help another player challenged to stay on task pace themselves and avoid impulsive behaviors. Allowing peers to explain drills in their own words often offers a more understandable explanation, gives them time to settle and understand the objective.
- Use repetition and correct hands-on practice. For example, Coach Melody uses short, replicated drills (three quick rounds of the same gymnastic drill) with breaks, helping athletes who lose attention build trust and confidence in the skill. After each repetition she checks for understanding (e.g., "show me your starting position, hand position").
- Use methods to reduce anxiety, increase routines, and build appropriate social skills. For example, Charly struggles with social anxiety and is challenged to take turns and dislikes the

very noisy dugout in softball. Coach Jordan accommodates by showing the batting order with pictures of the players and creates a "quiet corner" with noise reducing headphones and a calming soft baseball stress "fidget" ball. He also plays a sensory friendly playlist with lower base and no erratic jumps in volume, and provides Charly a "practice buddy" that models the moves and reinforces movement side-by-side with him. This strategy provides Charly with a predictable structure and gives him a self-regulation opportunity.

Summary: Consideration of Performance Levels

As athletes progress to the competitive club level, their needs will continue to evolve. Coaches will likely be more experienced, having played themselves and/or received some level of training, but they will most likely not have received any training for coaching athletes with HDCs. Athletes with HDCs who have entered into this level may have developed some coping skills, but they might experience higher levels of anxiety particularly when situations are unknown, unfamiliar, or perceived to be difficult (Braun & Braun, 2015). The SPC can teach skills such as relaxation, visualization, and self-talk to assist with this anxiety (Braun & Braun, 2015) and continue to provide resources such as apps, learning communities, and workshops to coaches and athletes. When preparing training modules/workshops, the SPC should focus on impactful examples using videos, testimonies, and activities to illustrate the strengths and challenges of HDCs.

At the elite level, coaches have clear expectations to win and maximize the performance of their athletes. Athletes with HDCs competing at this level will almost certainly have developed strong coping mechanisms and supports, and coaches will have had more training, and likely more access, to resources. As well, at this level, manifestations of HDCs characteristics may not be behavioral, but may be more psychological (e.g., heightened anxiety, loss of confidence). The SPC should be flexible and meet regularly with coaches and athletes. When meeting with the coach, the SPC can encourage and help normalize regular, brief check-ins with athletes, provide concrete information, and might use a rating or scale (e.g., 1–5, green/yellow/red, thumbs up/sideways/thumbs down) to let the coach quickly know if any intervention is needed. Coaches can also help reinforce sport psychology techniques and performance routines in a targeted manner with SPC guidance. In conclusion, because athletes with HD have largely been ignored within coaching literature and coaching education (Thurston et al., 2021), the SPC has an opportunity to promote inclusion and inclusive coaching behaviors through sport psychology interventions such as promotion of communication, stress management, and educational workshops, beginning at the youth level. This is a critical time period as it develops the foundation for future athletic endeavors, and when not inclusive, can elevate levels of attrition for both athletes and coaches. Continuing education, both for the SPC, and the coach, around HDCs will also be necessary.

EDITORS' TAKEAWAYS

In my (Lauren) opinion, we've spent more time—though also likely not enough—talking about athletes with physical disabilities and how to support them and not nearly enough discussion on this important and growing population. This chapter is packed full of essential insights and resources for all of us in the field as it is highly likely that we all at any given point in time are working with at least one client who has a hidden disability. Understanding more about this population and how to effectively work with them —such as the different types of HDCs, strategies for adapting our interventions to best suit their needs, consulting with coaches to create optimal environments for teams who have one or more athletes with HDCs, and their unique strengths—should probably be more formal and requisite parts of our education and competency development as practitioners. After reading this chapter, I have more of an understanding of how to approach providing services to this group of athletes (people)—as well as the various individuals who support them—and much more to learn and develop competency in so that I can effectively and ethically support this group of performers.

RECOMMENDED EXERCISES

1. What did you know or think about athletes with HDCs before reading this chapter? What has stayed the same or changed about your understanding of how to effectively and ethically provide SEPP services to this population?
2. Reflect on the unique challenges that athletes with SLDs, ADHD, or ASD might encounter in sport environments.
   a. How can you, as a SEPP practitioner, help create an inclusive setting that recognizes these challenges while also fostering athletes' strengths?
   b. This chapter notes that individuals with HDCs are at higher risk for anxiety and depressive symptoms. How might these mental health concerns further complicate their experiences in social, academic, and athletic contexts? What can you do to support their overall well-being?
3. How would you use self-regulatory techniques (e.g., mindfulness, self-talk) to help athletes with ADHD stay focused, manage impulsivity, and improve performance in high-pressure situations?
4. How would you adapt your teaching to support athletes with SLD in learning and applying psychological skills?
5. What strategies could you use to create consistency, address sensory sensitivities, and support social engagement for athletes with ASD?
6. Identify challenges an athlete with HDCs might experience in the youth or competitive sports environment and describe strategies from this chapter that could assist the athlete and coach.
7. How would you explain to a coach that UDL strategies benefit all athletes—not only those with HDCs? How would you guide coaches to structure practices and games that lower anxiety and promote positive social interactions?
8. What strategies would you teach an elite athlete to help them manage sensory challenges that affect learning and performance?

REFERENCES

Braun, R., & Braun, B. (2015). Managing the challenges of hidden disabilities in youth sport: A look at SLD, ADHD, and ASD through the sport psychology lens. *Journal of Sport Psychology in Action, 6*(1), 28–43. https://doi.org/10.1080/21520704.2014.991051

Braun-Trocchio, R., Rosenblatt, K., Frates, A., & Jackson, H. (2024). Preparation and attitudes of sport psychology consultants toward working with athletes with hidden disabilities. *Journal of Sports and Games, 6*(1), 43–51. https://doi.org/10.22259/2642-8466.0601005

Chapman, R., & Botha, M. (2023). Neurodivergence-informed therapy. *Developmental Medicine & Child Neurology, 65*(3), 310–317. https://doi.org/10.1111/dmcn.15384

Dwyer, P. (2022). The neurodiversity approach(es): What are they and what do they mean for researchers? *Human Development, 66*(2), 73–92. https://doi.org/10.1159/000523723

Flores, M. M., Vargas, T. M., & Beyer, R. (2017). *Effective coaching for all athletes within youth recreational sports.* FIT Publishing.

Forber-Pratt, A. J., & Lyew, D. A. (2020). A model case: Specialized group home for girls with disabilities in India. *Child and Adolescent Social Work Journal, 37*(3), 315–327. https://doi.org/10.1007/s10560-019-00633-8

Grigorenko, E. L., Compton, D. L., Fuchs, L. S., Wagner, R. K., Willcutt, E. G., & Fletcher, J. M. (2020). Understanding, educating, and supporting children with specific learning disabilities: 50 years of science and practice. *American Psychologist, 75*(1), 37–51. https://doi.org/10.1037/amp0000452

Judge, J. P., & Morgan, K. N. (2020). Video modeling: Strategies to support physical activity in children with autism spectrum disorder. *Palaestra, 34*(2), 28–32.

Lai, M. C., Kassee, C., Besney, R., Bonato, S., Hull, L., Mandy, W., ... & Ameis, S. H. (2019). Prevalence of co-occurring mental health diagnoses in the autism population: A systematic review and meta-analysis. *The Lancet Psychiatry, 6*(10), 819–829. https://doi.org/10.1016/S2215-0366(19)30289-5

Lelong, M., Zysset, A., Nievergelt, M., Luder, R., Götz, U., Schulze, C., & Wieber, F. (2021). How effective is fine motor training in children with ADHD? A scoping review. *BMC Pediatrics, 21,* 1–21. https://doi.org/10.1186/s12887-021-02916-5

Mammarella, I. C., Ghisi, M., Bomba, M., Bottesi, G., Caviola, S., Broggi, F., & Nacinovich, R. (2016). Anxiety and depression in children with nonverbal learning disabilities, reading disabilities, or typical development. *Journal of Learning Disabilities, 49*(2), 130–139. https://doi.org/10.1177/0022219414529336

Martinussen, R., & Major, A. (2011). Working memory weaknesses in students with ADHD: Implications for instruction. *Theory Into Practice, 50*(1), 68–75. https://doi.org/10.1080/00405841.2011.534943

Oliver, M. (2013). The social model of disability: Thirty years on. *Disability & Society, 28*(7), 1024–1026. https://doi.org/10.1080/09687599.2013.818773

Sanfilippo, J., Ness, M., Petscher, Y., Rappaport, L., Zuckerman, B., & Gaab, N. (2020). Reintroducing dyslexia: Early identification and implications for pediatric practice. *Pediatrics, 146*(1), 1–8. https://doi.org/10.1542/peds.2019-3046

Sherlock-Shangraw, R. (2013). Creating inclusive youth sport environments with the universal design for learning. *Journal of Physical Education, Recreation & Dance, 84*(2), 40–46. https://doi.org/10.1080/07303084.2013.757191

Stanley, C., & Baghurst, T. (2023). *Reach every athlete: A guide to coaching players with hidden disabilities and conditions.* Jones & Bartlett Learning.

Thurston, R. J., Alexander, D. M., & Michaud, M. (2021). Practical considerations for coaching athletes with learning disabilities and neurodevelopmental disorders. *International Sport Coaching Journal, 9*(2), 244–251. https://doi.org/10.1123/iscj.2021-0008

United Nations. (2006). *Convention on the rights of persons with disabilities.* https://www.un.org/disabilities/documents/convention/convoptprot-e.pdf

Vargas, T. M., Beyer, R., Bittner, M., & Flores, M. M. (2022). Recreation leaders' perceptions of athletes' behaviors and proposed resultant pedagogical strategies. *Palaestra, 37*(1), 5–11.

Vargas, T. M., Beyer, R., & Flores, M. M. (2018). Coaching athletes with hidden disabilities: Using universal design for learning to effectively coach all athletes. *International Sport Coaching Journal, 5*(2), 176–182. https://doi.org/10.1123/iscj.2018-0021

Vargas, T. M., Flores, M. M., & Beyer, R. (2012). Coaching athletes with hidden disabilities: Recommendations and strategies for coaching education. *Strategies: A Journal for Physical and Sport Educators, 25*(3), 32–33. https://doi.org/10.1080/08924562.2012.10592150

Wiersma, L. D., & Sherman, C. P. (2005). Volunteer youth sport coaches' perspectives of coaching education/certificates and parental codes of conduct. *Research Quarterly for Exercise and Sport, 76*(3), 324–338. https://doi.org/10.1080/02701367.2005.10599299

Wylie, K., McAllister, L., Davidson, B., & Marshall, J. (2013). Changing practice: Implications of the World Report on Disability for responding to communication disability in underserved populations. *International Journal of Speech-Language Pathology, 15*(1), 1–13. https://doi.org/10.3109/17549507.2012.745164

3 Working with Athletes with Physical Disabilities

In this chapter, we continue to explore specific sport settings—now focusing on athletes with physical disabilities. While the world stage at the Paralympic Games provides a spotlight and nowadays much public attention, of course much work goes into the preparation for and the process of performance development as a paralympic athlete. And obviously, as in Olympic sports, not all athletes make it to this world stage event—or even aspire to… Importantly, our diverse group of authors includes individuals that can speak authentically about the physically disabled athlete experience. Michael Whitehead was a dedicated multi-sport athlete who sustained a spinal cord injury and subsequently joined the Canadian wheelchair rugby team—representing Canada at six Paralympic Games. Derek Zike is a wheelchair user who identifies as a person with an acquired disability. He is a disabled emerging scholar who earned his PhD in 2025 at the University of Wisconsin-Milwaukee. Authentically, our author groups highlight key considerations for sport, exercise, and performance psychology professionals when working with athletes with physical disabilities, including a person-centered approach as well as communication and language best-practices.

PEOPLE FIRST: MENTAL PERFORMANCE CONSULTING IN PARA SPORT

Sommer Christie, Michael Whitehead, & Penny Werthner

Para sport has grown significantly over the years and continues to demonstrate that it is a top-tier sporting event that requires the same attention and support as non-disabled sports. This contribution outlines key challenges in para sport and considerations for supporting athletes with disabilities. It is essential to mention that although we articulate the uniqueness of working with athletes with disabilities, we avoid making assumptions that suggest they have significantly different needs and experiences from non-disabled athletes (Dieffenbach & Statler, 2012).

When supporting para athletes, getting to know the person first and developing a trusting relationship should be a primary goal. A person-centered approach emphasizes the athlete's autonomy, recognizing them as the experts in their own experience and allowing them to lead the direction of your work together (Rogers, 1959). This approach offers a foundational lens for support, grounded in empathy and respect. Applying this mindset begins with learning about the sport itself and extends to understanding each athlete's distinct context and needs.

Para sport includes a wide range of disciplines (e.g., para ice hockey, boccia), each with a distinct set of rules, adaptive techniques, and equipment. Although the rules of some sports might be similar to those of non-disabled sports, others are entirely unique, such as wheelchair

DOI: 10.4324/9781003781486-3

rugby and Goalball. To appropriately support athletes, it is essential to learn about the sport (e.g., rules, equipment, structure) and the specific needs of each athlete (e.g., guides, adaptive equipment). You might, for example, need to work with both an athlete and their guide on mental performance skills.

A common misconception is that para athletes embody what is characterized as a *supercrip* identity, whereby they are proud to be seen as someone who has overcome their disability in ways that are seen as inspiring to a non-disabled population. The supercrip identity is nuanced and can be seen as "offering both a disempowering and an empowering experience for people with disabilities" (Berger, 2008, p. 647); thus, it is crucial to understand the individual athlete's perspective before relying on assumptions. Para athletes are not simply athletes who "inspire" others due to their disabilities; they are skilled competitors who should be recognized for their athleticism, not simply for overcoming adversity. Practitioners should continuously reflect on their own biases, cultural assumptions, and beliefs about disability, as these will shape their approach to working with athletes.

Another key consideration when working in para sport is the language practitioners use. The use of person-first language (e.g., "athletes with disabilities" rather than "disabled athletes") is encouraged by many associations, including the International Paralympic Committee (IPC). Para athlete and para sport are also acceptable (IPC, 2021). When referring to an athlete's disability, it is important to use the appropriate terminology (e.g., athlete with a vision impairment). It is also important to avoid terms that imply individuals with disabilities are experiencing suffering or have a diminished quality of life (e.g., "suffers from" or "wheelchair-bound"). Ultimately, individuals may have personal preferences for how they self-identify, and if you are unsure, you can respectfully ask them. In our experience, para athletes prefer honest and open interactions without excessive concern over terminology. Each consultant should take time to learn about the environment and the athletes to develop an effective communication strategy and build rapport.

In practice, effective communication also depends on how practitioners position themselves, demonstrate respect, and tailor their approach to the individual needs of each athlete. This includes maintaining eye-level interaction, speaking in clear and straightforward language, and being mindful of different learning styles, particularly when working with athletes who may have a cognitive impairment. Depending on the athlete's impairment, you may also need to adapt your counseling skills. For example, you may need to adjust your active listening skills (e.g., nodding) when working with an athlete with a visual impairment (Bawden, 2006). Depending on the nature of the disability, you may also interact with an interpreter or personal support worker. In this scenario, it is important that you speak directly to the athlete.

Classification is a distinctive feature of para sport aimed at ensuring fair competition for athletes with disabilities. It involves categorizing athletes into classes based on the degree to which their impairment impacts the basic activities of their specific sport (IPC, 2015). The classification process is often experienced as a highly stressful event (Miller et al., 2024). The class assigned to an athlete can significantly impact their pathway (e.g., fast-tracking favorably classed athletes or lost opportunities for unfavorably classed athletes) and ability to succeed in sports (Martins Patatas et al., 2020), and can sometimes lead to being "classed out" of their sport altogether. Classification has been heavily critiqued over concerns such as power imbalances, subjectivity, fairness, and system accuracy, leaving athletes highly vulnerable to the process and the classifiers with the power to execute it (e.g., Lawson et al., 2023). Given the psychological and performance implications of classification, practitioners must approach this process with sensitivity and support. When supporting athletes through classification, mental performance consultants should work collaboratively with coaches and integrated support team (IST) members to provide holistic care before, during, and after classification (Christie et al., 2025). This includes helping athletes manage stress, maintain focus, and process the emotional impact of the experience (Christie et al., 2025).

While athletes with disabilities share many of the same challenges as their non-disabled counterparts (e.g., performance expectations, risk of injury), they also encounter distinct barriers that require careful consideration. Accessibility is a central concern, as athletes might face challenges with travel (e.g., navigating airports, finding accessible transportation), accommodation (e.g., inaccessible rooms, carpeted floors that hinder wheelchair access), and venue accessibility (e.g., access to ramps, elevators, or bathrooms). Daily activities, such as sightseeing or navigating the competition venue, can also present significant hurdles. This is particularly important in competition when athletes aim to peak physically and maximize rest and recovery. To ensure your consulting environment is accessible, you must consider factors like room access (stairs, doorway width), room layout (space for a wheelchair or extra chair for interpreter), and your position (eye-level interaction).

Creating an accessible consulting environment is only one part of offering inclusive support. When working with athletes with a disability, avoid making the assumption that an athlete needs assistance. Be mindful that athletes with disabilities may take longer to complete tasks, but rushing to help them can undermine their independence. Asking the athlete directly how to help before acting respects their autonomy and independence. A simple "I'm here if you need anything" goes a long way in letting athletes know you are available without overstepping.

While mental performance consultants do not manage injury or illness, it is crucial to understand the possible psychological effects from medical and physiological considerations when working with athletes with disabilities, as their bodies might respond differently to exercise and environmental conditions. For example, athletes with spinal cord injuries (SCIs) may experience lower heart rates, impaired breathing, and difficulty regulating body temperature. Disability-related injuries, like pressure sores, urinary tract infections, and shoulder injuries in wheelchair users, can interfere with daily functioning and training and can cause additional stress and time away from training (e.g., Fagher et al., 2020). These challenges, if not properly managed, can lead to increased stress and anxiety and affect both training and competition.

Another important consideration is adapting mental skills interventions to align with the athlete's abilities. For example, when working on imagery, practitioners should be mindful of the language and examples they use, as some athletes may have limited capacity to visualize (e.g., due to visual impairment), may not have limbs (e.g., amputees), or may lack sensation in certain areas of the body (e.g., individuals with SCI). Similarly, when implementing skills such as breathing, relaxation, or biofeedback, it is essential to note that heart rate, respiration rate, and blood pressure may vary depending on the athlete's disability. As a result, techniques may need to be adjusted accordingly. Additionally, competition plans may require a greater focus on accessibility considerations (e.g., transport, elevators, wheelchair ramps) and competition needs (e.g., guides, equipment). The practitioner must continually reflect, adapt, and innovate to tailor mental skills training to their athletes.

In conclusion, working with athletes with disabilities requires a person-centered approach (Rogers, 1959), emphasizing their identity as people first. These athletes should be seen as performers with specialized skills and determination, rather than defined by their disability. The culture of para sport is one of inclusion, perseverance, and mutual respect, and those working in the field will find it deeply rewarding to be part of this empowering environment. By prioritizing the needs of the athletes, fostering inclusivity, and applying principles of mental performance consulting with sensitivity and expertise, practitioners can help these athletes thrive both on and off the field.

WORKING WITH ATHLETES WITH ACQUIRED PHYSICAL DISABILITIES

Derek M. Zike

Athletes with acquired physical disabilities face a host of unique challenges in their participation and performance in sport, particularly when transitioning from non-disabled sport. When consulting with these athletes, it is essential to understand those challenges and how to effectively address them to provide adequate support. Acquired physical disabilities are impairments that develop during the lifespan, often resulting from accidents, injuries, or other medical conditions. Individuals with such disabilities might experience various physical limitations (e.g., mobility, dexterity, and other functions; Bengtsson, 2008) and psychosocial barriers (e.g., social stigma, emotional distress, and restricted opportunities for peer interaction; Stucki et al., 2002) that can profoundly affect their social participation, athletic identity, and relationship with sport (Perrier et al., 2014; Zike et al., 2025). Collectively, the research highlights the need to understand an athlete's cognitive, affective, and behavioral responses to acquired physical disability. As an author with a physical disability acquired through SCI from a sporting accident, I have drawn on this lived experience in my research with athletes with acquired physical disabilities, and it has greatly informed the development of this chapter contribution. I present a brief case study to highlight some important considerations when working with athletes transitioning from non-disabled to adaptive sport after acquiring a physical disability. This case study will be used to offer key insights into the challenges, resources, and role of consultants when supporting athletes with acquired physical disabilities.

Case Summary: Jasmine

Jasmine, 18, competed nationally as a hockey player until ten months ago, when she acquired a SCI in a car accident. Jasmine is now a disabled young woman living with paraplegia, which prevents her from participating in non-disabled hockey as she once did. This has been devastating because she had invested a great deal of time and effort into her athletic career, viewing success in sport as her primary identity, and aspiring to earn a scholarship to play hockey in college. She found her sport experience deeply fulfilling and gained great confidence in herself through her athletic accomplishments. She also took great pride in her athletic physique and her physical capabilities.

Since her injury, Jasmine has struggled with feelings of loss. Without hockey, she feels that her identity has been taken away. She has also expressed deep insecurity about her body, feeling disconnected from it. She perceives her body as broken and misaligned with what she believes an athletic body should look like, which makes it hard for her to see herself as an athlete. Jasmine's family and sport connections continue to encourage her to explore options for restoring her body to how it once was, even though her progress has plateaued despite her rehabilitation efforts. While returning to non-disabled sport might seem unrealistic, she feels both external and internal pressure to hold on to her athletic life before SCI and restore her body.

Jasmine has expressed a desire to explore options for returning to sport in some way. However, she lacks awareness of adaptive sport options and is reluctant to try them. She is struggling to move past her preconceptions of what sport and performance "should" look like, believing that adaptive sport will not satisfy what she values from sport, nor will it make her an athlete again. Jasmine has also shared that she tries to distance herself from people with disabilities and avoids social situations with them. She wants to minimize visible association with disability to fit in with non-disabled people and avoid appearing abnormal.

Case Insights

The Challenges. This case highlights multiple challenges that athletes with acquired physical disabilities may face as they transition from non-disabled sport to adaptive sport. Jasmine's case emphasizes how individuals who tell a "nonathlete" narrative (Perrier et al., 2014) often experience a foreclosure of their athletic identity due to bodily changes associated with their impairments. Athletes like Jasmine tend to hold rigid attachments to their previous embodied athletic identities, and the constant comparison between their past and present bodies prevents the development of a new athletic identity (Perrier et al., 2014). This underscores the influence of disability stigma. The disabled body, which is often seen as weak, passive, and dependent (DePauw, 1997), does not align with dominant cultural standards of the ideal athletic performative body (Hardin, 2003). Internalizing this stigma can make it difficult for athletes like Jasmine to reclaim their athletic identity and pursue meaningful athletic endeavors.

Jasmine's case also exemplifies a restitution narrative (Frank, 1995), which conveys hope for recovery after illness or injury. In the context of acquired disability, its core storyline is, "Yesterday I was able-bodied, today I'm disabled, but tomorrow I'll be able-bodied again" (Smith & Sparkes, 2005, p. 1096). This narrative is prevalent in Western cultures, and those who share these stories often aim to return to their previous embodiment and lifestyle (Zike, 2025; Zike et al., 2025). Jasmine's social network reinforces this narrative, and because she has no connections with other athletes with disabilities, she has not been introduced to alternative narratives about acquired disability and perspectives on living with disability. Consequently, she lacks an awareness and understanding of adaptive sport, and her assumptions about adaptive sport, rooted in disability stigma, remain unchallenged.

The Resources. To support athletes with acquired physical disabilities, it is crucial to provide appropriate resources to help them navigate these challenges. Participating in adaptive sport has been shown to assist with adapting to acquired physical disabilities (Zike, 2025). Athletes with SCIs report that involvement in adaptive sport helped them cope by reducing stress through play and aiding their acceptance of injury. To help athletes benefit from adaptive sport participation, there are many resources available to connect them with. Numerous organizations, such as the Challenged Athletes Foundation (challengedathletes.org), currently support athletes with physical disabilities by providing a variety of resources, including grants for adaptive equipment, financial aid for training and competitions, and access to sports programs, enabling athletes to lead active lifestyles through physical fitness and competitive sports. Organizations like the Kelly Brush Foundation (kellybrushfoundation.org) specifically support athletes such as Jasmine who have SCIs.

The Role of Consultants. As a sport psychology consultant, there are some practices you can engage in to help support athletes with acquired physical disabilities.

Treat Them Like an Athlete. Focus on the athlete, not the disability. Work with your athlete to identify their athletic purpose and goals for participating in sport. Find out what they already know and what they want to learn about adaptive sport. Talk about their present sport behaviors and what aspects of the sport experience bring them joy. Develop strategies to help them find renewed joy and reach their athletic purpose and sport goals. Research has shown that individuals with acquired physical disabilities who focus on their present sport behaviors and future sport goals share stories that align with a "the present self as athlete" narrative (Perrier et al., 2014). Athletes who shared this narrative demonstrated restored athletic identity and found renewed purpose and joy in their athletic pursuits (Zike, 2025). For an individual like Jasmine, who is unable to pursue their non-disabled sport goals, it is crucial to facilitate the development of future adaptive sport goals.

Normalize Disability in Athletics. Assist athletes in developing an understanding of how someone with a disability can also be an athlete. This may be achieved through repeated exposure to stories of athletes with disabilities. Research indicates that having opportunities to speak to those athletes and see them participating in sports or engaging in everyday activities can help normalize disability, counter disability stigma, and introduce alternative social narratives that facilitate participation in sport (Zike, 2025). These narratives can challenge an athlete like Jasmine's preconceptions about what someone with a disability can do and what defines an athlete. This practice can help reshape their understanding of what it means to be an athlete and better align the meanings of disability and athlete, allowing both to coexist. Athletes who tell a "present self as athlete" narrative do not consider athletes with disabilities as fundamentally different from non-disabled athletes (Perrier et al., 2014). Instead, what they view as the true characteristics of an athlete, regardless of whether they have a disability, is a commitment to sport and making the sacrifices needed to excel. Helping athletes with acquired physical disabilities recognize these characteristics can aid in normalizing athletes with disabilities and their participation in sports.

Conclusion

Jasmine's case highlights the complex challenges athletes encounter when transitioning from non-disabled sport to adaptive sport after acquiring a disability. The struggle to redefine athletic identity amid disability stigma and personal loss is a major obstacle for many, emphasizing the need for comprehensive support systems. By understanding the narratives that athletes share during this transition and how these narratives influence their adaptation, we can better address the challenges they face with the strategies and resources necessary to navigate their new realities.

SUPPORTING ATHLETES WITH DISABILITIES: A SINGAPOREAN PERSPECTIVE

Hansen Bay

The Landscape of Disability Sport in Singapore

Singapore has made progress in creating inclusive sports opportunities, mainly through the government's "Sport without Boundaries" initiative. However, the expansion of disability sports continues to face challenges, which can be broadly classified as intrinsic and environmental barriers. Intrinsic barriers include a lack of awareness about available sports opportunities among persons with disabilities (PwDs) and their caregivers. Environmental barriers stem from inaccessible sports facilities, social attitudes, and infrastructure limitations (Committee for Disability

Sports, 2016). Despite these challenges, opportunities exist to improve awareness, upgrade infrastructure, and reduce financial and transport-related barriers. To address these ongoing challenges and facilitate participation, the government introduced the Disability Sports Master Plan (DSMP) as a strategic framework to advance inclusive sports development.

The Disability Sports Master Plan

The DSMP, initiated after the 8th ASEAN Para Games in 2015, focuses on increasing grassroots participation in disability sports. Its core principles include ensuring inclusive participation opportunities, adopting a life-cycle approach to support PwDs of all ages, and leveraging partnerships across the people, private, and public sectors to maximize impact. Since its launch, the DSMP has achieved several key milestones: Participation of PwDs in community sports programs has increased (Singapore Disability Sports Council, 2023), and inclusive facilities such as the Enabling Village and ActiveSG gyms have been developed (MSF, 2022; Sport Singapore, 2022). Adaptive physical education has also been expanded to more schools (MSF, 2022). The implementation of the DSMP is largely driven by key organizations, with the Singapore Disability Sports Council (SDSC) taking the lead in operationalizing its objectives and helping to grow disability sports nationwide.

The Singapore Disability Sports Council

The SDSC, as the national body for disability sports, provides a structured sports development pathway for PwDs from grassroots participation to elite competition. SDSC offers programs in 18 sports and supports athlete development for local and international competitions. Working closely with other organizations, such as Special Olympics Singapore, the Deaf Sports Association, and Tan Tock Seng Rehabilitation Centre, SDSC organizes key events such as the National Para-Swimming Championships and supports the development of athletes for international competitions, including the Paralympic Games and ASEAN Para Games.

One such initiative is Goalball, a team sport for the blind introduced by SDSC in 2015. In the next section, I share my experience coaching the Women's Goalball Team for the 11th ASEAN Para Games in 2022, focusing on the integration of psychological skills and the challenges of supporting a diverse group of athletes with visual impairment.

Case Study: Psychological Skills Support for the Women's Goalball Team

My involvement with the women's Goalball team began in 2015 through a broader national initiative under the DSMP. In 2022, the SDSC appointed me to prepare the Women's Goalball Team for the 11th ASEAN Para Games held in Surakarta, Indonesia. While I served as coach, my primary occupation is as a mental performance consultant to national sports associations.

Goalball teams consist of five players. The team I worked with was diverse in terms of socioeconomic background, ethnicity, sporting experiences, commitment levels, and type and degree of visual impairment. The diversity posed challenges in fostering a unified approach to training and competition, especially when some players were more dedicated or experienced than others. I had to ensure that these differences did not hinder team cohesion, and that each player felt supported, valued, and motivated to contribute to the team's success.

Although I am qualified as a mental performance coach, I remained mindful of potential challenges that might arise from my dual role as both coach and psychologist, particularly regarding boundaries and conflicting interests. Consequently, I made it clear that my focus would be on coaching the sport and facilitating group psychological skills sessions. Additionally, a certified athlete counselor based in the United States provided individual online support, which was critical, as several players had a history of mental health challenges.

Program Description

Given the team's diversity, a strong sense of unity was important for developing psychological attributes like confidence, motivation, and resilience (Paradis & Martin, 2012). I facilitated cohesion sessions that encouraged players to share challenges and personal goals, and guided reflections on each other's strengths and uniqueness. These sessions highlighted how individual differences could support or limit team goals, fostering mutual support and alignment with shared values. While the cohesion sessions are similar to those for able-bodied athletes, players with visual impairment (VI) often require more attention. For example, those with lower or no vision needed additional support, such as help navigating to training and during practice. Some also felt less valued than better-sighted teammates, increasing the need for inclusive communication and validation.

Bronfenbrenner's Ecological Systems Theory (2006), particularly the microsystem, which highlights how peers, coaches, family, and workplaces shape resilience and development, informed most of my interventions. I organized social activities like hikes and casual lunches to build relationships and encourage shared responsibility among players, volunteers, officials, and employers. This support network helped address practical challenges identified during cohesion sessions. Teammates and volunteers began coordinating transport or accompanying each other, improving attendance. Involving families and employers also increased understanding and schedule flexibility, supporting players' training commitment. I would like to think that this stronger sense of community helped reduce feelings of inequality.

Additionally, the regular Goalball training sessions were integrated with the development of psychological skills such as goal-setting and attentional control. For example, I would vary practice conditions to simulate pressure (Davids et al., 2008) and facilitate discussions to enhance players' awareness of distractions and their ability to refocus on process goals.

Brief Summary of Results

The program's focus on team cohesion was key to the team's success at the 11th ASEAN Para Games. Players learned to manage interpersonal differences and resolve conflict constructively. This was especially important in Goalball, where athletes with visual impairment rely heavily on trust and clear communication.

Providing technical coaching alongside psychological skills training was advantageous as my familiarity with the athletes and training context allowed me to integrate psychological skills with technical and tactical practice sessions, enhancing their application during competitions. The athlete counselor provided individual online support to maintain appropriate boundaries and ensure individual concerns were addressed confidentially. Given that athletes with disabilities often face higher rates of mental health challenges compared to their able-bodied peers (Zabala-Dominguez et al., 2023), this additional layer of psychological support was especially valuable. Improved support from families, employers, and volunteers also helped reduce logistical pressures and strengthened emotional support. This allowed players to commit more fully to training and competition.

Together, these elements helped the players to perform better under pressure. In the semi-finals against host nation Indonesia, the team secured victory with a golden goal in extra time. They went on to win the silver medal, marking Singapore's first podium finish in Goalball at the ASEAN Para Games.

EDITORS' TAKEAWAYS

We are very grateful that we were able to solicit contributions from two authors that actually can share lived experiences as athletes and performers with physical disabilities for this chapter. Being able to engage with a first-person, lived experience is always powerful. As such Christie, Whitehead, and Werthner's contribution is such a helpful reminder that athletes with physical disabilities are people first and foremost—just as able-bodied athletes. For sport, exercise, and performance psychology professionals (SEPPPs), then it is essential to embrace a person-centered, not a disability-centered approach when working with such clients as well as be aware of personal biases and explore blind spots one might have. Zeke builds on the wealth of helpful insights into specific experiential aspects and challenges one might have to consider and explore when working with athletes with disabilities shared by Christie and colleagues, and brings them to life with his case study focused on athletes navigating adjusting their personal and athletic identity after acquiring SCI. A key message he shares: You as the SEPPP are not alone in this with your client, and you should actively engage other key stakeholders. Bay, sharing his Singaporean perspective, again builds on this notion. He presents another case example where he highlights using Bronfenbrenner's Ecological Systems Theory to guide context-specific program creation. The insights he shares about the development of the national sporting landscape for para sport athletes from an organizational, structural, and governmental level serve as a good reference point for readers to research how the landscape might look in one's own national context.

RECOMMENDED EXERCISES

1 Reflect on your assumptions about athletes with disabilities. Write down any preconceived notions or biases and explore how they might shape your approach to working with these athletes. How can you challenge yourself and overcome these biases to provide more empowering support?
2 Consider a scenario where you are helping an athlete with a physical disability prepare for a competition. List potential accessibility issues they might face pertaining to travel, accommodations, or competition venues. How would you ensure that these challenges are addressed? What kind of support can you offer to make their experience as smooth and empowering as possible?
3 Athletes with the same disability might have different needs. How will you determine each athlete's unique needs and individualize your support?
4 Consider a situation where you might be working with an athlete with a sensory disability (e.g., hearing or visual impairment). How would you adapt your communication style to ensure effective interaction? What changes would you make to your body language, tone, or use of assistive tools?
5 Reflect on a mental skills technique you commonly use (e.g., visualization, relaxation). How might you adapt this technique for an athlete with a disability? For instance, how

would you modify imagery exercises for an athlete with a visual impairment or an athlete with a high-level SCI? What considerations would be important to ensure the intervention is effective and respectful of their unique needs?

6 Using the same mental skills technique from question 5, reflect on how you would adapt the technique for an athlete with a different disability. What considerations would be important to ensure the intervention is effective and respectful of this athlete's unique needs?
7 What potential stressors or emotional challenges might arise for an athlete going through the classification process? How could you, as a consultant, support them in navigating this process in a way that promotes confidence and reduces anxiety?
8 Think about how you would feel if you were an athlete going through the classification process. What support would you want in navigating this process in a way that promotes confidence and reduces anxiety?

REFERENCES

Bawden, M. (2006). Providing sport psychology support for athletes with disabilities. In J. Dosil (Ed.), *The sport psychologist's handbook: A guide for sport-specific performance enhancement* (pp. 665–683). John Wiley & Sons. https://doi.org/10.1002/9780470713174.ch29

Bengtsson, S. (2008). *Handicap og samfundsdeltakelse 2006 (Disability and participation 2006)*. SFI-rapport 08:18. Socialforskningsinstituttet.

Berger, R. J. (2008). Disability and the dedicated wheelchair athlete: Beyond the "supercrip" critique. *Journal of Contemporary Ethnography, 37*(6), 647–678. https://doi.org/10.1177/0891241607309892

Bronfenbrenner, U. (2006). *The ecology of human development: Experiments by nature and design*. Harvard University Press.

Christie, S., Côté, P., McRoberts, M., & Smith, S. (2025, October 15–18). Classification in parasport: An integrated approach to support [Workshop session]. In *Association for Applied Sport Psychology (AASP) Annual Conference,* Montréal, Québec, Canada. https://appliedsportpsych.org/annual-conference/

Committee for Disability Sports. (2016). *Disability sports master plan (Full report)*. Ministry of Culture, Community and Youth, Singapore.

Davids, K., Button, C., & Bennett, S. (2008). *Dynamics of skill acquisition: A constraints-led approach*. Human Kinetics.

DePauw, K. (1997). The (in)visibility of disability: Cultural contexts and "sporting bodies." *Quest, 49*(4), 416–430. https://doi.org/10.1080/00336297.1997.10484258

Dieffenbach, K. D., & Statler, T. A. (2012). More similar than different: The psychological environment of Paralympic sport. *Journal of Sport Psychology in Action, 3*(2), 109–118. https://doi.org/10.1080/21520704.2012.683322

Fagher, K., Dahlström, Ö., Jacobsson, J., Timpka, T., & Lexell, J. (2020). Prevalence of sports-related injuries and illnesses in Paralympic athletes. *Physical Medicine and Rehabilitation Clinics of North America, 12*(3), 271–280. https://doi.org/10.1002/pmrj.12211

Frank, A. W. (1995). *The wounded storyteller*. University of Chicago Press.

Hardin, M. (2003). Marketing the acceptably athletic image: Wheelchair athletes, sport-related advertising and capitalist hegemony. *Disability Studies Quarterly, 23*(1), 108–125. https://doi.org/10.18061/dsq.v23i1.403

International Paralympic Committee. (2015). *Athlete classification code*. https://www.paralympic.org

International Paralympic Committee. (2021, August). *IPC guide to para and IPC terminology*. https://www.paralympic.org/sites/default/files/2021-08/IPC%20Guide%20to%20Para%20and%20IPC%20Terminology.pdf

Lawson, J. A., Williams, T., & Latimer-Cheung, A. E. (2023). Exploring athletes' and classifiers' experiences with and understanding of classification in Para sport. *Qualitative Research in Sport, Exercise and Health, 15*(4), 516–531. https://doi.org/10.1080/2159676X.2022.2152084

Martins Patatas, J., De Bosscher, V., Derom, I., & De Rycke, J. (2020). Managing parasport: An investigation of sport policy factors and stakeholders influencing para-athletes' career pathways. *Sport Management Review, 23*(5), 937–951. https://doi.org/10.1016/j.smr.2019.12.004

Miller, B., Barker, J. B., Hunton, E., & Plateau, C. R. (2024). Understanding experiences of and influences on well-being in elite para-sport: A qualitative exploration of U.K. para-athletes. *Sport, Exercise, and Performance Psychology, 13*(2), 126–143. https://doi.org/10.1037/spy0000342

Ministry of Social and Family Development. (2022). *Enabling Masterplan 2030 report: Empower, engage, enable.* https://www.msf.gov.sg/docs/default-source/enabling-masterplan/emp2030-report-(final2).pdf?sfvrsn=8032eb4d_3

Paradis, K. F., & Martin, L. J. (2012). Team building in sport: Linking theory and research to practical application. *Journal of Sport Psychology in Action, 3*(3), 159–170. https://doi.org/10.1080/21520704.2011.653047

Perrier, M. J., Strachan, S. M., Smith, B., & Latimer-Cheung, A. E. (2014). Narratives of athletic identity after acquiring a permanent physical disability. *Adapted Physical Activity Quarterly, 31*(2), 106–124. https://doi.org/10.1123/apaq.2012-0076

Rogers, C. R. (1959). The essence of psychotherapy: A client-centered view. *Annals of Psychotherapy, 1*, 51–57.

Singapore Disability Sports Council. (2023). *Annual report 2022.* https://www.sdsc.org.sg/wp-content/uploads/2024/04/2022-2023-Annual-Report.pdf

Smith, B., & Sparkes, A. C. (2005). Men, sport, spinal cord injury, and narratives of hope. *Social Science & Medicine, 61*(5), 1095–1105. https://doi.org/10.1016/j.socscimed.2005.01.011

Sport Singapore. (2022). *Empowering persons with disabilities to live better through sport.* https://sportcares.sportsingapore.gov.sg/files/Update%20on%20DSMP_25%20May%202022.pdf

Stucki, G., Cieza, A., Ewert, T., Kostanjsek, N., Chatterji, S., & Üstün, T. B. (2002). Application of the International Classification of Functioning, Disability and Health (ICF) in clinical practice. *Disability and Rehabilitation, 24*(5), 281–282.

Zabala-Dominguez, O., Rubio Florido, I., Lázaro Fernández, Y., & Borrajo Mena, E. (2023). Life satisfaction and psychological capital in athletes with physical disabilities. *Behavioral Sciences, 13*(12), 1010. https://doi.org/10.3390/bs13121010

Zike, D. M. (2025). *Having, being, and living: Stories of disability by women athletes after spinal cord injury* (Publication No. 32117503) [Doctoral dissertation, University of Wisconsin–Milwaukee]. ProQuest Dissertations & Theses.

Zike, D. M., Hansen, M. A., & Arvinen-Barrow, M. (2025). Psychosocial factors associated with athlete adaptation to spinal cord injury: A systematic review. *Disability and Rehabilitation, 47*(11), 2735–2747. https://doi.org/10.1080/09638288.2024.2406981

4 Working in Youth Sport

Working with youth athletes is a unique and rewarding area of sport psychology practice, requiring sport, exercise, and performance psychology professionals (SEPPPs) to tailor their approaches to the developmental, cognitive, and emotional needs of young performers. Youth sport presents distinct challenges and opportunities, as athletes are still forming their identities, learning fundamental skills, and navigating the social dynamics of peers, coaches, and parents. Effective service delivery in this context often involves balancing performance enhancement with broader goals of personal growth, enjoyment, and long-term engagement in sport. As such, we must adapt our communication, interventions, and expectations to align with the athlete's stage of development while collaborating closely with key stakeholders to create a supportive environment. To help us navigate these dynamics, we have solicited three author groups with expertise in youth populations to help provide some practical service delivery strategies.

TRANSCONTINENTAL SUCCESS FACTORS FOR DOING SPORT PSYCHOLOGY WITH YOUTH: STAKEHOLDER ENGAGEMENT AND PRIORITIZING FUN IN SERVICE DELIVERY

Amanda J. Visek & Lindsey C. Blom

Youth athletes represent the largest population of sport participants worldwide—and doing sport psychology with them requires distinct considerations given their ongoing development and the complex systems surrounding them. To navigate the multiple interacting systems, the youth sport consulting model developed by Visek and colleagues (2009) offered sport psychology practitioners the first athlete-centered framework for addressing unique characteristics of youth sport from planning to implementing to evaluating service delivery. Building on this, Arvinen-Barrow and Visek (2025) highlighted how ecological systems and post-pandemic realities shape youth athlete experiences and service delivery today. They identified service delivery success factors for sport psychology practitioners to consider in today's post-pandemic era. This chapter examines two of those success factors, relevant within the early planning and implementation phases of service provision, that are universally pertinent when working with youth athletes: (1) involving adult stakeholders, and (2) making it fun. We discuss these factors drawing on our applied experiences working in youth sport across North America, Europe, Africa, and Asia, with an emphasis on approaches that transcend cultural and geographical boundaries.

DOI: 10.4324/9781003781486-4

Involve Adult Stakeholders

Working with youth athletes inevitably requires engaging adult stakeholders, primarily sport parents/caregivers, sport coaches, and occasionally sport administrators, who play critical roles in the athletic ecosystems involving minors (Blom et al., 2013). The youth athlete is at the center of these interacting relational dynamics—and maintaining an athlete-centered approach is key to the success of the athlete. While there are numerous ways to involve adult stakeholders, effective involvement must be intentional, collaborative, and culturally sensitive. What follows are approaches we have taken to engaging and maintaining adult stakeholders' involvement.

In the early phase of service delivery, define each stakeholder's role in supporting the youth athlete. In our experiences, parents and coaches are often eager to learn what they can do to support and contribute to the growth and success of their youth athlete(s). Offering guidance on how they can reinforce mental skills, such as using shared language from sessions (e.g., self-talk phrases, focus cues) and how they can model healthy coping strategies are tangible ways they can contribute. Alongside role clarity, it is important to seek athlete input on the involvement of referent others. In other words, encourage the youth athlete to express how much involvement they want from parents and coaches. This gives the youth athlete a voice by honoring their autonomy. In turn, this can strengthen the athlete's engagement and concurrently respect their growing sense of independence and agency, especially among older adolescent athletes. Likewise, foster two-way communication by inviting parents and coaches to share observations and concerns. Open communication among adult stakeholders that co-informs and co-educates is instrumental in establishing and maintaining healthy partnerships (Blom et al., 2013). This helps sport psychology practitioners triangulate information for a fuller context, and in turn, sport psychology practitioners can offer context-specific strategies. For example, if a coach notices an athlete shutting down under pressure or after a forced error, the sport psychology practitioner can guide the coach in how to navigate those instances, sharing emotion regulation and self-talk tools tailored to that situation that (re)focuses the athlete.

In parallel to promoting a culture of open communication, maintaining ongoing communication with adult stakeholders helps coaches and parents feel informed, empowered, and aligned with the sport psychology practitioner's efforts. Creative communication channels for doing this can include brief digestible resources such as infographics summarizing key mental skills, newsletters with tips on how to support youth athletes, and short videos or podcasts explaining psychological concepts and their application in sport. Curating these resources, or leveraging existing resources on the market, is useful for connecting adult stakeholders to content that can foster further buy-in of the benefits of sport psychology and bolster understanding and knowledge. Subsequently, enhanced understanding and knowledge will increase the chances that the mental skills being taught to athletes are reinforced in practices and competitions, as well as in home settings (Moore et al., 2021). This can accelerate athletes' learning while providing opportunities for real-time trial, error, and correction in supportive environments with adult stakeholders. For example, in a youth soccer program, we provided a slick sheet on focus cues that parents could reference during car rides home, while coaches were given laminated cards with reminders to reinforce team-wide self-talk routines during practice.

Involving adult stakeholders in intentional and collaborative ways enhances the quality and sustainability of the applied sport psychology work with youth athletes, and in turn, increases opportunities for athletes to internalize the new mental skills they are acquiring, apply them consistently, and remain engaged. That said, cultural norms will also influence the degree and nature of adult involvement. In some contexts, for instance, parents may step back during adolescence; in others, they may remain highly involved. In other instances, parents may have different expectations around gender participation at various developmental levels. Sport psychology practitioners should assess cultural norms early and adapt their engagement strategies accordingly in ways that balance both the athlete and adult stakeholders' needs simultaneously.

Make It Fun

The research is clear in sport: having fun fosters sustained participation, performance, and personal development. Further, fun is not trivial amusement or happen chance. It is a personally meaningful experience, marked by positive emotions, intrinsic motivation, satisfaction, and growth (Visek et al., 2015, 2023). Making sport psychology fun for youth athletes is an essential factor that is both a science and an art (Arvinen-Barrow & Visek, 2025). Originally undertaken to identify the full spectrum of fun determinants in organized sport settings, the fun integration theory (see Visek et al., 2015 for further reading) offers a highly adaptable, athlete-centered, evidence-based framework that sport psychology practitioners can embrace as a philosophical foundation of service delivery. What follows are approaches we have taken, grounded in fun integration theory, that make fun an intentional and core component of sport psychology practice. When considering the approaches described, it is important that sport psychology practitioners reflect on the youth populations they intend to serve and how cultural nuances might influence how fun is experienced in youth athletes' sport experiences. For example, consider the ways in which values and rituals rooted in individualism versus collectivism impact cultural aspects of social connections and fun priorities.

Globally, we have learned to first and foremost commit to fun as both a process and outcome of service delivery. Doing so includes actively listening to youth athletes and being responsive to what motivates and excites them (Visek et al., 2015). When youth athletes feel seen and heard, they are more likely to meaningfully engage in the process. Embedding fun in session design is about creating psychologically safe, autonomy supportive, and engaging learning environments that empower youth athletes through voice and choice. As an example, allowing them autonomy in the direction of the sport psychology work engages them in the co-creation of sessions that demonstrates their level of needs awareness, establishes a working alliance built on trust and collaboration, and facilitates self-expression. Illustrations of this could be: (1) prompting the youth athletes(s) to define what success or confidence or failure means in their own words; (2) giving them choice in how they express themselves, whether through writing, drawing, or metaphor; and (3) giving them agency in the creative materials and technologies they use (e.g., colored pens, sticky notes, tablet) that reflect their personality (Arvinen-Barrow & Visek, 2025). Couple this in response with purposeful humor and culturally relevant language that connects with artful storytelling and "sticky" allegory the athlete will remember easily.

Fun is also experiential. Design interactive, positive challenge-based learning activities that reinforce mental skills. For instance, gamified elements, such as timed challenges with creative constraints keep engagement high. Once skills like deep breathing and focused concentration are learned well independently, increase the challenge by combining mental skill applications. As an example, facilitate "pressure plays" where athletes use self-talk cues before executing a sport-specific skill under time constraints as a way to learn controlled breathing and focus. Moreover, in the process of in-session activities, or those given as out-of-session activities to complete, incorporate feedback loops with positivity and encouragement that allow for mistakes and errors as part of the learning process. Sport psychology sessions should serve as an exemplary model of communication—and feedback must be growth oriented. Toward that growth, involve youth athletes in goal setting, strategy development, and reflection. This will create mental skills training experiences that meet athletes' psychological needs, offer social connection, provide for skill mastery, and facilitate meaningful engagement that culminates in having fun acquiring the mental skills to thrive and grow.

TEACHING MENTAL SKILLS TO TWEENS

E. Earlynn Lauer, Larry Lauer, & Rebecca A. Zakrajsek

Sport plays a significant role in the lives of many children, with over 50% of youth aged 6–17 in the United States participating in organized activities (Youth Sport Facts, 2022). Tweens, typically aged 10 to 12–13, represent a substantial portion of these participants; yet, this group is often misunderstood. Tweens are in a transitional stage between childhood and adolescence, experiencing significant physical, psychological, and social developmental changes. Despite this, they are sometimes viewed as "little adults," with insufficient recognition of their ongoing growth and maturation (Flett et al., 2012). This developmental stage provides an ideal opportunity for mental performance coaches (MPCs) to teach tweens how to regulate their thoughts, emotions, and behaviors in sports (Lauer et al., 2020; Zakrajsek et al., 2017). However, the field of sport psychology has historically focused on college-aged athletes, leaving a gap in research and applied practice with youth athletes, including tweens. As a result, many MPCs in training are underprepared to address the unique characteristics of this population.

This chapter will explore three key areas essential for working with tweens in sport: (1) developmental considerations that include cognitive, emotional, and environmental factors, (2) ways to build rapport with tweens, and (3) strategies for working with tweens. By addressing these topics, readers will gain an understanding of the unique challenges and opportunities in supporting tweens through their mental skills development.

Developmental Considerations for Tweens

Tweens are on the cusp of several developmental changes associated with puberty and adolescence. Cognitively, capacities such as abstract reasoning begin to emerge, allowing tweens to start to think beyond concrete concepts and consider possibilities, hypothetical scenarios, and broader implications. It is important to note, however, that these abilities are typically still in their infancy, and tweens may still struggle to critically understand and, perhaps more importantly, apply abstract concepts. Tweens are often still prone to thinking concretely (e.g., thinking, "If I win once, then I should be able to win again") or in extremes (e.g., thinking "I'm terrible" or "I'm amazing"). MPCs need to be aware of this oscillation between concrete and abstract thinking that often occurs with this age group.

Emotionally, tweens are in the beginning stages of hormonal shifts that coincide with puberty; therefore, they may experience large swings in their emotions that they struggle to understand. Socially, tweens tend to overemphasize comparisons with their peers, often using simplistic, concrete markers (e.g., rankings, lineups) to understand their sporting abilities. Frustratingly, aspects of the sport environment are also often changing for tweens as these developmental shifts are starting to occur, creating even more potential disruptions to their sport experience. As tweens transition to higher competitive levels, characterized by more deliberate practice and skill development, they may face pressures to improve their skills to stay competitive with their peers. These pressures might even be purposefully or implicitly exacerbated by tweens' coaches. For example, coaches, often with good intentions, might compare young athletes to peers or role models to encourage improvement. However, tweens may still struggle to reason with this information because of their tendency to think concretely (e.g., thinking, "If I'm not the example, then I'm not good enough") and overemphasize the significance of the comparison (e.g., "Coach will only like me if I'm the example"). These comparisons can even lead tweens to adopt conditional self-worth, causing them to treat themselves based on perceived external judgments (see McHenry et al., 2021). These challenges might explain high sport dropout rates during this stage. Helping tweens manage these stressors can enhance their motivation and engagement in sport participation, thereby reducing attrition.

Building Rapport with Tweens

Working with tweens requires several consulting and teaching skills specific to this age group. Below are several suggestions for effectively building rapport with tweens.

Speak Their Language

Use language that is direct and simple to understand. Avoid using academic jargon and instead create simple, specific terms that you can use with tweens (e.g., instead of "pre-performance routine," simply use "routine"). Similarly, avoid using terminology to describe the process of mental performance work. For example, it is better to say "In this first session, we'll just get to know each other" instead of saying "In this first session, we'll complete a client intake."

Ask Age-Appropriate Questions

Tweens tend to be "in-between" abstract and concrete thinking. One way to help tween athletes make abstract concepts (e.g., confidence, focus, resilience) more concrete is by asking them to provide observable behaviors for each concept. For example, a mental coach could ask, "What do resilient athletes do?" or, "What does confidence look like?" This can also help the MPC assess tweens' understanding of these concepts.

Use Narrative and Story

Using narrative and story can be a powerful way to engage with tween athletes. Asking them to "tell the story" of a particular experience might be easier than asking recall questions. MPCs can even ask tween athletes to create a story about a hypothetical experience (e.g., "Write a story about how you would react to making a mistake and then refocusing"). This approach can tap into tweens' imaginative abilities while allowing them to apply their mental skills, knowledge, and strategies in a real-world way.

Be Authentic and Engaged

Tweens can lack a social filter and tell you exactly what they think. Be authentic in your interest in tweens' experiences and points of view. Listen actively and use reflecting and summarizing skills to demonstrate genuine engagement. Provide positive reinforcement and demonstrate positive regard when they share their experiences. Avoid patronizing tweens (e.g., using sarcasm, belittling tweens' experiences, using overly simple language) as it can cause them to disengage and lose interest.

Teaching Mental Skills to Tweens

Effective MPCs use a variety of teaching methods, such as discussions, goal-setting exercises, and exploratory activities with tweens to maintain their engagement and maximize learning and retention. Tweens appreciate interactive and dynamic approaches, especially when these methods align with their developmental stage. Below are some strategies for effectively teaching mental skills to tweens.

Promote Positive Comparisons

Tweens tend to overemphasize the outcome. Encourage tweens to compare their progress to their own past performance rather than to their peers by setting process goals for practices and competitions. Teach tweens the differences between process and outcome goals and how to effectively use goals to create a mastery-oriented mindset.

Build Intentionality

Use reflective practices to help tweens develop purposeful thinking and engagement in practice. For example, using a journal can help tweens build both planning (e.g., setting process goals before a practice) and reflection (e.g., evaluating their process goals post-practice or monitoring goal achievement over time) skills.

Normalize Stress and Anxiety

Help tweens understand that stress and anxiety are a normal part of sport. Openly discuss stress and anxiety using stories of tweens' lived experiences in sport. Use these exercises as opportunities to teach strategies such as breathing and imagery within simple routines.

Make Mental Skills Practical

Collaborate with tweens to determine how best to make mental skills "sticky" using catchy phrases (e.g., "Breathe and Believe," see Lauer et al., 2020). In addition, create clear plans for using mental skills during performance (e.g., take a diaphragmatic breath after a mistake).

Conclusion

Tweens occupy a unique developmental stage that presents challenges and opportunities for mental performance coaching in sport. Their cognitive, emotional, and environmental transitions require tailored approaches that align with their developmental needs. By addressing these considerations, building meaningful rapport, and using age-appropriate teaching methods, MPCs can foster important mental skills. Strategies such as focusing on process goals, building reflective skills, normalizing stress, and collaborating on practical strategies can help tweens navigate the demands of sport while equipping them with skills for lifelong growth and well-being.

SPORT PSYCHOLOGY SERVICE THAT SUPPORTS COACHES IN THEIR ROLE AS CULTURAL LEADER USING HOLISTIC ECOLOGICAL WORKING MODELS

Louise Kamuk Storm, Jacob Vinholt, & Kristoffer Henriksen

The youth sport coach has many roles; one of them is as a cultural leader. Youth sport has the potential to have a positive impact on young people. Not only does it provide opportunities for athletic development, but it also plays a vital role in building character, life skills, coherent groups, and positive experiences. However, to realize this potential, it is essential to foster a good environment and a culture that is supportive of all participants. A cultural leader is

> the professional and social role of a person who has legitimacy (is in the position) and responsibility to develop, maintain, and (if needed) attempt to change the culture of a group of learners, such as pupils or athletes, in the service of good.
>
> (Storm et al., 2024, p. 4)

Cultural leadership is a meta-function. This means that at the same time as they are setting up exercises, instructing, and giving feedback, coaches are also always leading culture and developing the environment (Henriksen et al., 2018). With this role comes a special responsibility to facilitate and maintain an environment that is caring and where the outcome is positive experiences and continued involvement in youth sport (Fry & Gano-Overway, 2010). In this chapter, we suggest that a key role for sport psychology professionals (SPPs) in youth sport is to help coaches accept, understand, and develop their role as cultural leaders. We describe how SPPs can support a coach to analyze their own environment, share a four-step process grounded in holistic ecological models with specific exercises, and illustrate how sport psychology services can adopt holistic ecological approaches to help coaches grow as cultural leaders and support them in developing quality youth sport environments.

Phase 1: Understanding the Youth Sport Coach's Own Motives

Cultural leadership starts with the coach becoming more aware of their own values and approaches to youth development. This phase draws on existential psychology (striving for an authentic life in which people take responsibility for their decisions; Nesti, 2004) and prompts the coaches to become aware of their own tacit knowledge, values, and assumptions that influence what they say and do. The coach's basic assumptions are questioned and explored. Good questions to stimulate such discussion in a team of coaches include: "What is important and meaningful to me/us to perform and thrive?" "What do I/we want our athletes to learn beyond sport-specific skills?" and "What do I/we have a 'taste' for?" Specific for engendering a quality youth sport environment is to also stimulate a discussion of what the coach perceives as "talent" (Henriksen et al., 2024) and ask the coaches to describe this as a *persona* with attributes, behaviors, and skills. We often use the metaphor of a flower in the sun and a flower in the shadow to understand young athletes' chances of flourishing in the environment. The coaches imagine themselves being the sunlight and the young athletes being the flowers. In a group, they are encouraged to challenge each other regarding who their light is shining on (i.e., giving more attention, positive feedback, etc.). This exercise helps them to become aware of who they acknowledge and give the most attention to and is an opportunity to discuss how their assumptions impact the athletes' development and shape the culture.

Phase 2: Analyzing the Environment

To evolve as a cultural leader, coaches must understand the system in which they are operating and in which the athletes are developing. Our work is grounded in the holistic ecological approach, its working models, and in the ideas that we cannot understand athletes' development without understanding their environment, and that improving the sport environment is a core mission of modern sport psychology (Henriksen & Stambulova, 2023). The athletic talent development environment working model (ATDE; Henriksen et al., 2010) and the dual-career development environment working model (DCDE; Henriksen et al., 2020) are well-suited frameworks to support this work. The models have the youth athletes at the center and illustrate how they are embedded in various life domains (e.g., sport, study, and private life), at various levels (micro and macro). A good and holistic analysis considers all these levels and domains. We typically provide the coaches with empty versions of the model (either ATDE or DCDE depending on what type of environment they identify as) and ask

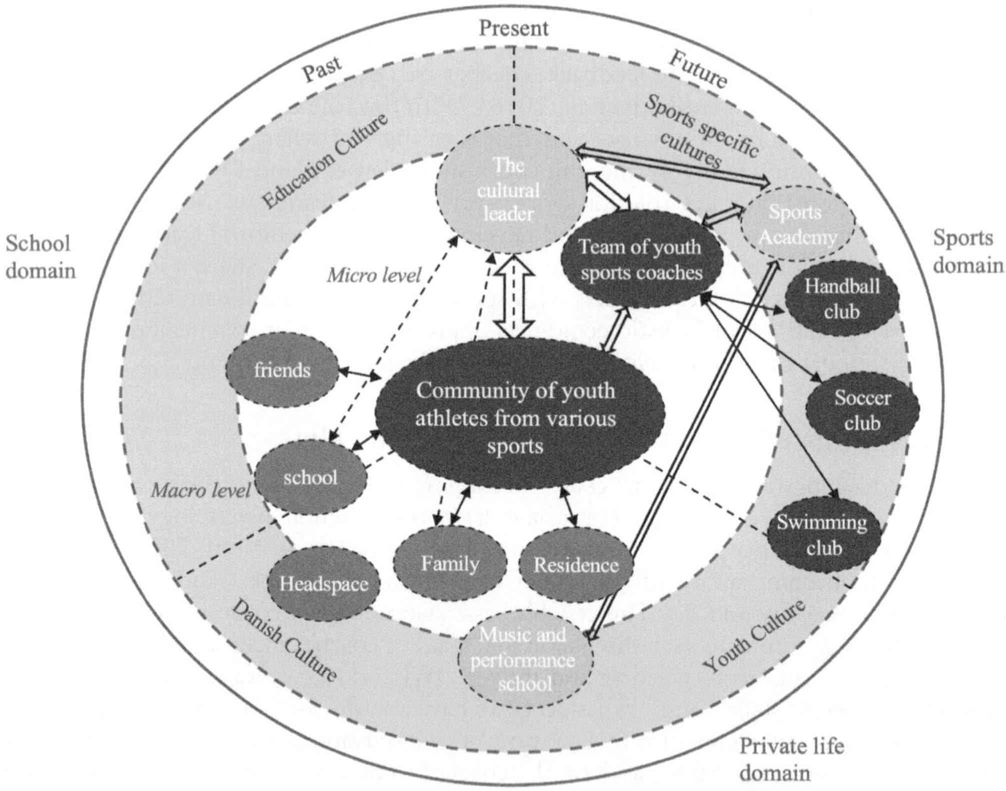

Figure 4.1 The Athletic Talent Development Environment Model completed by a team of coaches.

them to draw key components and illustrate different roles and relations within the environment as well as highlight what they can impact and what they have to navigate (Figure 4.1 is a model filled out by a team of coaches).

After analyzing the structure, we move on to analyzing and discussing the culture of the environment. Inspired by the environment success factors (ESFs) model (Henriksen et al., 2010), we discuss: What is the overall purpose of my team/club/environment (e.g., to have many members, to win competitions, to develop competent senior athletes)? What does it take for the team/club/environment to "survive"–and how does this shape everyday life (i.e., what does the organization make money from)? Who are formal and informal leaders, and what types of power do they have? What is rewarded or ignored?

Phase 3: Development of a Shared and Coherent Philosophy

Building upon the self-reflection (phase 1) and the analysis of the environment (phase 2), coaches are then introduced to a list of features of successful talent development environments (Henriksen & Stambulova, 2023; e.g., long-term development focus, integrated efforts, role models, sharing knowledge). The team of coaches scores their own environment based on this list. After this exercise they discuss the features that are present and absent in their environment, and select two or three specific features they would like to develop, and actually have the legitimate power to improve in their environment. Key questions are: What tells you that your environment is good and supportive? What can be improved? What can you change? What do you have to accept and navigate? In this phase the SPP offers observations of practices. After this exercise, and based on the previous phases, the SPP supports the coaches to formulate shared values related to the environment and decide on how to improve the selected features. The SPP helps the coaches to act as a cultural leader and lead the positive features of the environment. For example, the coaches might agree to facilitate peer relationships between youth athletes to stimulate a culture of responsibility for their own learning.

Phase 4: Ongoing Evaluation and Reflection

Working with the environment and the coach as a cultural leader never stops and the SPP embed themselves in the environment (i.e., engaged but not overly identified with the team to be able to shift between an insider and an outsider position, which is helpful for the process of supporting the coaches in their role as cultural leaders). Environments are dynamic and evolve even when coaches are not intentionally trying to shape them in a specific manner. Therefore the phases presented here should be seen as a spiral of continuous work. The SPP should help coaches constantly act and reflect on their role as a cultural leader and the degree to which their daily environment matches their vision and philosophy. In conclusion, creating a quality youth sport environment takes purposeful effort from both coaches and SPPs. Coaches can learn to consider their role from a holistic and ecological perspective, and pay attention not only to the individual athlete but also to the whole environment. We invite SPPs to reflect, adapt, and inspire coaches in their role as cultural leader.

Conclusion

A good youth sport environment supports the long-term motivation and development of its athletes. However, good environments don't emerge by coincidence—they must be carefully nurtured and facilitated, mainly by the coaches. With that said, while coaches have many roles, one of the most important is being a cultural leader. This includes facilitating the norms and values of the group and developing the entire social environment. Embracing this role requires self-reflection and keeping in mind essential features of a successful talent development environment (see Table 4.1). While Table 4.1 highlights shared features of successful talent development environments in sport, we encourage you to also use it as a framework to assess your own youth sport environment and how it aligns with successful talent development features. To enable you to do so, Table 4.1 contains the positive characteristics, which are also explained with an "opposite" negative pole. You should read each pair as a continuum. Use it as a framework to reflect on what characterizes your own environment. Evaluate your own environment based on the statements and circle the number that you think characterizes your environment. "0" divides the scale into two parts, positive and negative. In each part, "1" means "almost not applicable" and "5" means "very applicable." We hope this provides you with a good starting point on your journey toward creating and fostering sustainable positive youth sport environments.

Table 4.1 Features of a Successful Talent Development Environment

Features	*Descriptors*	*Evaluation*	*Opposite Pole*
Training groups with supportive relationships.	Opportunities for inclusion in a training community. Supportive relationships and friendships within the group, despite performance level.	5 4 3 2 1 0–1-2-3-4–5	Individualized training programs at an early stage; training alone; low cohesion in the group; inter-group rivalry.
Proximal role models.	Opportunities to train with elite athletes who are willing to pass on their knowledge.	5 4 3 2 1 0–1-2-3-4–5	Boundaries between athletes at different levels. Elite-level athletes keep their secrets.
Openness and sharing knowledge.	Coaches and athletes sharing knowledge inside the environments. Open cooperation with experts and other clubs.	5 4 3 2 1 0–1-2-3-4–5	Secrecy among coaches and athletes. Others are only seen as rivals.
Support of sporting goal by the wider environment.	Opportunities to focus on the sport, school, family, friends; People acknowledge and accept the athletes' dedication to sport.	5 4 3 2 1 0–1-2-3-4–5	Non-sport environment shows a lack of understanding of elite sport.
Holistic skill development.	Opportunities to develop competences that are of benefit outside sport, considering athletes as whole human beings.	5 4 3 2 1 0–1-2-3-4–5	Focus solely on winning at any cost; excessive control from coaches; focus not on personal improvement but on relative performance level, which devalues learning and development.

(*Continued*)

Table 4.1 (Continued)

Features	*Descriptors*	*Evaluation*	*Opposite Pole*
Training that allows for diversification.	Opportunities to sample different sports during early phases; integration of different sports in the daily routines; appreciation of versatile sports profiles and basic sport skills.	5 4 3 2 1 0–1-2–3-4–5	Promoting early specialization and sport-specific skills only, considering athletes' interest in trying different sports to be rivalry and potential threat.
Room for free initiative.	Opportunities to organize training and playing at own initiative across age- and training groups.	5 4 3 2 1 0–1-2–3-4–5	Lack of access to facilities. Athletes cannot train or "play" High training loads demotivate athletes to train outside formal training.
Focus on long-term development.	Focus on long-term development of the athletes rather than early success; age-appropriate amount and content of training.	5 4 3 2 1 0–1-2–3-4–5	Focus on short-term success; kids are seen as miniature elite athletes.
Integration of efforts.	Coordination and communication between sport, school, family, and other components; athletes experience synergy.	5 4 3 2 1 0–1-2–3-4–5	Lack of communication; conflicting interests; athletes experience contradicting demands.
Coherent organizational culture.	Coherence between espoused values and actions. Culture provides stability to the group and supports a learning environment.	5 4 3 2 1 0–1-2–3-4–5	Fragmented culture in which espoused values do not correspond to actions; uncertainty and confusion.

EDITORS' TAKEAWAYS

Reading these contributions, we were struck by how little weight we often give to the complexities of working with youth. Too often, graduate students "practice" with youth clients simply because they are often more readily accessible and available, especially when services are unpaid. Yet this chapter highlighted the importance of intentionally preparing practitioners for this work, given the substantial impact we can have on young people's well-being, confidence, and even their desire to continue participating in sport. We were also reminded of the need for cultural humility. Youth are understood and valued differently across cultural contexts shaped by religion, socioeconomic conditions, politics, and tradition. While this was briefly acknowledged in the first contribution, it feels crucial that readers recognize how cultural research and awareness inform our ability to work effectively with young athletes and support their development.

RECOMMENDED EXERCISES

1 Reflect on your intrapersonal and interpersonal strengths. How might these support your work with youth sport athletes across different locations, contexts, and cultures?
2 Reflect on your intrapersonal and interpersonal areas of opportunity. How might these create barriers in your work with youth athletes across locations, contexts, and cultures? What additional competencies or knowledge areas could you acquire that would help you work effectively in youth sport?
3 Identify a country or community in which you are interested in working. Learn about the sport structure at the community, school, and elite youth levels. How could you integrate applied sport psychology services into those settings?
4 Identify a mental skill approach or exercise you have used with adult athletes. How could you adapt it creatively to make it engaging and developmentally appropriate for youth?
5 Think back to your own tween years. How did you handle challenges and emotions in sports or activities? How might a mental performance consultant have supported you then?
6 Observe (or recall) a tween-focused practice or game. Identify moments of concrete thinking, emotional fluctuation, or social comparison. How would you respond to these as a mental performance consultant?
7 Conduct a retrospective fun audit of a session you recently delivered to a youth athlete or team. This can be both a self-reflective exercise or one in which the athlete(s) are asked to provide this assessment.

   a On a scale of 1–10, how fun was that session for the athlete?
   b What elements contributed to, or limited, the fun?
   c Design a 30-min sport psychology session for the youth athlete that intentionally integrates fun as both a process and outcome. Include one to two core mental skills (e.g., focus, confidence) and at least two approaches (e.g., active listening, autonomy, gamification, creativity).

8 Reflect on Table 4.1 and how it applies to a current youth environment you are working with (e.g., a youth sport team you are providing sport, exercise, and performance psychology services to), are familiar with (e.g., a youth sport team a youth athlete family member is a part of), or a youth sport team you were a part of (e.g., your club sport team when you were a youth athlete).

   a Evaluate the environment you have chosen to reflect on based on the features described in the table, and circle the number that you think characterizes your environment.
   b What stands out to you about your evaluation (e.g., strengths of the environment, areas that need improvement)?
   c Based on your evaluation, how would you work with coaches as cultural leaders to improve the sport environment?
   d How would you define success and handle challenges in that collaboration?

REFERENCES

Arvinen-Barrow, M., & Visek, A. J. (2025). The subtleties of doing sport psychology with post-pandemic youth athletes. In B. Hemmings, T. Holder, & S. Winter (Eds.), *Professional skills in sport psychology consultancy: Personal and interpersonal dynamics.* Routledge.

Aspen Institute Project Play. (2022). *Youth sport facts: Participation rates.* https://projectplay.org/youth-sports/facts/participation-rates

Blom, L. C., Visek, A. J., & Harris, B. (2013). Triangulation in youth sport: Healthy partnerships among parents, coaches, and practitioners. *Journal of Sport Psychology in Action, 4*(2), 86–96. https://doi.org/10.1080/21520704.2012.763078

Flett, M. R., Gould, D., & Lauer, L. (2012). A study of an underserved youth sports program using the Youth Program Quality Assessment. *Journal of Applied Sport Psychology, 24*(3), 275–289. https://doi.org/10.1080/10413200.2011.641061

Fry, M. D., & Gano-Overway, L. A. (2010). Exploring the contribution of the caring climate to the youth sport experience. *Journal of Applied Sport Psychology, 22*(3), 294–304. https://doi.org/10.1080/10413201003776352

Henriksen, K., Larsen, C. H., & Storm, L. K. (2024). *All you need to know about talent development in sport.* Athlete Insight Press.

Henriksen, K., & Stambulova, N. (2023). The social environment of talent development in youth sport. *Frontiers in Sports and Active Living, 5,* 1127151. https://doi.org/10.3389/fspor.2023.1127151

Henriksen, K., Stambulova, N., & Roessler, K. K. (2010). Holistic approach to athletic talent development environments: A successful sailing milieu. *Psychology of Sport and Exercise, 11*(3), 212–222. https://doi.org/10.1016/j.psychsport.2009.10.005

Henriksen, K., Storm, L. K., Kuettel, A., Linnér, L., & Stambulova, N. (2020). A holistic ecological approach to sport and study: The case of an athlete friendly university in Denmark. *Psychology of Sport and Exercise, 47,* 101637. https://doi.org/10.1016/j.psychsport.2019.101637

Henriksen, K., Storm, L. K., & Larsen, C. H. (2018). Organisational culture and influence on developing athletes. In C. Knight, C. Harwood, & D. Gould (Eds.), *Sport psychology for young athletes* (pp. 159–170). Routledge. https://doi.org/10.4324/9781315545202-20

Lauer, E. E., Lerman, M., Zakrajsek, R. A., & Lauer, L. (2020). Creation of a mental skills training program in elite youth tennis: A coach-driven approach to developing resilient, confident competitors. *International Sport Coaching Journal, 7*(1), 74–81. https://doi.org/10.1123/iscj.2019-0012

McHenry, L. K., Cochran, J. L., Zakrajsek, R. A., Fisher, L. A., Couch, S. R., & Hill, B. S. (2021). Elite figure skaters' experiences of harm in the coach-athlete relationship: A person-centered theory perspective. *Journal of Applied Sport Psychology, 33*(4), 420–440. https://doi.org/10.1080/10413200.2020.1800862

Moore, M., Blom, L. C., Califano, K., Hussey, K., Farello, A., Vasiloff, O., & Gabler, T. (2021). Redesigning a youth soccer program: Holistic development of athletes. *Child and Adolescent Social Work Journal, 38*(4), 409–421. https://doi.org/10.1007/s10560-021-00770-z

Nesti, M. (2004). *Existential psychology and sport: Theory and application* (1st ed.). Routledge. https://doi.org/10.4324/9780203483435

Storm, L. K., Svendsen, A. M., Stambulova, N., Barker, D., Ronkainen, N., Bjørndal, C. T., … & Henriksen, K. (2024). Cultural leadership in physical education and youth sport: Consensus from a Nordic Think Tank. *Scandinavian Journal of Sport and Exercise Psychology, 6,* 1–9. https://doi.org/10.7146/sjsep.v6i.141284

Visek, A. J., Achrati, S., Mannix, H. M., McDonnell, K., Harris, B. S., & DiPietro, L. (2015). The fun integration theory: Toward sustaining children and adolescents' sport participation. *Journal of Physical Activity & Health, 12*(3), 424–433. https://doi.org/10.1123/jpah.2013-0180

Visek, A. J., Harris, B. S., & Blom, L. C. (2009). Doing sport psychology: A youth sport consulting model for practitioners. *The Sport Psychologist, 23*(2), 271–291. https://doi.org/10.1123/tsp.23.2.271

Visek, A. J., Ivarsson, A., Putt, G., & Learner, J. (2023). To have fun: What it means and its significance in sport. In M. Toms & R. Jeanes (Eds.), *Routledge handbook of coaching children in sport* (pp. 51–61). Routledge.

Zakrajsek, R. A., Lauer, E. E., & Bodey, K. J. (2017). Integrating mental skills and strategies into youth sport training: A tool for coaches. *International Sport Coaching Journal, 4*(1), 76–89. https://doi.org/10.1123/iscj.2016-0078

5 Working with Coaches

Coaches occupy a unique position within the sport environment, serving not only as leaders, decision-makers, and motivators but also as influential intermediaries between sport, exercise, and performance psychology professionals (SEPPPs) and athletes. As performers in their own right, coaches benefit from sport psychology services aimed at enhancing their own performance—such as leadership under pressure, effective communication, and resilience in the face of setbacks. At the same time, coaches are often the most consistent and trusted figures in athletes' day-to-day training, placing them in an ideal position to model psychological skills, reinforce mental performance strategies, and help integrate sport psychology principles into the team culture. In this dual role, coaches can be both beneficiaries and facilitators of sport psychology, with their development directly influencing the well-being and performance of the athletes they lead.

BUILDING EFFECTIVE ENVIRONMENTS FOR DEVELOPMENT AND PERFORMANCE SUCCESS IN SPORT: WORKING WITH AND THROUGH COACHES

Svenja Wachsmuth, Rebecca A. Zakrajsek, Donna O'Connor, & Oliver Höner

Recent research (e.g., Brown et al., 2024) has demonstrated that sport environments must (and can) be shaped in ways that foster thriving, that is, promoting both sustainable performance and well-being. Herein, coaches represent important leaders who carry a significant responsibility for shaping a culture that protects athletes from harm and fosters performance excellence (Junggren et al., 2018). Building environments that enable optimal development (including well-being) and performance is easier said than done and requires elite coaches to encompass sound professional skills as well as outstanding inter- and intrapersonal skills (Côté & Gilbert, 2009). Informed by a well-crafted coaching philosophy, coaches thus need to develop and implement athlete-tailored training and competition programs, attend to organizational and administrative duties, provide guidance and leadership to their team, and build trusting relationships with and among athletes and staff—all while also engaging in self-reflection, self-improvement, and self-care. Given these wide-ranging demands, it is evident that coaches need to be resilient performers themselves who can cope with the challenges of elite sport. Yet, it may be called into question whether coaches generally receive sufficient support to develop the competences needed to skillfully manage professional responsibilities. The provision of sport psychology services can offer an opportunity to work with coaches for their own

DOI: 10.4324/9781003781486-5

professional development as well as through coaches for the purpose of building effective development and performance environments.

To work with coaches as an effective sport psychology practitioner (SPP), it is essential to understand the complexity of the coaching role and to form quality relationships. Such working alliances build on trust and offer coaches the space to be vulnerable, and thus, to openly share concerns and feelings. At the same time, they enable the SPPs to ask challenging questions and voice critical reflection with the intent to support coaches' development. Given the leadership role of the coach, power dynamics can challenge such close bonds due to a fear of negative consequences, where SPPs might be concerned about their (job) dependency on the coach, or a coach's worry about losing face, authority, and impact (Wachsmuth et al., 2022). Thus, crafting such quality relationships will take time and commitment; it requires SPPs to be present and available, ask curious questions and listen closely, have thoughtful (and often immediate) answers to coaches' help seeking approaches, and importantly, be aware of and remain within their competence area and role. SPPs might also experience challenges related to their positioning in the environment. For example, SPPs might be viewed as closer to the coaching staff, the athletes, or somewhere in between, or even as an "external insider" and all these constellations can impact the levels of trust in the respective working relationships. In terms of helping coaches build a nourishing environment, SPPs can face the challenge of being "part of the system" and, as such, might be blind to (difficult) social dynamics or even reinforce (destructive) assumptions, beliefs, and values in the way they behave.

Notwithstanding these challenges, SPPs can assist coaches in mastering *professional skills* by helping to refine their coaching philosophy, value-driven engagement, and attitudes toward self and others. As a critical friend, SPPs may also foster *intrapersonal skills* linked to professional practice by encouraging reflection of daily coaching practices and their alignment with coaches' overarching values and objectives. SPPs might further help develop self-referential cognitions and skills such as building self-regulation strategies to deal with the pressures of performance sport or fostering self-care to prevent overwork and health concerns. Finally, SPPs may work with coaches on *interpersonal skills* such as improving communication and conflict management skills or promoting leadership behaviors that align with coaches' goal pursuits and philosophy. By enhancing coaches' inter- and intrapersonal as well as professional skills, SPPs can add significant value to shaping a nourishing sport environment. Grounded in their work with coaches, SPPs are then in a position in which they can facilitate positive social dynamics and act as guardians of a constructive culture. We provide three examples on how SPPs may work with and through coaches.

Example 1: Developing an Attitude of Unconditional Positive Regard

SPPs are encouraged to work with coaches to develop a foundational attitude (i.e., *way of being*) with self and others that is reflective of unconditional positive regard (UPR; i.e., respect, acceptance, engagement, belief in, and challenge *through* success and failure) with authenticity and empathic understanding (McHenry & Zakrajsek, 2023). Engaging coaches in intra- and interpersonal self-reflective exercises is an effective approach to helping coaches shift their understanding and use of UPR. For instance, SPPs can help coaches gain self-awareness of their own, often unintentional, use of UPR opposites (e.g., conditional regard, negative regard, or disregard). A description of activities in a professional development program that aimed to facilitate coaches' learning and use of UPR can be found in McHenry and Zakrajsek (2023). For coaches to develop an attitude of UPR, they could be asked to (a) create a list of athlete behaviors that they love and a list of athlete behaviors that irritate them, (b) reflect on how they react to each athlete behavior, and (c) seek feedback from athletes and colleagues to learn about how their reactions to those behaviors are perceived by others. SPPs can also help coaches identify their own interactions as moving *away from* (i.e., disregard), *against* (i.e., negative regard), *toward* (i.e., disregard for potential via over-accommodation or control), or *with* athletes (i.e., UPR with authenticity and empathic understanding; McHenry & Zakrajsek, 2023). Through consistent self-reflection coaches can learn to catch themselves prior to reacting with negative regard or disregard and instead pause, reflect, and choose to respond in alignment with UPR. It is important to remember that any positive shift in coaches' *way of being*, however minor, is a shift toward an environment that supports athletes' well-being and performance.

Example 2: Acting as a Critical Friend

As a critical friend, SPPs can facilitate coaches' process of self-reflection and thus be an invaluable resource to a coach by offering constructive feedback and fostering reflective practice in a supportive yet challenging manner. This relationship involves providing honest, balanced insights into the coach's strategies, behaviors, and decision-making processes, prompting them to critically examine their approach, become more self-aware, and consider new perspectives. An essential part of this role is the ability to listen and use open-ended, thought-provoking questions to facilitate the coach's self-reflection. By asking questions like, "What impact do you think that strategy had on your athletes?", "How does your behavior align with your coaching philosophy and values?" or "How might you approach this situation differently in the future?" The SPP as a critical friend guides the coach to explore their assumptions, experiment with new ideas, and arrive at their own conclusions. However, being a critical friend comes with challenges as it requires maintaining a delicate balance between support and critique. The critical friend must be sensitive to the coach's needs, ensuring that feedback is both specific and actionable without being overly critical or demotivating. Building trust is vital, as the coach must feel safe to be vulnerable and open to critique. Importantly, a critical friend must also continuously reflect on their own biases and approach to feedback, ensuring that their insights are grounded in a genuine desire to facilitate the coach's development rather than impose their own viewpoint. Thus, SPPs could ask "Have I invited feedback on my role as a critical friend—what have I learned from it, and how have I responded?" or "What assumptions am I making about the coach's ability and way of learning—how could this be influencing the way I support or challenge them?"

Example 3: Mediating Difficult Situations Between Coaches, Athletes, and Staff

Especially in times of conflict or when dealing with (supposedly) difficult athletes, acting as a critical friend can be challenging and SPPs may be at risk to act as messengers between two emerging fronts or even be demanded to pick sides; circumstances which in most cases are little conducive to positive interpersonal relationships in any given setting. In those situations, SPPs may make a conscious decision to engage (as) an active mediator that can enable coaches and athletes to bridge the gap within their relationships (Wachsmuth et al., 2022).

To be effective, it is desirable for SPPs to take a neutral stance with the purpose of achieving the best possible outcomes for both sides as well as for the entire environment (i.e., guardian of culture). Rather than fixing symptoms of a problem and agreeing on short-sighted compromises, SPPs may lead individual and joint conversations which offer the space to attend to the core concern(s) of a conflict and respective underlying individual needs. Identifying those needs often enables conflict parties to open up their minds to think about and develop new, mutually desirable solutions, thus, leading to more sustainable and potentially even closer working relationships. At the same time, witnessing such constructive management of interpersonal difficulties will increase others' confidence in the relationships and culture in their environment.

To conclude, SPPs can contribute to building an optimal sport environment and as such offer great value to the well-being, development, and performance of athletes as well as coaches. However, from our perspective it seems that many neophyte practitioners might not yet receive education and training needed to work with coaches. It is thus important to include coach-specific expertise (e.g., leadership, cultural development, coaching ethics) in SPPs' training routes, accompanied by sound supervision and opportunities to specialize in that area of work (e.g., coach development).

EMPOWERING LEADERS: WORKING WITH THE COACH AS A PERFORMER

Kristen Dieffenbach & Melissa Thompson

When you think about sport coaching, it is easy to conjure images shaped by the media—the loud, intense figure pacing the sideline or delivering fiery speeches. However, modern coaching is far more complex with individuals being responsible for an increasing list of expectations and responsibilities (Lara-Bercial et al., 2020). As a future sport and exercise psychology professional (SEPP), our hope is that this chapter will help you understand that coaching today demands deep sport science knowledge, psychological acumen, and leadership across increasingly complex environments. In taking a proactive, collaborative, and evidence-informed approach, you can support coaches both as leaders of athletes and as high-performing individuals.

Professionalization of Sport Coaching

The coach operates in a complex sport ecosystem. The American system is notably decentralized, encompassing a wide array of independent organizations operating at various levels (Dieffenbach, 2019). Unlike many countries with government-led sport systems, the United States relies on a mix of non-profit organizations, educational institutions, national governing bodies, and private enterprises to develop its coaching workforce. This structure presents both opportunities and challenges for coach preparation and professionalization.

At the youth and developmental levels, volunteer coaches dominate the workforce, often with limited formal training (Gould & Carson, 2007). In contrast, collegiate and professional levels generally employ full-time, salaried coaches who often possess more formalized education and certifications. However, in your work with coaches you will encounter a wide variety of educational backgrounds, so it's critical to take time to explore each coach's personal developmental pathway to help you assess their needs.

Frameworks Guiding Coaching Practice

Increasingly in recent years, both scholars and sport organizations have begun to advocate for the recognition of coaching as a legitimate profession, emphasizing the need for evidence-based education, accreditation, and ongoing professional development (North et al., 2018), with emphasis being placed on systemic development strategies. While athlete performance has always been central in coach education, calls for competency-based development focused on supporting long-term development (Walters et al., 2020) have emphasized the need to prepare both "what to" knowledge as well as the "how to" knowledge, highlighting the role of coach as teacher. The *International Sport Coaching Framework* (ICCE, 2013) offers a comprehensive overview of the coaching role, categorizing the essential professional areas of skills and knowledge within the field into four areas: core (e.g., personal values), intrapersonal (e.g., self-awareness), interpersonal (e.g., communication), and contextual knowledge (e.g., training science).

Within the United States, a structured understanding of the expectations and responsibilities associated with coaching was first developed in 1995, with the 3rd edition of *The National Standards for Sport Coaches (NSSC)* being published by SHAPE America in 2019. The NSSC outlines competencies related to fostering athlete development, promoting ethical behavior, ensuring safety, and supporting holistic well-being. Additionally, the *United States Olympic & Paralympic Committee's* (2020) *Quality Coaching Framework* emphasizes the importance of athlete-centered coaching, aligning with principles from positive youth development and long-term athlete development models with coaching behaviors. These leadership documents collectively position the coach not only as a facilitator of athletic excellence but also as a guardian of athlete well-being.

For SEPPs, familiarity with these frameworks is essential for recognizing how sport and exercise psychology fits within the sport coaching education conversation when designing interventions, workshops, or collaborative initiatives aimed at enhancing coaching effectiveness. More importantly, these documents identify coaches as peers in the evolving conversation around professional roles and responsibilities in the sport landscape; this highlights the need for SEPPs to carefully examine opportunities to support the well-being and performance of coaches.

Coaches as Performers in the Sport Setting

Coaching at any level—youth, collegiate, or professional—involves exposure to scrutiny, performance evaluation, and emotional labor. Increasingly, coaches are being recognized as performers who experience similar pressures and psychological demands as athletes (Sheehy et al., 2019b). This shift reframes how SEPPs might approach support strategies. Rather than viewing coaches merely as conduits to athlete development, SEPPs should consider the psychological skills, coping mechanisms, and mental preparation that coaches themselves need in order to thrive in high-pressure environments.

Support Into the Profession

One emerging area in coaching preparation is the transition from athlete to coach. Often, this shift occurs without formal training in leadership, psychology, or sport science, leaving individuals underprepared for the role's complexity (Chroni et al., 2020). As a SEPP, you can support this within-sport transition by promoting reflective practice, addressing identity shifts, and offering targeted transition programs. The International Coach Developer Framework (Crisfield & Bales, 2024) outlines ways SEPPs can collaborate with coach education systems to enhance readiness and well-being. Whether working individually or within organizations, SEPPs play a vital role in ensuring more effective, confident, and well-supported early career coaches.

Building Collaborative Relationships

Collaborative relationships between SEPPs and coaches are key. Building trust and open communication enables you to work "with" and "through" coaches, enhancing both coach and athlete development (Sharp & Hodge, 2013). As a SEPP, you can work with coaches to collaborate on athlete training plans by reinforcing psychological principles during physical preparation phases. Embedding mental skills training directly into the athletes' broader training schedule ensures greater consistency and effectiveness. Through the construction of a strong relationship, the SEPP can also support the coach. SEPPs can help coaches navigate the profession's challenges by guiding them toward professional development resources, mentoring opportunities, and peer support networks.

Enhancing Coach Well-Being

As a SEPP, your role includes promoting the long-term sustainability of coaching careers. Coaches are at high risk for burnout due to workload, emotional demands, and role ambiguity (Honttä et al., 2024). SEPPs can support coaches' well-being through interventions focused on stress management, resilience, and work-life balance (Sheehy et al., 2019a). Kenttä et al. (2024) recommend strategies such as mindfulness training, peer support networks, and one-on-one consultations. These approaches not only protect individual mental health but also enhance the overall quality of the sport environment. Supporting coaches' mental health is both an ethical responsibility and a key contributor to effective athlete development. Further, when considering the coach as a performer, it's necessary to educate coaches on how their own well-being impacts their coaching.

Facilitating Access to Professional Developmental Resources

Finally, SEPPs can play a key role in guiding coaches toward and through professional development opportunities that support their ongoing development of inter- and intrapersonal skills such as self-awareness, conflict management, and communication. SEPPs with a background in educational psychology, pedagogy, andragogy, and curriculum development, can facilitate the development of professional peer learning groups (e.g., communities of practice), and mentorship programs. By connecting individuals with "just in time" resources to suit their current coaching challenges, SEPPs empower them to continually grow their skills and better navigate the challenges of their profession.

Conclusion

As the professionalization of coaching continues, organizations like the United States Center for Coaching Excellence and the ICCE that are working to raise the standards for coach education and certification can be valuable resources. For SEPPs, applying a science-practitioner framework offers an effective strategy for supporting coaches within this complex environment. By understanding the landscape of professionalization, leveraging leadership frameworks, recognizing coaches as performers, and developing collaborative relationships, as an SEPP you can significantly enhance both coach and athlete experiences. Ultimately, supporting the well-being and professional development of coaches strengthens the foundation of sport itself.

PROMOTING WELLBEING OF HIGH PERFORMANCE SPORT NEW ZEALAND COACHES: SHAPING SYSTEMS AND INTEGRATING PRINCIPLES

Antoinette Minniti & Daryl Gibson

This chapter provides the perspective of a sport psychologist (Antoinette) working at a systems level within High Performance Sport New Zealand (HPSNZ) in the role of Wellbeing and Engagement Lead (WBE Lead), alongside ongoing collaboration with the Head of High Performance Coaching (Daryl) to collectively shape systems and structures that enhance coach wellbeing. A brief overview of the high-performance sport landscape in New Zealand will be shared as it relates to coaching and the implementation of HPSNZ's wellbeing framework. We will identify practical applications for coach support and educational programming along with future directions and opportunities.

Brief History of High Performance Sport in New Zealand and HPSNZ Coaching

HPSNZ was established as an entity in 2011–2012 as a subsidiary of Sport New Zealand. As outlined by Sport New Zealand (n.d.), the nature and focus of high-performance sport were represented by several key stages which influenced shifts in high-performance coaching. For example, the Hillary Commission (1995–2001) marked the beginning of increased government involvement in sport, and this essentially fostered a ***generalized coaching approach***. The Commission's work was followed by a series of shifts in the way that high-performance sport and athletes were funded. The current HPSNZ 2032 strategy has extended the organization to include a new Wellbeing and Leadership pillar which has allowed for heightened attention to promote athlete and coach wellbeing, thus supporting a ***hybrid approach with coaching consultancy and educational programming***. Whilst recognizing the government funding driver of achieving medals, this organizational shift is an acknowledgment of HPSNZ's values to take care of all our people in the system ("he tangata"), whereby consultancy and educational opportunities support coaches in pursuit of striving for the remarkable ("mahi toa").

This history provides important context for understanding the evolution and developments related to coach wellbeing within the current landscape of high-performance sport in New Zealand. The varying extent of government engagement and support alongside the degree of emphasis placed on medal tallies has arguably led to direct and indirect effects on New Zealand's approach to high-performance sport and coaching (Sport New Zealand, n.d.)., which in turn can be mapped across to coach wellbeing needs.

Developing Our Well-being Framework and Guidelines for All

The HPSNZ Wellbeing Programme was recently established within the Wellbeing and Leadership pillar as part of a strategic shift to further elevate the importance of wellbeing for all parties within high-performance environments. In my role as WBE Lead, it was fundamental to ensure extensive consultation and partnership with stakeholders, and as a non-native New Zealander this proved especially valuable for systems development. Potentially related to the increased demands and focus on performance and medal hauls, coach wellbeing was consistently a topic of discussion as part of the aforementioned consultation.

Breadth and depth of discussion across sports led to the recently published policy, HPSNZ Wellbeing Framework and Guidelines (HPSNZ, 2023), which explicitly indicates wellbeing as everybody's right and responsibility, including athletes, coaches, and support staff. Wide-ranging stakeholder engagement was central to this key tenet, and it was clear that both coach wellbeing *and* coaches promoting wellbeing were critical components. Whilst acknowledging the reviews that have importantly outlined the critical need to attend to athlete wellbeing (e.g., Cottrell, 2018; Muir & Rooney, 2020), it is equally paramount to understand and support coach wellbeing as essential to underpinning the care that coaches can provide to themselves (e.g., DeWolfe & Dithurbide, 2022) and others (e.g., Bissett et al., 2020).

Contextual Challenges in High Performance Sport

It is worth noting that the nature of HPSNZ's partnership with sports means that policy implementation is sport-led. Given the variations across sports (e.g., de/centralization, domestic/overseas location, full-time/part-time coaches), there are substantial logistical challenges in connecting with and supporting coaches, thus necessitating collaborative approaches to promote wellbeing of coaches and their respective environments such as those provided in the next section.

Exploring Practical Ways to Support High-Performance Sport Coaches

Our collaborative work spans across a range of individual (I), technical (T), and educational (E) dimensions to support high-performance sport coaches amidst the nuances of high-performance sport environments. We conduct regular meetings that include Daryl, Toni, and the HPSNZ Head of Discipline for Psychology to identify and address topical issues that can benefit from aligned discussions with both the HPSNZ Wellbeing and Psychology teams. Several initiatives have emerged as a result of these meetings, including:

- bespoke support resources developed for coaches to utilize for their own wellbeing, recognizing that coaches are also performers (I),
- collaboration on educational programming focused on supporting coach wellbeing (I, T, E),
- partnership in the development of mental health referral training to support coaches with situations that require referral (T, E), and
- promotion of principles from empirical research that support healthy environments (T, E).

In light of the focus of this chapter, we will briefly expand on a couple of these items, beginning with the mental health referral training. Fundamentally, collaboration with the Wellbeing, Psychology, and Coaching teams has been essential to ensure alignment with the coaching strategy and wider HPSNZ 2032 strategy. As a joint group, there has been a deliberate and targeted approach to ensure that this offering is contextualized and relevant for high-performance sport coaches. Coaching case study examples are incorporated and form key points of discussion for the training. Remote/hybrid training is conducted to support overseas coaches and domestic coaches unable to attend in-person trainings. Of note, feedback from coaches led to the eventual title "Training to Refer" (rather than "mental health referral training") to promote clarity and an emphasis on coaches knowing *how to refer* rather than needing to be counselors. Importantly, the training is supported by coaching leadership as an essential initiative for all high-performance coaches to attend, as it importantly promotes health, wellbeing, and performance of coaches and their athletes.

Reflecting on one example related to promoting wellbeing research for coaches and their environments, Gibson and O'Connor (2022) highlighted the importance of normalizing social support mechanisms, such as wellbeing checks, by proactively embedding such strategies so that these are in place regardless of performance outcome. This recommendation is a simple addition that, when consistently included, speaks to the value for both coach *and* athlete wellbeing when embedding such principles into systems and structures. Importantly, this work is supported by sport psychologists via individual consultancy work with coaches, as well as educational programming with not only coaches but also athletes and other support staff who form the ecosystem of the high-performance environment.

Future Directions and Opportunities

The HPSNZ Coaching Team recently conducted a strategic refresh which included identifying feasible and sustainable opportunities that support coaches' wellbeing and their capacity to promote wellbeing in their respective high-performance environments. In my WBE Lead role, I was invited to provide input to the refresh process, which included recommendations for an enhanced focus on embedding systems and structures to promote wellbeing. In line with current research recommendations (e.g., Cassidy et al., 2024; O'Connor et al., 2024), future strategic directions are focused on a portfolio of targeted research initiatives to better understand coach wellbeing, individualized and group consultancy work to support coach wellbeing, and ongoing review and development of educational programming that is contextualized, culturally responsive, and embeds wellbeing both implicitly and explicitly.

There is always more work to be done in this space, but this journey has affirmed the importance of collaboration and ongoing discourse, while maintaining a clear sense of purpose and persistence to keep the work progressing despite challenges that naturally occur within high-performance environments.

EDITORS' TAKEAWAYS

Many coaches find themselves "lonely at the top," and as Wachsmuth and colleagues point out, this creates a valuable opportunity for sport, exercise, and performance psychology professionals (SEPPPs) to support coaches in developing their professional, intrapersonal, and interpersonal skills. As the authors emphasize throughout, the foundation of this support is trust—the essential linchpin in the coach-SEPPP relationship. Perhaps the greatest benefit, beyond the coach's own growth, is the modeling it provides to athletes, who witness firsthand the value of building a strong working alliance with a SEPPP. Building on Dieffenbach and Thompson's insights about facilitating coach-to-coach peer groups, I (Andrew) recall one of my first roles as a SEPPP after completing my master's degree—facilitating roundtable discussions for our provincial Canada Games coaches. It was an eye-opening experience. I remember simply posing questions to the group and the coaches enthusiastically exchanged ideas for hours! That moment underscored for me how much experiential knowledge coaches already have about the mental game, and how, at times, our role as SEPPPs is simply to bring them together and let them learn from each other's wisdom. A key takeaway from Minniti and Gibson's contribution is their recognition of the contextual challenges within high-performance sport—namely, that policy implementation must be sport-led. As they note, training and competition logistics can vary greatly from one sport to another. It is encouraging to see HPSNZ administrators acknowledge these differences and commit to bespoke collaborations with coaches to ensure policies align with each sport's unique demands.

RECOMMENDED EXERCISES

1 What key challenges do coaches face in their environments, and what skills are needed to manage them effectively?
2 How might your current views of coaching rely on stereotypes, and how could that limit your effectiveness when collaborating with coaches?
3 Under what circumstances would you feel able to have an honest conversation with coaches where you may challenge them and ask difficult questions (e.g., during guided self-reflection or when mediating conflict)? What do you need to do to be able to have conversations like this with coaches?
4 Reflect on your work with coaches, or imagine future work with this population.

   a Under what circumstances did or would you "move away from" (i.e., disregard) them?
   b Under what circumstances did or would you "move against" (i.e., negative regard) them?
   c Under what circumstances did or would you "move toward" (i.e., disregard for potential via over-accommodation or control) them?
   d Under what circumstances did or would you "move with" (i.e., UPR with authenticity and empathic understanding) them?
   e What differences do you notice regarding the circumstances and outcomes of these interactions?

5 How can you support the psychological well-being and identity development of coaches transitioning from athlete roles or entering high-pressure settings?
6 How can sport psychology professionals promote coach well-being across different sports and cultural contexts?

   a In what areas would you feel prepared to support coaches in professional development or in support of well-being?
   b In what areas might you need additional training or insight?

7 How can you help coaches foster athlete well-being in everyday training and competition environments?
8 Imagine a day in the life of a coach. Or, alternatively reach out to a coach to interview them to further your understanding. Pick a particular coaching context (e.g., youth volunteer coach, high school head coach, college assistant coach, professional coach).

   a Do some research and outline a week in the life of a coach in that context, including responsibilities, stressors, and decision-making challenges.
   b Narrate a "day in the life" from the coach's perspective, describing emotions, decisions, interactions with athletes, parents, and administrators.
   c Reflect on the following:

      i What psychological challenges did the coach face?
      ii How could a SEPPP have constructively supported this coach?
      iii What specific interventions or frameworks could be applied?

REFERENCES

Bissett, J. E., Kroshus, E., & Hebard, S. (2020). Determining the role of sport coaches in promoting athlete mental health: A narrative review and Delphi approach. *BMJ Open Sport & Exercise Medicine, 6*(1), e000676. https://doi.org/10.1136/bmjsem-2019-000676

Brown, D. J., Passaportis, M. J. R., Wagstaff, C. R. D., & Arnold, R. (2024). Systems that promote thriving in sport. In L. Davis, S. Jowett, & R. Keegan (Eds.), *Social psychology in sport* (2nd ed., pp. 335–348). Human Kinetics.

Cassidy, T., Byrne, G., Mallett, C. J., & Bloom, G. A. (2024). Coach development curriculum. In *The Routledge handbook of coach development in sport* (pp. 208–221). Routledge.

Chroni, S., Peterson, S., & Dieffenbach, K. (2020). Going from athlete-to-coach in Norwegian winter sport: Understanding the transition beyond the change of title. *Sport in Society, 23*(4), 751–774. https://doi.org/10.1080/17430437.2019.1631572

Côté, J., & Gilbert, W. (2009). An integrative definition of coaching effectiveness and expertise. *International Journal of Sports Science & Coaching, 4*(3), 307–323. https://doi.org/10.1260/174795409789623892

Cottrell, S. (2018). *Elite athletes' rights and welfare.* Sport New Zealand.

Crisfield, P., & Bales, J. (2024). *International coach developer framework.* International Council for Coaching Excellence.

DeWolfe, C. E., & Dithurbide, L. (2022). Beware of the blues: Wellbeing of coaches and support staff throughout the Olympic Games. *International Journal of Sports Science & Coaching, 17*(6), 1243–1257. https://doi.org/10.1177/17479541221116880

Dieffenbach, K. (2019). Frameworks for coaching education and development. In K. Dieffenbach & M. Thompson (Eds.), *Essential coaching education.* Human Kinetics.

Gibson, D., & O'Connor, D. (2022). Leading while losing: Elite coaches' perspectives of losing streaks. *International Sport Coaching Journal, 10*(1), 42–53. https://doi.org/10.1123/iscj.2021-0054

Gould, D., & Carson, S. (2007). Personal development through sport. In O. Bar-Or & H. Hebestreit (Eds.), *The young athlete* (Vol. 13, pp. 287–301). Wiley-Blackwell. https://doi.org/10.1002/9780470696255.ch2

High Performance Sport New Zealand. (2023). *HPSNZ wellbeing framework and guidelines.* https://hpsnz.org.nz/wp-content/uploads/2024/04/HPSNZ-Wellbeing-Framework-and-Guidelines.pdf

International Council for Coaching Excellence. (2013). *International coach developer framework.* Human Kinetics.

Junggren, S. E., Elbæk, L., & Stambulova, N. B. (2018). Examining coaching practices and philosophy through the lens of organizational culture in a Danish high-performance swimming environment. *International Journal of Sports Science & Coaching, 13*(6), 1108–1119. https://doi.org/10.1177/1747954118796914

084Genttä, G., Dieffenbach, K., Bentzen, M., Thompson, M., Côté, J., Mallett, C., & Olusoga, P. (2024). Position paper: Rationale for a focused attention on mental health of high-performance sports coaches. *International Sport Coaching Journal, 11*(3), 457–465. https://doi.org/10.1123/iscj.2022-0123

Lara-Bercial, S., Bales, J., & North, J. (2020). Coaching around the world: On becoming a profession. In *Coaching for human development and performance in sports* (pp. 93–121). Springer. https://doi.org/10.1007/978-3-030-63912-9_6

McHenry, L. K., & Zakrajsek, R. A. (2023). Thriving in elite athletes. In I. Nixdorf, R. Nixdorf, J. Beckmann, S. Martin, & T. MacIntyre (Eds.), *Routledge handbook of mental health in elite sport* (pp. 12–30). Routledge. https://doi.org/10.4324/9781003099345

Muir, P., & Rooney, J. (2020). *Complaints management and/or dispute resolution service for NZ sport: Feasibility study.* Simpson Grierson.

North, J., Piggott, D., Lara-Bercial, S., Abraham, A., & Muir, B. (2018). The professionalisation of sport coaching. In *Professional advances in sports coaching* (pp. 3–21). Routledge. https://doi.org/10.4324/9781351210980-2

O'Connor, D., Bennett, B., Perry, K., Fyall, G., Rogers, A., & Morley, D. (2024). Coach development in Australia and Aotearoa New Zealand: Evolutions and current directions. In *The Routledge handbook of coach development in sport* (pp. 22–44). Routledge.
SHAPE America. (2019). *National standards for sport coaches* (3rd ed.). SHAPE America – Society of Health and Physical Educators.
Sharp, L. A., & Hodge, K. (2013). Effective sport psychology consulting relationships: Two coach case studies. *The Sport Psychologist, 27*(4), 313–324. https://doi.org/10.1123/tsp.27.4.313
Sheehy, T., Zizzi, S., Dieffenbach, K., & Sharp, L. A. (2019b). "...Didn't only change my coaching, changed my life": Coaches' use of sport psychology for their own development and performance. *The Sport Psychologist, 33*(2), 137–147. https://doi.org/10.1123/tsp.2018-0061
Sheehy, T. L., Dieffenbach, K., & Reed, P. (2019a). An exploration of coaching research in *Journal of Applied Sport Psychology* from 1989 to 2017. *Journal of Applied Sport Psychology, 31*(3), 352–365. https://doi.org/10.1080/10413200.2018.1494642
Sport New Zealand. (n.d.). *Evolution of government agency for sport and recreation*. https://sportnz.org.nz/resources/evolution-of-government-agency-for-sport-and-recreation/
United States Olympic & Paralympic Committee. (2020). *Quality coaching framework 2020* (2nd ed.). Human Kinetics.
Wachsmuth, S., Jowett, S., & Harwood, C. G. (2022). Third party interventions in coach-athlete conflict: Can sport psychology practitioners offer the necessary support? *Journal of Applied Sport Psychology, 34*(2), 178–203. https://doi.org/10.1080/10413200.2020.1723737
Walters, S., Rogers, A., & Oldham, A. R. H. (2020). A competency-based approach to coach learning: The Sport New Zealand coach developer program. In B. Callary & B. Geary (Eds.), *Coach education and development in sport: Instructional strategies* (pp. 154–165). Routledge.

6 Working with Exercisers

You might think: Why a separate chapter on exercise? Isn't all exercise sport—and thus haven't we already covered "exercisers" in the last few "sport" chapters? Indeed, there are many folks that don't consider themselves athletes and wouldn't say they are participating in "sport" when engaging in physical activity. However, any form of physical activity, movement, or play is part of exercising—and doesn't necessarily involve sport-specific aspects. As such, people engaging in these forms of exercise can also benefit from sport, exercise, and performance psychology support—even if there are no competitions involved as in most sporting contexts. In today's day and age where physical inactivity, obesity, and cardiovascular conditions are prevalent issues among aging societies there are a host of potential clients out there. Let our authors take you on the journey where one thing is for sure: There are many, many "regular" folks out there who could benefit from sport, exercise, and performance psychology professionals (SEPPPs) helping them engage and maintain physically active lifestyles.

WORKING IN THE WORLD OF APPLIED EXERCISE PSYCHOLOGY

Isabella Cacciatore & Clara Swedlund

What Is Applied Exercise Psychology?

Applied exercise psychologists use psychological principles to help individuals from all walks of life develop a healthy and sustainable relationship with physical activity (PA) and other health behaviors (e.g., diet) with the aim of improving their physical and mental health (Watson, 2023). Although an exercise psychologists' role is typically associated with PA promotion, it encompasses a much broader range of support provision in the context of health and well-being, which we will further explore in this chapter.

Contexts of Applied Work

Whilst applied exercise psychology is still a fairly new and evolving field, there are many different contexts that applied exercise psychologists currently work in. Perhaps the first context that comes to mind is fitness, where they can support individuals in setting value-based goals (Harris, 2019), planning and periodizing exercise in a contextually informed way (e.g., using formulation to inform decisions), and monitoring both objective and subjective engagement. Here, a key focus of the applied exercise psychologist would be to help clients work through any unhelpful or uncomfortable thoughts, feelings, sensations, or urges that might interfere

DOI: 10.4324/9781003781486-6

with sustainable and meaningful participation in PA, irrespective of whether their goal is to increase, maintain, or reduce their activity levels.

Applied exercise psychologists may also work within the sports industry, supporting athletes who struggle with their relationship with food, exercise, and body image, as well as helping coaches create environments that promote a healthier approach to these issues. Competitive bodybuilding is one such context where applied exercise psychology can be particularly beneficial. This appearance-based sport demands that athletes pay close attention to their PA and nutritional intake, and coaches instruct them in the process of optimizing these to develop a more muscular physique (Alwan et al., 2022). Given the associated psychological risks to rigidly and meticulously monitoring one's exercise, diet, and body (Alwan et al., 2019), an applied exercise psychologists' support could be instrumental in mitigating these (Willmott et al., 2023).

Within the context of cardiac prevention and rehabilitation, applied exercise psychologists can work within multidisciplinary teams providing psychological support to clients. This can include supporting them to address any psychological or emotional barriers that may be causing avoidance of PA, and unhelpful eating behaviors that may be contributing to cardiac issues. For example, some rehabilitating from a cardiac event might have a fear of exercise.

When working in the context of weight management or diabetes prevention, applied exercise psychologists can provide psychological support to clients to help them make behavior changes around PA and diet. Body dissatisfaction is prevalent among individuals who are overweight or obese (Weinberger et al., 2016) and can act as a barrier to making lifestyle changes (e.g., avoiding PA). Therefore applied exercise psychologists can also support clients to move toward body neutrality and address weight stigma.

Applied exercise psychologists can also provide support to clients who are prenatal. For example, pregnancy can lead to the development of gestational diabetes, a type of diabetes that can lead to health problems in both the parent and baby. A risk factor for gestational diabetes is physical inactivity and treatment can include making changes around diet and PA. Therefore, applied exercise psychologists can support pregnant people to address certain psychological and emotional barriers that could get in the way of these behavior changes. Additionally, throughout pregnancy, people's bodies go through physical changes that can have a significant impact on their body image (Hodgkinson et al., 2014). This can influence their eating and PA behavior as well as their mental health. Applied exercise psychologists can thus provide psychological support to help clients move toward body neutrality with the aim of improving physical and mental health.

As highlighted, applied exercise psychologists can work in various contexts, with common themes emerging across them. Thus, it is crucial for practitioners to develop specific knowledge and skills.

Knowledge and Skills Required for Applied Work

It has been our collective experience that when working in the field of applied exercise psychology, we commonly come into contact with clients who are struggling with disordered eating, exercise dependence, and negative body image. Therefore, we recommend that applied practitioners develop their knowledge around these topics, including awareness about the limits of their own skills and potentially relevant (clinical) referrals. Nonetheless, exercise psychologists are often well placed to support clients presenting with these issues at subclinical levels. To do so, we believe that it is crucial that applied exercise psychologists develop a clear practitioner philosophy that enables them to train and become skilled in philosophically-congruent counseling frameworks and approaches that will help them to support their clients (e.g., by formulating a clients' presenting issues, to facilitate the planning, delivery, monitoring, and evaluation of an intervention). Examples of some of the approaches that we have found useful when working with some of these presenting issues include Acceptance and Commitment Therapy (ACT) and Cognitive Behavioral Therapy (CBT).

Acceptance and Commitment Therapy

ACT is a third wave of CBT that promotes acceptance of uncomfortable thoughts, sensations, and emotions in service of committing to actions that align with one's values. ACT posits that experiential avoidance (i.e., avoiding or escaping uncomfortable thoughts, feelings, and sensations) can be problematic when the strategy an individual uses to achieve avoidance is costly, unhealthy, or takes the individual away from their values. For example, Cathy (pseudonym) is a mother of two who recently found out from her doctor that she is at risk of developing cardiovascular disease. Cathy works long hours in a sedentary office job and has been struggling with emotional eating. Through a shared case formulation it becomes apparent that when Cathy experiences feelings of anxiousness and the physical sensations that accompany this (e.g., a pit in her stomach which she cannot tolerate), she reaches for chocolate and will consume a large amount. Whilst this behavior relieves these feelings and sensations in the short term, she then tends to feel secondary feelings of guilt and shame which leads to temporary restriction throughout the next day followed by overeating in the evening. Additionally, Cathy is disconnected from her values and has not really thought about what a meaningful life looks like to her before. Moving forward, this shared formulation informed the development of an intervention that helped Cathy connect with her values, further explore the workability of her current emotion regulation strategies, and develop alternative strategies such as acceptance and defusion.

Cognitive Behavioral Therapy

Clients who experience body image concerns tend to engage in over-evaluation of shape and weight, and judge their self-worth predominantly on this and their ability to control it. From a CBT lens, in order to address body image concerns, it is important to understand present cognitions and behaviors that maintain the over-evaluation of shape and weight. For example, Eddie (pseudonym) is a semi-professional rugby player. He has a core belief that he is not good enough and has developed an intermediate belief that being smaller will help him run faster and perform better—a common belief in his sport. Eddie also engages in other distorted thinking patterns such as mind reading and has a misperception about the size of his body. This leads to automatic thoughts such as, "I'm bigger than most of my teammates" and "Everyone is going to judge me in the changing room." As a result, he engages in safety behaviors such as body checking (weighing himself multiple times per day), avoidance (e.g., avoiding mirrors), and body comparison (with teammates and on social media). Whilst these safety behaviors help him to relieve anxiety in the short term, they increase focus on weight and shape and prevent his negative body perception from being reality tested, thus maintaining his body dissatisfaction in the long term. Based on this shared formulation the intervention designed for Eddie focused on empathically challenging assumptions and using behavioral techniques to address his safety behaviors, with the aim of helping him to develop body neutrality.

We hope that these brief summaries and examples outline the core psychological competency of case formulation that is expected of an applied exercise psychologist to be able to competently work with these, and many other, presenting issues.

Concluding Remarks

Whilst the future of the field of applied exercise psychology is promising, there are ongoing challenges for both trainees and qualified practitioners. Training to become an applied exercise psychologist is costly and once qualified, it is often up to the practitioner to develop their own working opportunities. Despite these challenges, the field is growing and heading in a promising direction, with applied exercise psychologists being employed in private practices, setting up independent practices, and working on more strategic levels of health promotion. Being an applied exercise psychologist near the beginning of the field's conception comes with its challenges; however, it is also exciting and means that we can have a voice in the growth and development of the field moving forward.

CONSIDERATIONS WHEN WORKING WITH ELDERLY EXERCISERS

Urska Dobersek & David Pargman

The global population is aging at an unprecedented rate, with projections indicating that by 2050, the number of people aged 60 and older will reach 2.1 billion—more than double since 2020 (WHO, 2022). Given that the prevalence of the elderly is growing, maintaining physical and mental health via exercise is essential for prolonging functionality and quality of life. However, less than 15% of Americans aged 65 years and older meet the federal guidelines for PA (CDC, 2023b). Consequently, the elderly population should be of interest to many sport and exercise psychology professionals to increase the clientele's understanding of the changes that occur during the aging process, the benefits of exercise, and how exercise can mitigate these developmental changes.

The Aging Process

Aging is a process associated with a wide range of physiological, structural, psychological, and social changes. Specifically, a reduction in muscle mass, bone density, and strength (sarcopenia) can lead to reduced mobility and a greater risk of falls and fractures. By the age of 80, approximately 50% of people have some type of motor impairment (Louis & Bennett, 2007). Additionally, given the loss of elasticity in ligaments and tendons during aging, agility and flexibility are undermined. Because of decreased overall movement, cardiovascular efficiency declines, reducing stamina and increasing vulnerability to heart disease.

Aging is also associated with reduced brain volume, especially in temporal and frontal cortices and hippocampus (Sele et al., 2021). As a result, the elderly show deteriorations in many cognitive functions—memory, attention, and processing speed. Furthermore, the aging process often involves significant life transitions, which can result in changes in individuals' social networks and support systems. Elderly individuals might face social isolation due to retirement from the workforce, the loss of family members/friends, and reduced mobility which makes it more challenging for the elderly to maintain an active lifestyle. Cumulatively, these developmental changes can contribute to feelings of loneliness, depression, and a reduced sense of purpose and meaning in life.

"Reversing" the Aging Process

While aging is an inevitable process, engagement in regular exercise can play a significant role in slowing down or even partially "reversing" some aspects of aging. For instance, resistance training can increase muscle mass and strength, even in individuals in their 80s and 90s (Marzuca-Nassr et al., 2023). Aerobic exercise (walking, cycling) can improve cardiovascular health, increase stamina, and reduce the risk of heart disease, allowing older individuals to maintain independence and quality of life.

Psychologically, exercise can reduce depression and anxiety, improve mood, and increase overall well-being (Windle et al., 2010). By participating in group exercise, older individuals can build and maintain social connections, which can reduce feelings of isolation and loneliness (Almonacid-Fierro et al., 2021). Finally, engagement in regular exercise is associated with improved cognitive function, enhanced memory, attention, and executive function (Pereira et al., 2019).

Recommendations for Sport Psychology Consultants Working with the Elderly

Individuals who are 65 or older should engage in 150 minutes of weekly aerobic PA and two days per week of strength training, along with the exercises that improve balance (CDC, 2023a). While biopsychosocial changes in the aging body are normal, elderly individuals might face a number of barriers associated with aging to meet the minimal exercise requirements. These include lack of knowledge, energy, motivation, confidence, enjoyment, fear of falling, joint pain, and limited financial resources and access to facilities. As such, sport psychology consultants (SPCs) can support elderly clients in various ways that go beyond performance enhancement. Their role could be promoting PA, mental resilience, adherence to rehabilitation, and increasing or maintaining quality of life. Given that the elderly have different needs than college and professional athletes, SPCs should adopt a holistic approach—considering the biopsychosocial aspects of aging.

After developing a trusting working alliance, SPCs should assess clients' knowledge about exercise, its benefits, and educate them on how exercise can mitigate their developmental changes. Using motivational interviewing strategies, SPCs can address individuals' ambivalence, readiness, motivation, mental, emotional, and physical challenges, and other idiosyncratic needs. For example, if a client is hesitant about exercising due to a lack of confidence or fear of injury, the SPC could explore their ambivalence by stating, "It sounds like part of you wants to stay active because you know it's healthy, and another part of you is worried about getting hurt. Can you tell me more about that?"

Additionally, SPCs should build clients' confidence by setting realistic goals, which can help the elderly overcome a fear of injury and increase motivation to engage in regular PA. For instance, in collaboration with clients, the SPC could explore their personal goals and support their autonomy by asking, "You know yourself best. What kind of PA feels manageable and meaningful to you right now?" Exploring clients' goals while offering self-determination can strengthen their intrinsic motivation to exercise.

Encouraging a positive and growth mindset and emphasizing the benefits of exercise for mental well-being can also enhance adherence to exercise. This could be done by eliciting change talk by exploring clients' positive experiences and the benefits of exercise with a question like: "What are some of the benefits you have noticed when you stick with the exercise, even a little bit?" and maybe following up with a reflection or reinforcement, "Feeling stable seems to be important to you. It also shows that your effort to go to the gym is really paying off and that you're seeing some changes."

Ideally, SPCs should work closely with a medical team or primary care physician to maintain clients' safety and ensure that the exercise program is tailored to the individual's health status and physical capabilities. Using physical assessments, such as balance, strength, and cardiovascular fitness, SPCs can monitor clients' progress and adjust exercise regimens when needed. Given that the elderly might be conservative about exercise rigor due to fear of injury and pain, SPCs must determine an appropriate intensity level for each client. This can be done by using tools, such as target heart rate, metabolic equivalent task, and rate of perceived exertion (see Pargman & Dobersek, 2024).

From a social perspective, encouraging participation in group activities or community-based exercise programs can provide opportunities for social interaction and support to combat loneliness and enhance overall well-being. Finally, SPCs should be sensitive to the cultural and individual needs of elderly clients, recognizing that social support and community engagement can take many forms depending on the client's background and preferences.

To get involved in working with elderly clients, SPCs could explore a number of venues, depending on their preferences. For example, SPCs could partner with senior centers, assisted living facilities, or community health organizations to offer workshops on mental skills for active aging (goal-setting, staying motivated, managing anxiety). They could also collaborate with mental health professionals, such as occupational and physical therapists, to integrate psychological support into their rehabilitation programs. Finally, SPCs could provide services to master's athletes focusing on injury, motivation, and identity-related concerns.

Conclusion

Aging is a multifaceted process that affects individuals physiologically, psychologically, and socially. Nevertheless, engagement in regular exercise can slow down many aspects of the aging process and improve the overall quality of life for older individuals. As such, SPCs play a vital role in supporting elderly clientele by providing safe, effective, and holistic exercise programs that address the unique developmental challenges of aging. Consequently, they can help individuals maintain physical function, a positive outlook on life, and, more importantly, independence as they age.

WORKING WITH EXERCISE PARTICIPANTS

Michael L. Sachs, Selen Razon, & Jerry Holt

Of the more than eight billion people on this planet, only a few million are elite athletes. This means that there are billions of "regular people" out there waiting for your help in adopting and maintaining a lifestyle encompassing exercise. The bad news is that most of them have decided, at least for the moment, not to exercise or be physically active on a regular basis (USDHHS, 2018). This is a major concern in that physical inactivity, or the "sedentariness epidemic," is one of the primary public health challenges of our time (López-Valenciano et al., 2020). However, this seemingly grim news comes with amazing opportunities for you to change the lives of billions of individuals by working with them to become more physically active and to exercise on a regular basis. So how can you achieve this lofty goal?

First, you need to decide if this is a population you want to work with—regular people who are either sedentary or exercise irregularly. Perhaps your goal is to work with Olympians, and that's where your heart is. In that case, "go for the gold" and let others work with regular folks. But if your goal is to really change people's lives (and exercise can do that), then continue reading. In working with this population, you will be contributing greatly to the individual health of your clients. Additionally, you will also be contributing to the health of your community. As exercise professionals, it is gratifying for us to see healthy people, healthy families, and healthy communities. It is doubly gratifying if we know that we have contributed to the overall health of these individuals and groups. We are in the business of helping people establish healthy patterns of behavior. These patterns include proper nutrition, sleep, mental health, and, of course, exercise. As an exercise professional, you should help your clients establish and maintain these healthy behavior patterns, so that the individual and community health benefits outlined above can be realized. Unfortunately, a large percentage of the population that we will work with are reluctant to "do what it takes" to establish and maintain a lifestyle that will result in more healthful living. But that's where we come in.

Second, you will need to develop competence. Your university classes probably focused primarily on sport (and maybe performance) psychology, but hopefully you had a class (or at least part of a class) on exercise psychology. If you didn't, start with some excellent textbooks on exercise psychology and learn all about what we do as exercise psychologists (e.g., Andersen & Hanrahan, 2015; Berger et al., 2015; Buckworth et al., 2013). If you did have such classes, but it has been a while, refresh your memory with these resources. What are some of the skills you will need as an exercise psychology professional? Tod et al. (2024) offered a partial list of important characteristics, based on a review of traits that exercisers themselves perceived to be helpful in a good exercise psychology professional. These include the ability to develop rapport with clients, form relationships based on openness and realistic perceptions, inspire positive expectations and hope, help clients engage in helpful actions, and fit within the context in which the professional is operating.

Next, your pursuit of competence can extend to textbooks within applied exercise psychology (e.g., Razon & Sachs, 2024), and then texts specifically dealing with exercise as therapy (especially for anxiety and depression; e.g., Hays, 1999; Sachs & Buffone, 1984) or even the darker side of exercise, such as exercise addiction (e.g., Szabo & Demetrovics, 2022). Additional competency will include knowledge about decisional balance scales and the Transtheoretical Model of Behavior Change, as well as other theories of behavior change (e.g., found in Berger et al., 2015). As Razon and Sachs (2024) pointed out, getting your clients to adhere to their newly established exercise regimen is often a difficult task for the exercise professional, but with proper preparation and a mindset of encouragement for your clients, you can accomplish the task. You will then learn about the numerous excuses people make for not exercising ("excusercise") and how to help people overcome these barriers to increase exercise participation (Cohen & Sachs, 2023). Indeed, behavior change is the bottom line—changing from sedentary behavior to regular exercise behavior, and then maintaining that desired exercise behavior for the long term (i.e., exercise adherence).

Another important consideration is that you, as a competent practitioner, will work with your clients on performance and process goals, and maybe an occasional outcome goal (Weinberg & Gould, 2023). Perhaps your older client wants to win a medal in their age group at a local 5k race. Their performance goal might be running a 29:50 5k, and the process goals will involve regular runs, weightlifting, and stretching. The outcome goal of winning a medal will depend on competitors, but the performance is what really matters. For most of your clients who need help in adopting a physically active lifestyle, you will focus on the most important ingredient, enjoyment. You will help your clients select an activity (or set of activities) that they enjoy and are, therefore, that much more likely to adhere to and maintain for their lifetime.

As an exercise professional, you will learn various ways to help your clients experience the joys of exercise. Again, your familiarity with the literature is important. There are numerous resources upon which you can draw to construct exercise programs for your clients that are enjoyable for them (e.g., Nesti, 2016). For example, the British Heart Foundation (2021) suggests some approaches to exercise that will increase the "fun factor" for exercising, such as: Ask others to join you, add some entertainment, be a big kid, make exercise a game, move for a cause, and reward yourself. In this regard, getting to know your clients is an important consideration. In consultation with them, you can determine what they like in terms of PA, and together you can build a program that will keep them exercising (Hagberg et al., 2009). As the American College of Sports Medicine's (ACSM) Action Guide for Exercise Professionals states:

> Your ultimate goal is to build your client's self-efficacy, so they continue to integrate physical activity into their lives long after their engagement with you has ended. You want them to feel so good about their experience with exercise that they can say "I'm the kind of person who is physically active because it's part of who I am now – and I actually enjoy it!"
> (ACSM, 2022, p. 7)

It is also important to note that having a basic knowledge of exercise physiology effects–frequency, intensity, time, and type (FITT), would give you an edge. You do not need to become a certified personal trainer, but you should have the basic knowledge (such as information on activity and nutrition in Bushman, 2017) to be a well-rounded practitioner in behavior change. And you should also have some great personal trainers on your contact list for referrals for your clients who need that assistance in meeting their exercise goals.

An additional important consideration is knowing that you are not alone in your effort to help people become exercisers and maintain an exercise program. You will have a support system of fellow exercise professionals who will help you with suggestions, shared stories, anecdotes, and research information. An organization such as the Association for Applied Sport Psychology (AASP) is a great source of information and support. AASP's Exercise Psychology and Wellness Special Interest Group includes dozens of other professionals and other interested persons who have the same interests as you in terms of wellness and exercise. Networking with them is a great opportunity for both socialization within the field as well as for receiving valuable information to use in your practice. There are also numerous opportunities for continuing education activities that will help you keep abreast of new ideas and approaches. Professional organizations (e.g., ACSM) and companies such as Human Kinetics, are great sources of information and of continuing education opportunities.

Third, along with this general competence, you will want to develop specific competence/expertise in working with the populations with whom you will engage. There are differences in working with a 36 year old and a 76 year old, with women and men, individuals of different ethnicities, ability status, etc. Known as cultural competence or cultural humility (Lekas et al., 2020), even though you recognize that each of your clients is an individual, this quality indicates that you are knowledgeable about general issues related to that person's characteristics that will better inform your work with them.

Finally, you will decide where you will connect with your clients. Perhaps you will do so as part of your education, but afterwards you may do so as part of a private practice. Maybe your private practice will focus primarily on exercise clients. You may also make connections with local fitness centers or health clubs, etc., to offer exercise psychology services to their members. Rest assured that your entrepreneurial skills will be put to good use in building and sustaining your client base.

And, of course, don't forget to practice what you preach. On an intuitive basis, exercise professionals themselves should maintain their own health and wellness by engaging in an ongoing program of exercise. Moreover, when clients see their exercise leaders maintaining a healthy lifestyle through exercise, they are further motivated to maintain their own exercise program. Exercise professionals serve as role models and sources of information for the exercising public. Further, their exercise behaviors serve as sources of increased self-efficacy when they are working with clients (Newsome et al., 2024). When exercise professionals are seen as embodying the values they promote, this builds trust, rapport, and credibility with clients—a critical component in sustaining long-term behavior change.

EDITORS' TAKEAWAYS

Cacciatore and Swedlund's point about applied exercise psychology being in its relative infancy highlights both its challenges and opportunities. While growing pains are inevitable, this early stage means there is still room for our perspectives and innovations to shape the field. The examples throughout this chapter, and the entire book, show the hurdles ahead for new SEPPPs, but these challenges also invite us to influence and improve practice. For those willing to engage, the potential for meaningful impact is significant—leave it to exercise psychologists to find optimism through reappraisal. We were also struck by Dobersek and Pargman's emphasis on developing a strong working alliance with elderly clients. Building such relationships may require different approaches than with younger athletes, including attending more closely to life history, health needs, and social contexts. Adapting our methods in this way can foster stronger, more supportive connections. Finally, Sachs and colleagues' reminder about making exercise enjoyable stood out. Gyms often promote "no pain, no gain" mindsets that can discourage participation. Yet people are far more likely to continue an activity when they genuinely enjoy it. The task for exercise psychology professionals is to design sound programs that are also engaging—where fun becomes a foundation for consistency and positive behavior change.

RECOMMENDED EXERCISES

1 Have your thoughts on what applied exercise psychology "is" changed after reading this chapter?

   a If so, how?
   b What areas of applied exercise psychology interest you, and why?
   c What are some additional contexts applied exercise psychology practitioners can work in? Think outside of the box!

2 Imagine a client asks what you do and how applied exercise psychology can help. What would your brief elevator pitch be?
3 Think about your personal relationship with exercise across your life.

   a What experiences shaped your attitudes toward physical activity?
   b Have you ever struggled with motivation, confidence, or consistency?
   c How might these experiences influence how you support exercisers?

4 Imagine you are working with a "difficult" exercise client (e.g., skips workouts or mental skills sessions, loses motivation, feels guilty if they don't exercise but doesn't use that as motivation).

   a What emotions arise in you when someone doesn't follow through, in general as well as particularly when it comes to exercise? Frustration? Sympathy? Judgment?
   b How might these reactions influence your effectiveness?
   c What beliefs do you hold about "motivation" that might need revisiting?

5 Reflect on your beliefs about aging.

   a How might these shape your motivation to exercise or to encourage physical activity in yourself and others as you age?
   b How might these shape your service delivery with exercisers?

6 Create a simple one-week exercise plan (considering duration, frequency, and intensity) that meets physical and social needs. After completing it, reflect on changes in mood, energy, sensations, and social interactions.

7 Increase your familiarity with and understanding of the relationship between exercising and aging.

   a Join a group exercise session with older adults and observe the social dynamics. Reflect on how group activity may support psychological and social well-being.
   b To get a sense of aging, add kernels into your shoes, wear glasses with one eye patched and weights (on your ankles, wrists, and body), and put earplugs in your ears. Then, attempt to walk and talk to a colleague at the same time and reflect on the experience.

8 Think about the tone or style you want to bring to work with exercisers (e.g., encouraging, structured, gentle, motivational, collaborative, accountability-focused).

   a Which helping style feels most natural to you?
   b Which one might exercisers need from you—even if it is not your default?
   c How might you adapt your style for someone who needs a different approach?

REFERENCES

Almonacid-Fierro, A., Vargas-Vitoria, R., De Carvalho, R. S., Fierro, M. A., & Valdés-Badilla, P. (2021). Social representation of older people in relation to physical activity and health at old age: A qualitative study. *Journal of Physical Education and Sport, 21*(1), 36–45. https://efsupit.ro/images/stories/ianuarie2021/Art%205.pdf

Alwan, N., Moss, S. L., Davies, I. G., Elliott-Sale, K. J., & Enright, K. (2022). Weight loss practices and eating behaviours among female physique athletes: Acquiring the optimal body composition for competition. *PLoS One, 17*(1), e0262514. https://doi.org/10.1371/journal.pone.0262514

Alwan, N., Moss, S. L., Elliott-Sale, K. J., Davies, I. G., & Enright, K. (2019). A narrative review on female physique athletes: The physiological and psychological implications of weight management practices. *International Journal of Sport Nutrition and Exercise Metabolism, 29*(6), 682–689. https://doi.org/10.1123/ijsnem.2019-0037

American College of Sports Medicine. (2022). *Exercise professional's action guide.* Exercise is Medicine. https://www.exerciseismedicine.org/wp-content/uploads/2021/02/Exercise-Pros-Action-Guide-clickable-links.pdf

Andersen, M. B., & Hanrahan, S. J. (2015). *Doing exercise psychology.* Human Kinetics.

Berger, B. G., Weinberg, R. S., & Eklund, R. C. (2015). *Foundations of exercise psychology.* Fitness Information Technology.

British Heart Foundation. (2021). *Fun exercises: 6 ways to make exercise more enjoyable*. https://www.bhf.org.uk/informationsupport/heart-matters-magazine/activity/fun-exercises

Buckworth, J., Dishman, R. K., O'Connor, P. J., & Tomporowski, P. D. (2013). *Exercise psychology* (2nd ed.). Human Kinetics.

Bushman, B. (Ed.). (2017). *Complete guide to fitness & health* (2nd ed.). American College of Sports Medicine.

Centers for Disease Control and Prevention. (2023a). *Older adult activity: An overview*. https://www.cdc.gov/physical-activity-basics/guidelines/older-adults.html

Centers for Disease Control and Prevention. (2023b). *Physical activity guidelines for Americans mid-course report: Implementation strategies for older adults*. https://odphp.health.gov/our-work/nutrition-physical-activity/physical-activity-guidelines/current-guidelines/midcourse-report

Cohen, B., & Sachs, M. L. (2023). *Excusercise: Inexcusable excuses for not exercising*. Excusercise.

Hagberg, L. A., Lindahl, B., Nyberg, L., & Hellénius, M. L. (2009). Importance of enjoyment when promoting physical exercise. *Scandinavian Journal of Medicine & Science in Sports, 19*(5), 740–747. https://doi.org/10.1111/j.1600-0838.2008.00844.x

Harris, R. (2019). *ACT made simple: An easy-to-read primer on acceptance and commitment therapy*. New Harbinger Publications.

Hays, K. F. (1999). *Working it out: Using exercise in psychotherapy*. American Psychological Association. https://doi.org/10.1037/10330-000

Hodgkinson, E. L., Smith, D. M., & Wittkowski, A. (2014). Women's experiences of their pregnancy and postpartum body image: A systematic review and meta-synthesis. *BMC Pregnancy and Childbirth, 14*, 330. https://doi.org/10.1186/1471-2393-14-330

Lekas, H.-M., Pahl, K., & Fuller Lewis, C. (2020). Rethinking cultural competence: Shifting to cultural humility. *Health Services Insights, 13*, 1–6. https://doi.org/10.1177/1178632920970580

López-Valenciano, A., Mayo, X., Liguori, G., Copeland, R. J., Lamb, M., & Jimenez, A. (2020). Changes in sedentary behavior in European Union adults between 2002 and 2017. *BMC Public Health, 20*, 1–10. https://doi.org/10.1186/s12889-020-09293-1

Louis, E. D., & Bennett, D. A. (2007). Mild parkinsonian signs: An overview of an emerging concept. *Movement Disorders, 22*(12), 1681–1688. https://doi.org/10.1002/mds.21598

Marzuca-Nassr, G. N., Alegría-Molina, A., SanMartín-Calísto, Y., Artigas-Arias, M., Huard, N., Sapunar, J., Salazar, L. A., Verdijk, L. B., & van Loon, L. J. (2023). Muscle mass and strength gains following resistance exercise training in older adults 65–75 years and older adults above 85 years. *International Journal of Sport Nutrition and Exercise Metabolism, 34*(1), 11–19. https://doi.org/10.1123/ijsnem.2023-0087

Nesti, M. S. (2016). Exercise for health: Serious fun for the whole person? *Journal of Sport and Health Science, 5*(2), 135–138. https://doi.org/10.1016/j.jshs.2016.01.001

Newsome, A. N. M., Kilpatrick, M., & Dedrick, R. F. (2024). Exercise prescription practices among mental health professionals on college campuses: Testing the information–motivation–behavioral skills model. *International Journal of Behavioral Medicine*, 1–13. https://doi.org/10.1007/s12529-024-10266-6

Pargman, D., & Dobersek, U. (2024). Exercise and aging. In *Applied exercise psychology* (pp. 258–274). Routledge.

Pereira, T., Cipriano, I., Costa, T., Saraiva, M., Martins, A., & ALConsortium. (2019). Exercise, ageing and cognitive function: Effects of a personalized physical exercise program in the cognitive function of older adults. *Physiology & Behavior, 202*, 8–13. https://doi.org/10.1016/j.physbeh.2019.01.012

Razon, S., & Sachs, M. L. (Eds.). (2024). *Applied exercise psychology: The challenging journey from motivation to adherence*. Routledge.

Sachs, M. L., & Buffone, G. W. (Eds.). (1984). *Running as therapy: An integrated approach*. University of Nebraska Press.

Sele, S., Liem, F., Mérillat, S., & Jäncke, L. (2021). Age-related decline in the brain: A longitudinal study on inter-individual variability of cortical thickness, area, volume, and cognition. *NeuroImage, 240*, 118370. https://doi.org/10.1016/j.neuroimage.2021.118370

Szabo, A., & Demetrovics, Z. (2022). *Passion and addiction in sports and exercise.* Routledge.

Tod, D., Slade, K., & Lafferty, M. (2024). The sport and exercise psychology practitioner's contribution to service delivery outcomes. *International Journal of Sport and Exercise Psychology, 23*(5), 791–808. https://doi.org/10.1080/1612197X.2024.2351444

U.S. Department of Health and Human Services. (2018). *Physical activity guidelines for Americans* (2nd ed.). Author.

Watson, P. M. (2023). What it means to be an applied exercise psychologist: Reflections from 2003 to 2023. *Case Studies in Sport and Exercise Psychology, 7*(1), 122–134. https://doi.org/10.1123/cssep.2023-0038

Weinberg, R. S., & Gould, D. (2023). *Foundations of sport and exercise psychology* (8th ed.). Human Kinetics.

Weinberger, N. A., Kersting, A., Riedel-Heller, S. G., & Luck-Sikorski, C. (2016). Body dissatisfaction in individuals with obesity compared to normal-weight individuals: A systematic review and meta-analysis. *Obesity Facts, 9*(6), 424–441. https://doi.org/10.1159/000454837

WHO. (2022). *Ageing and health.* World Health Organization. https://www.who.int/news-room/fact-sheets/detail/ageing-and-health

Willmott, E. F., Thrower, S. N., Williams, T. L., & Petróczi, A. (2023). The perfect storm: A meta-ethnography of the motivations, behaviours, and experiences of competitive bodybuilders. *International Review of Sport and Exercise Psychology,* 1–20. https://doi.org/10.1080/1750984X.2023.2263851

Windle, G., Hughes, D., Linck, P., Russell, I., & Woods, B. (2010). Is exercise effective in promoting mental well-being in older age? A systematic review. *Aging & Mental Health, 14*(6), 652–669. https://doi.org/10.1080/13607861003713232

7 Working in Esports

Over the last few years, the emergence of esports as a relevant, organized competitive realm for esports athletes and teams has certainly been quite notable. Even the International Olympic Committee (IOC) started to embrace esports back in 2018. Following the organization of the Olympic Esports Week 2023 in Singapore in 2024 the 142nd IOC session decided to create the Olympic ESport Games. In 2026, the Asian Games will take place in Japan with several esports title events taking part as official medal contribution to the respective winning nations. Also, 2026 will be the inaugural year of the first Esports Nations Cup, a multi-title international esports tournament where players can represent their home countries. Evidenced by this development of esports within the Olympic movement, clearly esports is here to stay—and grow. As such, it is also a relevant field for research and practice for sport, exercise, and performance psychology professionals across the globe and our global teams of esports experts will share their experiences working with these performers.

LEVEL UP: BUILDING A MENTAL PERFORMANCE CAREER IN ESPORTS

Eric LeNorgant, Alessandro Quartiroli, Claudio Godoi, & Jackson Jin

Esports, or electronic sports, have rapidly grown in popularity and are increasingly recognized as a legitimate career path for professionals in sport, exercise, and performance psychology (SEPP) (Anderson et al., 2018). What began as recreational entertainment has since transformed into a lucrative industry, fueled by multi-million dollar competition prize pools, millions of viewers, and significant corporate investment into franchise infrastructure (Mangeloja, 2019). Champion competitors are often the product of rigorous training regimens and comprehensive support systems designed to maximize their chances of success (Carrani et al., 2022). This brief introduction into the world of esports intends to provide several insights for practitioners looking to engage with this dynamic industry.

The rise of esports is attributed to early video games evolving over time from standalone arcade titles to popular collaborative and competitive internet-based platforms (Bányai et al., 2018). As these video games grew into social, cultural, and economic markets, interest from stakeholders and spectators surged. This led to more organized competitions, increasing the demand placed on players to seek and achieve higher levels of performance (Martin-Niedecken & Schättin, 2020). Esports' rising popularity is driving increased investment in tournaments, teams, and player development, creating a growing demand for industry professionals.

DOI: 10.4324/9781003781486-7

Preparing for a Career in Esports

For SEPP professionals interested in entering the esports performance domain, several practical considerations are essential (Shynkaruk et al., 2021). While formal training in SEPP is foundational; understanding and educating oneself in esports-specific elements, such as psychological demands, organizational structures, and cultural aspects, is also crucial for success (Anderson et al., 2018; Horne et al., 2024). Beyond formal education as a critical starting point, early immersion in the esports setting and culture, through observation and hands-on exposure, is invaluable for practitioners. Scholars have emphasized the steep learning curve faced by those entering the esports domain (Swettenham & Whitehead, 2022), particularly for professionals transitioning from traditional sport (Brain et al., 2024a). To develop effective, context-sensitive practice (Stambulova & Schinke, 2017), practitioners should invest time in learning game-specific demands and, where possible, seek pre-season engagement to build relationships with key stakeholders. A major adjustment lies in working primarily within virtual environments (Brain et al., 2024b). Esports performance context is inherently and primarily a digital environment, which enables practitioners to support individuals or teams regardless of location. This remote structure contributes to culturally diverse rosters and introduces unique communication challenges (Brain et al., 2024c). Expanding the scope of engagement, especially through remote roles, can offer meaningful insight into the industry's structures and pressures (Brain et al., 2024a). Academic institutions provide a promising entry point. As esports becomes integrated across educational levels, from primary schools to universities, these programs offer valuable in-person exposure and a foundation for developing skills suited to more complex performance environments (Jenny et al., 2017).

Aside from early exposure, it is essential for SEPP professionals to understand the psychological and contextual demands of esports. Competitors operate in high-pressure environments with shifting game dynamics, year-round competition, and few structured breaks (Brain et al., 2024a). Many young athletes train between three and ten hours daily (DiFrancisco-Donoghue & Balentine, 2018), a level of commitment that contributes to high burnout and turnover rates (Meng-Lewis et al., 2022). Practitioners also face challenges associated with remote work, including limited proximity and reduced access to non-verbal cues, which can hinder engagement with players and coaches (Brain et al., 2024a). A strong understanding of these demands is critical. Supporting competitors in navigating constant performance expectations, rapid change, cross-cultural dynamics, and mental health pressures distinguishes effective practitioners (Cottrell et al., 2019). With investment in education, experience, and contextual awareness, professionals can make a meaningful contribution to the esports organizations as well as to the entire esports industry.

Becoming an Effective Performance Practitioner in Esports

To effectively and ethically work within the esports performance domain, aspiring SEPP practitioners must develop a robust set of key competencies. First, practitioners must have a clear understanding of their own abilities and limitations. This foundational self-awareness is not only vital for ethical decision-making but also essential for establishing boundaries and expectations, ensuring they operate within the scope of their expertise and the role they were hired to fulfill (Brain et al., 2024a). Esports organizations are primarily focused on their players, leading to substantial investment in resources aimed at enhancing competitive success. These resources often include a wide range of supporting staff, such as social media marketing teams, as well as strength and nutrition professionals. For a psychology practitioner, integrating into this layered infrastructure demands not only technical expertise but also a commitment to interdisciplinary collaboration. Supporting a holistic performance system involves balancing psychological specialization with clear communication and mutual respect across professional roles, all in service of sustainable player development. However, most organizational structures lack the financial capacity to maintain fully staffed interdisciplinary teams, which can lead to a blurring of responsibilities for the practitioner. For example, some practitioners have reported being asked to weigh in on roster decisions or provide advice on nutrition and physical training (Brain et al., 2024b, c). While being well-versed in the broader performance landscape can be valuable, organizations do not always recognize either the full scope of their athletes' psychological needs or the limitations of what practitioners are ethically permitted to provide. Brain et al. (2024a) highlighted the tension practitioners may face when shifting between addressing organizational performance goals and supporting the individual well-being of players and coaches. Practitioners can sometimes find themselves caught between an organization's drive for success and their professional obligation to prioritize mental health and holistic development. This dual accountability can create ethical dilemmas, particularly when organizational decisions may conflict with the psychological needs of players (Brain et al., 2024c). Practitioners must remain vigilant, upholding professional ethics while navigating complex demands and continually adapting to esports' rapidly evolving landscape, refining their practice, pursuing new opportunities, and responding to the shifting needs of players, coaches, and organizational leaders, to achieve and sustain a successful career within the esports performance domain.

This includes keeping pace with technological advancements, platform changes, and evolving team structures that influence how performance support is delivered. Networking is a powerful tool for this purpose, as building connections with established professionals in esports can provide valuable insights and open doors to new opportunities. Strong communication skills are equally important, as they enable practitioners to work effectively with both players and organizational staff. As the designated expert in psychology, practitioners must confidently guide their collaborators, offering informed recommendations grounded in best practices and careful observation. The ability to translate psychological knowledge into accessible, actionable strategies is key to fostering trust and legitimacy within high-performance esports settings. Esports performance environments share many core features with traditional athletic settings, including training demands, team dynamics, competitive pressure, and career instability (Pizzo et al., 2018). By adapting evidence-based practices and structural insights from conventional sport, practitioners can better address challenges such as burnout, career longevity, and identity development in this still-emerging field. Yet, it is essential to remain aware of the unique characteristics and nuanced demands of the esports performance domain which may not align neatly with traditional sport models. In doing so, practitioners position themselves not only as responsive professionals but also as pioneers shaping the future of esports. Cultivating these competencies may enable aspiring practitioners to contribute meaningfully to the ethical, effective, and sustainable growth of the domain.

Conclusion

In conclusion, building a career in esports requires careful navigation of ongoing challenges. The authors recommend gaining early experience in accessible settings such as local academic institutions, as these are often players' first exposure to organized esports. Such environments offer valuable learning opportunities for practitioners, players, and coaches alike. However, limitations in time and proximity to players remain common challenges. Practitioners are therefore encouraged to stay flexible with mental performance sessions and make them as engaging as possible to promote buy-in and reduce distractions. New challenges will continue to emerge throughout a practitioner's journey, especially given the rapid evolution of the esports performance domain. By striving to maintain deliberate engagement with both organizations and the broader performance landscape, practitioners can develop and sustain a successful and meaningful career within esports.

OPENING THE DOORS OF ESPORTS: EXPECTATIONS VERSUS REALITY

Bernadette Ramaker, Lisa Musculus, & Ismael Pedraza-Ramirez

You might be offered a position in esports while your background is in sport and exercise psychology (SEP) within traditional performance settings. It is reasonable to ask whether that training is sufficient for the distinctive demands of esports and as highlighted by Horne et al. (2024), entering in esports could feel overwhelming and intimidating. Thus, based on the rising interest in SEP and our combined experience of over a decade in professional esports, we highlight key challenges that practitioners face when entering the esports scene. Unfortunately, we have seen many colleagues struggle to break in or remain in the industry, often because of misaligned expectations and the underdeveloped nature of the industry (Horne et al., 2024). Therefore, in this chapter, we provide a critical look at these challenges and offer practical suggestions to help bridge the gap between expectations and reality.

The Performance Coach: Roles, Boundaries, and the Multidisciplinary Ideal

Esports environments are high-pressure, fast-evolving performance settings characterized by intensive schedules, frequent game updates, and complex interpersonal dynamics (Pedraza-Ramirez et al., 2024). Accordingly, there is growing recognition that SEP practitioners can support mental health, optimize training culture, and foster sustainable high-performance. Traditional sport psychology principles (e.g., mental skills, motivation, resilience, team dynamics) apply in esports (Pedraza-Ramirez et al., 2025), with adaptations to a digitally mediated, cognitively demanding, and sedentary environment.

In traditional sports, SEP practitioners are often described as "wearing many hats" (see Jack-of-all-trades; Friesen & Orlick, 2011). Similar patterns appear in esports, where the field's infancy and the screen-based work create expectations that practitioners will assume duties beyond psychology (e.g., basic sleep and nutrition guidance, organizing routines, assisting media obligations). Given this breadth, practitioners should critically reflect on their scope of practice. The key question is not which hats must be worn, but rather which ones can be worn competently and ethically while still aligning with professional standards and boundaries.

Esports teams typically add SEP support in one of a few ways; some react mid-season when "the mental is missing," others hire a specialist from the start, and recently some game developers, responding to mental health concerns (Kegelaers et al., 2025), have established requirements for mental health support (Riot Games, 2024). This trend has led many organizations to establish a "performance coach" role (Watson et al., 2021) covering all out-of-game performance factors.

Ideally, organizations would avoid implementing a single practitioner as a multi-role solution and instead invest in multidisciplinary teams (e.g., sport psychology, nutrition, physiotherapy, strength and conditioning) that collaborate to meet diverse demands (Zentgraf et al., 2024). In reality, however, most esports organizations operate in survival mode. Because budgets prioritize player salaries and media production (to satisfy sponsors), teams often survive with only one practitioner covering multiple support domains. In such situations, practitioners must navigate these gaps by upholding professional standards, ensuring sufficient time for core work, seeking collaboration or supervision in areas beyond their expertise, and committing to continuous professional development. Equally important is maintaining clear role boundaries, professional distance, and confidentiality, guided by a strong professional philosophy. Our experience suggests handling tasks closest to one's expertise (e.g., sleep patterns, basic nutrition) in collaboration with specialists (Ramaker & Pedraza-Ramirez, 2023), while referring players to qualified professionals for more distant areas (e.g., physical training, individualized nutrition).

Player Development Gaps: From Game Skill to Professional Skill

Esports lacks robust grassroots and academic systems that teach the craft of being a performer. Many players move directly from high school to professional teams, missing structured opportunities to develop life skills, self-regulation, and professional habits. Unlike traditional sports, dual-career pathways are rarely supported during or after an esports career. SEP therefore adds significant value by helping players build these foundational competencies.

A recurring challenge is the expectation, often shared by coaches, that players already possess a complete professional toolkit (e.g., structuring learning, feedback literacy, time and energy management, recovery routines, media conduct, teamwork). In reality, players may excel in-game yet still need to learn how to learn and sustain improvement. This gap can fuel overreliance on "grind," inconsistent behaviors, and stalled development (Abbott et al., 2022). Practitioners can bridge this gap by building players' capacity for self-directed growth, developing their metacognitive skills, goal-setting and reflection, deliberate practice habits, and healthy lifestyle routines, embedded within daily training and competition schedules. Organizations should engage accredited SEP practitioners; although accreditation pathways differ, they share core standards such as supervised practice, self-reflection, and continuing education that safeguard quality and ethical services.

Because many managers still seek a one-size-fits-all performance coach and are unaware of accreditation standards, role clarity, and fit often suffer. Practitioners may be the only highly trained experts in the room, responsible for life skills and performance development alongside logistics and career transitions. Under such conditions, practitioners must establish clear scope and boundaries, collaborate with other experts and prioritize high-impact activities, and carry out coach-the-coach interventions (Watson et al., 2021) that equip the staff to design learning-rich sessions with a clear purpose, implement constraint-based drills with structured feedback, model professional habits, and create a psychologically safe learning climate (Bubna et al., 2023). In parallel, practitioners should assess and shape the environment (i.e., training structures, schedules, players' obligations) to align with development goals (Pedraza-Ramirez et al., 2024). By upskilling coaches and optimizing the environment, even a single practitioner can foster durable improvements in players' learning, well-being, and performance.

The Quick-Fix Trap: Why Psychological Change Needs Time and Structure

Similar to traditional high-performance sports, esports teams are expected to perform early in the season to qualify for playoffs or other major events. Short seasons and frequent roster changes (Swettenham & Whitehead, 2022) leave little time for long-term development, fueling a search for "quick fixes" when results or team dynamics falter. This mindset conflicts with the timeline required for effective psychological training, as building performance-related habits requires understanding, repetition, and reinforcement (Laborde et al., 2020). Expecting a one-off sport psychology session to suddenly improve emotional control, change one's behavior, or improve motor-cognitive performance misrepresents what the field can deliver.

Meanwhile, ongoing psychological work is often disrupted by esports-specific demands (e.g., time-intensive tactical practice, press and content obligations, and constant social media engagement), which fragment players' focus and recovery. For sport psychology to add real value, teams must protect time and space for this work, aligning coaches on realistic timelines, and measuring adherence to training plans rather than expecting instant results.

From Grind to Design: Replacing Volume with Deliberate, Periodized Practice

Esports offers near-unlimited practice access. Players can play at any time—whether for fun, socializing, or improvement. Unlike many physical sports, where injury risk and fatigue impose daily training limits, esports training is constrained mainly by cognitive and fine-motor fatigue. These factors enable prolonged, continuous practice; continuous matchmaking and rank-based incentives further encourage high volumes of play. However, cognitive fatigue accumulates with excessive hours, reducing decision-making, motor precision, and learning efficiency.

Many teams favor an endless practice approach, leaving little space for practitioners to implement psychological interventions. The solution is not to cut practice indiscriminately but to periodize it by embedding goal-directed practice sessions, scheduling regular review and recovery periods, and setting stopping rules based on performance quality rather than hours. Balancing coaches' preference for repetition (Abbott et al., 2022) and players' desire for endless play with the need to integrate mental training is challenging. However, once such routines are accepted, they increase the perceived value and impact of sport psychology support. Practitioners can bridge this gap through psychoeducation, emphasizing that deliberate, high-quality practice enhances team performance more effectively than a constant, mindless *grind*.

Conclusion: Opening the Doors to Sustainable Esports Performance

Esports offers opportunities, but practitioners face the challenge of meeting expectations in demanding contexts. Moving away from the quick-fix and grind mindset and protecting the time to integrate psychological work, SEP practitioners can make a lasting impact. The ideal is multidisciplinary support, but the current reality is often still a single expert. Establishing a clear scope and standards, collaborating with others, and prioritizing a learning-centric environment will all support sustainable growth. All stakeholders must align on success as intra-individual and system improvement, measured by quality over quantity. By doing so, aligning expectations with reality, we open the doors of esports to sustainable performance and well-being.

A PRACTICAL GUIDE OF APPLIED SPORT PSYCHOLOGY IN ESPORTS

Rebecca Wong & Remco Polman

Research has indicated that esports players experience significant stress (e.g., Poulus et al., 2022a). Although many of the stressors experienced by esports players are similar to those experienced by traditional athletes, research has also indicated that they experience some unique stressors (e.g., anti-social behavior, technical issues, Poulus et al., 2022b). As such, esports players could benefit from psychological interventions similar to those used with traditional athletes (Poulus et al., 2020). To date, very few studies have examined the efficacy of psychological interventions in esports players. In one of the few studies, Poulus et al. (2024) showed that a coping intervention was successful in enhancing perceived coping effectiveness and subjective performance in professional esports players. However, more work is required to support the efficacy of sport psychological support in esports. One way to do this is by providing case studies through practitioners working in esports. This offers firsthand accounts of applied experiences and strategies for implementing psychological support in esports.

Case Study: Setting the Right Tone for the Team

I (first author) am sharing this case study based on sport psychology support provided to a five-player esports team. Despite prior engagements with multiple sport psychology practitioners (SPPs), the team continued to experience a performance gap. The organization's leadership perceived previous interventions as ineffective; as such I was invited to step into the role of SPP. Initial interactions revealed skepticism among team members regarding the efficacy of sport psychology services based on their past experiences (e.g., too much focus on group motivation, not really understanding the psychological demands for coaches and athletes). According to reports from the team manager and head coach, the players exhibited difficulties in managing in-game adversities effectively and demonstrated inconsistent execution of strategic plans, often due to breakdowns in communication. Preliminary observations during bootcamp visits further indicated that the team operated within an unstructured system, contributing to suboptimal coordination and performance. To address these issues, I proposed, developed, and implemented a high-performance program that included the following: two workshops approximately two months before the competitive season commenced, psychological skills sessions, and weekly meetings with the team manager and coaches.

The first workshop involved key stakeholders consisting of the head coach, assistant coach, captain, and team manager with the primary objective of establishing a shared vision for team culture and defining measurable competitive goals. This session aimed to develop a preliminary framework and align leadership perspectives before disseminating strategies to other team members. Unlike traditional sports systems, most esports stakeholders lack formal education or training in sport coaching and management. The first workshop also aimed to educate key stakeholders on how an effectively cultivated team culture fosters high levels of commitment and self-discipline among members. Leadership behaviors and role modeling by coaches, captain, and the team manager can positively influence team cohesion and performance, particularly during adversity. Consequently, a team alignment session holds significant importance in facilitating these outcomes.

The second workshop included the remaining team members (players). I facilitated discussions to promote ownership and accountability by encouraging every member to contribute their perspectives to shaping the team's vision. Research indicates that teams fostering accountability demonstrate improved communication and conflict resolution in high-pressure environments (Breitbach et al., 2017). To support open dialogue, I established a psychologically safe space, emphasizing that all opinions were valid. This was achieved through active questioning and shared reflection; while this potentially elicited vulnerability, it was deemed critical for fostering mutual understanding and acceptance. Given that the team trained and lived together, minimizing interpersonal conflict was essential (Poulus et al., 2022b). I facilitated discussions on behavioral expectations, encouraging members to articulate their preferences for interpersonal treatment within the team. Establishing these boundaries promotes professionalism while safeguarding mutual respect and individual privacy. Although "respect" was unanimously endorsed as a core value, sustained psychological safety remained fundamental for maintaining an environment conducive to open contribution from all members.

To establish a consistent understanding of psychological safety within the context of this case study, I introduced the concept to all participants during the workshop. Psychological safety, a relatively emergent construct within high-performance environments, is formally defined as

> the belief that one will not face punishment or humiliation for speaking up with ideas, questions, concerns, or mistakes. In psychologically safe environments, individuals perceive interpersonal risk-taking—such as seeking help or admitting errors—as free from negative social consequences.
>
> (Edmondson, 2018, p. 15)

I emphasized its crucial role in fostering team dynamics. Beyond alleviating the fear of negative repercussions for speaking up, promoting psychological safety was highlighted as a facilitator of enhanced team cohesion and dynamic adaptability. Furthermore, the discussion underscored the secondary benefits of psychological safety for mental health maintenance, noting its association with reduced anxiety and improved resilience within competitive contexts (Newman et al., 2017).

The workshop culminated in the establishment of a shared team goal and agreed-upon team culture characteristics, endorsed by all team members. This collective agreement fostered a clear and unambiguous understanding of mutual expectations, thereby promoting a unified, performance-oriented mindset. Additionally, I provided strategies for the implementation and ongoing reinforcement of the team culture. Like the acquisition of physical skills, the development of psychological competencies requires a dedicated commitment to practicing the relevant behaviors, attitudes, and skills (Weinberg & Gould, 2024). It fosters increased team cohesion and confidence not only among team members but also individually, ensuring the team is collectively prepared to face future challenges both in and outside the games.

To date, the relationship between mental states and performance in esports is still developing and is not well understood by both coaches and players (Poulus et al., 2023). As such, psychoeducation is essential to enhance its understanding. To this end and following from the workshops, several psychological skills sessions were provided on topics such as stress and its appraisal, mindfulness and breathing techniques, and visualization and mental pregame routine. I worked closely with the team manager and coaches to ensure these sessions helped close the performance gap. Additionally, a weekly meeting with the team manager and coaches was part of the high-performance program, aimed at identifying team and player issues and providing further intervention strategies to rectify those issues before it became chronic or complex. Ethically, these matters were discussed only after informed consent was obtained from the individuals involved. This practice reflects adherence to a professional code of ethics, recognizing that breaching confidentiality without appropriate grounds can compromise trust and therapeutic relationships between players and the SPP.

The persistent integration of team culture, open communication, and psychological skill development into daily training programs contributed to the team effectively managing the fluctuations of the season and ultimately reaching the grand-finals. Anecdotal evidence through observation and feedback by coaches and players suggested that the team developed high levels of resilience, both during competition and in response to external challenges such as tiring competition schedules when the team dropped to lower brackets, through to grand-finals. This was evidenced by their ability to persist and recover from difficult situations. Notably, an identical program was implemented in the following seasons, yielding nearly identical outcomes. The organization reached the grand-finals in three seasons, reflecting a consistent level of performance. Additionally, the organization was perceived as a safe and trusted environment, where performance, health, and well-being were closely aligned.

Current Challenges and Future Directions

There remains a significant gap in understanding the potential benefits SPPs can offer to esports teams (Watson & Pedraza-Ramirez, 2021). Despite a growing demand, there is also a lack of trained and accredited professionals due to the absence of formal training programs. It is essential to promote a better understanding of how SPPs can contribute to esports organizations, ranging from individual players to the broader esports ecosystem. Establishing clear definitions and theoretical foundations of the psychological aspects of esports performance is crucial (e.g., Poulus et al., 2024). Similar to traditional sports, SPPs can either work directly with team members or indirectly via coaches and other team officers (Watson & Pedraza-Ramirez, 2021). Integrating sport psychology into coaching can enhance training efficiency, performance, and well-being by creating a more effective and supportive training environment that fosters both individual and team success. There is also a need for more applied research adopting evidence-based approaches to support the development of esports (Watson & Pedraza-Ramirez, 2021). This is essential for navigating the complexities of this rapidly evolving field, as well as to provide the necessary tools and strategies for enhancing team performance and well-being in addition to contributing to the overall legitimacy and sustainability of esports as a competitive discipline.

EDITORS' TAKEAWAYS

LeNorgant and colleagues' contribution highlights the unique opportunity in esports to observe performance almost exactly as the performer experiences it. Because of its virtual nature, practitioners can see precisely what the performer sees and hear every word exchanged between teammates—an immersion rarely available in other performance domains. This level of access positions esports as a promising frontier for ethnographic research in performance psychology. Ramaker and colleagues remind us that for those entering esports, limited team resources may mean being asked to provide guidance beyond traditional sport psychology. Practitioners with a kinesiology background are well-positioned to draw upon that broader training, making use of knowledge from areas like nutrition, physiology, and strength training—while always staying mindful of professional scope of practice. In this way, what might once have felt like dormant undergraduate or graduate coursework can become a practical asset, offering value to teams while reinforcing the practitioner's versatility. We appreciated Wong and Polman's prioritization of psychological safety in their applied work with an esports team. One of the key benefits of a psychologically safe group is the freedom to engage in creative problem-solving without fear of ridicule or premature shutdown. In a performance context where strategies evolve rapidly, that freedom to experiment and take interpersonal risks is not just an interpersonal courtesy but a potential competitive advantage.

RECOMMENDED EXERCISES

1 After reading this chapter, what do you anticipate will be your initial challenge with esports, and what strategies could you implement to overcome it?
2 Given that esports players often meet online and may be geographically dispersed, how would you communicate effectively with them? What would coaching or training sessions look like, and how would you ensure psychological safety in online environments?
3 Considering the common training habits of logging many hours per day, what would you include or change to help players maximize their training sessions?
4 Esports teams can include diverse cultural backgrounds, ages, and native languages. How could these factors influence your work, and how would you approach team dynamics to be effective and inclusive?
5 If you created an action plan based on this chapter's practical guidance, what would your first three steps be?
6 What factors must be considered to ensure enough time and space for performance coaching within a professional esports team structure?
7 Similar to other sports and performance domains, esports consists of different genres. How might sport psychological support or interventions differ across different esports?
8 How could you navigate potential gaps in expertise as a practitioner while you are made the expert in the room regarding everything surrounding esports performance?

REFERENCES

Abbott, C., Watson, M., & Birch, P. (2022). Perceptions of effective training practices in *League of Legends*: A qualitative exploration. *Journal of Electronic Gaming and Esports, 1*(1). https://doi.org/10.1123/jege.2022-0011

Anderson, C. G., Tsaasan, A. M., Reitman, J., Lee, J. S., Wu, M., Steel, H., ... Steinkuehler, C. (2018). Understanding esports as a STEM career ready curriculum in the wild. *2018* In *10th international conference on virtual worlds and games for serious applications (VS-Games)* (pp. 1–6). IEEE. https://doi.org/10.1109/VS-Games.2018.8493445

Bányai, F., Griffiths, M. D., Király, O., & Demetrovics, Z. (2018). The psychology of esports: A systematic literature review. *Journal of Gambling Studies, 35*, 351–365. https://doi.org/10.1007/s10899-018-9763-1

Brain, J., Quartiroli, A., & Wagstaff, C. R. (2024a). Transitioning from traditional sport to esport: Exploring sport psychology practitioners' experiences. *The Sport Psychologist, 38*(4), 280–291. https://doi.org/10.1123/tsp.2024-0074

Brain, J., Wright, O., Quartiroli, A., & Wagstaff, C. R. D. (2024b). Supporting a national team during the Overwatch World Cup: Three confessional tales. *Case Studies in Sport and Exercise Psychology, 8*(S1), 28–35. https://doi.org/10.1123/cssep.2023-0034

Brain, J., Wright, O., Quartiroli, A., & Wagstaff, C. R. (2024c). Sport psychology practitioners' contributions to the drafting process of a professional esports team: A case study. *Case Studies in Sport and Exercise Psychology, 8*(1), 55–65. https://doi.org/10.1123/cssep.2023-0045

Breitbach, A. P., Reeves, S., & Fletcher, S. N. (2017). Health care as a team sport? Studying athletics to improve interprofessional collaboration. *Sports, 5*(3), 62. https://doi.org/10.3390/sports5030062

Bubna, K., Trotter, M. G., Watson, M., & Polman, R. (2023). Coaching and talent development in esports: A theoretical framework and suggestions for future research. *Frontiers in Psychology, 14*, 1191801. https://doi.org/10.3389/fpsyg.2023.1191801

Carrani, L. M., Riera, A. B., Altarriba-Bartés, A., Gil-Puga, B., Gonzalez, A. P., Piniés-Penadés, G., ... Peña, J. (2022). Are esports players comparable to traditional athletes? A cross-sectional study. *Aloma: Revista de Psicologia, Ciències de l'Educació i de l'Esport, 40*(2), 83–92.

Cottrell, C., McMillen, N., & Harris, B. S. (2019). Sport psychology in a virtual world: Considerations for practitioners working in esports. *Journal of Sport Psychology in Action, 10*(2), 73–81. https://doi.org/10.1080/21520704.2018.1518280

DiFrancisco-Donoghue, J., & Balentine, J. R. (2018). Collegiate esport: Where do we fit in? *Current Sports Medicine Reports, 17*(4), 117–118. https://doi.org/10.1249/JSR.0000000000000477

Edmondson, A. C. (2018). *The fearless organization: Creating psychological safety in the workplace for learning, innovation, and growth.* Wiley.

Friesen, A., & Orlick, T. (2011). Holistic sport psychology: Investigating the roles, operating standards, and intervention goals and strategies of holistic consultants. *Journal of Excellence, 14,* 18–42.

Horne, G., Burkill, R., Agarwal, A., & Swettenham, L. (2024). Should aspiring esports psychologists train in esports? Reflections of trainee sport and exercise psychologists. *Journal of Electronic Gaming and Esports, 2*(1), 1–12. https://doi.org/10.1123/jege.2024-0020

Jenny, S. E., Manning, R. D., Keiper, M. C., & Olrich, T. W. (2017). Virtual(ly) athletes: Where esports fit within the definition of "sport." *Quest, 69*(1), 1–18. https://doi.org/10.1080/00336297.2016.1144517

Kegelaers, J., Mairesse, O., Van Ruysevelt, L., Trotter, M. G., Watson, M., Pedraza-Ramirez, I., ... Van Heel, M. (2025). The mental health status of esports athletes. *Journal of Electronic Gaming and Esports, 3*(1), 1–10. https://doi.org/10.1123/jege.2025-0017

Laborde, S., Kauschke, D., Hosang, T. J., Javelle, F., & Mosley, E. (2020). Performance habits: A framework proposal. *Frontiers in Psychology, 11,* 1815. https://doi.org/10.3389/fpsyg.2020.01815

Mangeloja, E. (2019). Economics of esports. *Electronic Journal of Business Ethics and Organization Studies, 24*(2), 34–42.

Martin-Niedecken, A. L., & Schättin, A. (2020). Let the body'n'brain games begin: Toward innovative training approaches in esports athletes. *Frontiers in Psychology, 11,* 138. https://doi.org/10.3389/fpsyg.2020.00138

Meng-Lewis, Y., Wong, D., Zhao, Y., & Lewis, G. (2022). Understanding complexity and dynamics in the career development of esports athletes. *Sport Management Review, 25*(1), 106–133. https://doi.org/10.1016/j.smr.2020.08.003

Newman, A., Donohue, R., & Eva, N. (2017). Psychological safety: A systematic review of the literature. *Human Resource Management Review, 27*(3), 521–535. https://doi.org/10.1016/j.hrmr.2017.01.001

Pedraza-Ramirez, I., Ramaker, B., Mathorne, O. W., Watson, M., & Laborde, S. (2024). Behind the curtains of elite esports: A case study from a holistic ecological approach to talent development. *Case Studies in Sport and Exercise Psychology, 8*(S1), S18–S27. https://doi.org/10.1123/cssep.2023-0017

Pedraza-Ramirez, I., Sharpe, B., Behnke, M., Toth, A. J., & Poulus, D. R. (2025). The psychology of esports: Trends, challenges, and future directions. *Psychology of Sport and Exercise, 71,* 102967. https://doi.org/10.1016/j.psychsport.2025.102967

Pizzo, A., Baker, B., Na, S., Lee, M. A., Kim, D., & Funk, D. (2018). Esport vs. sport: A comparison of spectator motives. *Sport Marketing Quarterly, 27*(2), 108–121. https://doi.org/10.32731/SMQ.272.062018.04

Poulus, D., Coulter, T., Trotter, M., & Polman, R. (2020). Stress and coping in esports and the influence of mental toughness. *Frontiers in Psychology, 11,* 628. https://doi.org/10.3389/fpsyg.2020.00628

Poulus, D., Coulter, T., Trotter, M., & Polman, R. (2022a). Longitudinal analysis of stressors, stress, coping and coping effectiveness in elite esports athletes. *Psychology of Sport and Exercise, 60,* 102093. https://doi.org/10.1016/j.psychsport.2021.102093

Poulus, D., Coulter, T., Trotter, M., & Polman, R. (2022b). Perceived stressors experienced by competitive esports athletes. *International Journal of Esports, 1*(1), 73. https://www.ijesports.org/article/73/html

Poulus, D., Sharpe, B. T., Jackman, P. C., & Bennett, K. (2024). Defining elite in esports: A scoping review. *International Review of Sport and Exercise Psychology.* Advance online publication. https://www.ijesports.org/article/73/html

Poulus, D. R., Bennett, K. J. M., Swann, C., Moyle, G. M., & Polman, R. (2023). The effects of a coping intervention on coping effectiveness, resilience, mental health, and performance among elite esports players: A pilot study. *Psychology of Sport and Exercise, 69*, 102510. https://doi.org/10.1016/j.psychsport.2023.102510

Ramaker, B., & Pedraza-Ramirez, I. (2023). Everyone is figuring it out along the way: Diving headfirst into the world of esports. In *Navigating applied sport and exercise psychology* (pp. 84–99). Routledge. https://doi.org/10.4324/9781003263890-8

Riot Games. (2024). *Riot esports EMEA season review 2023*. https://cmsassets.rgpub.io/sanity/files/dsfx7636/news/c8d8d9e5ac3e99634c2a3561223689a9f2fe58f7.pdf

Shynkaruk, O., Byshevets, N., Iakovenko, O., Serhiyenko, K., Anokhin, E., Yukhno, Y., … Stroganov, S. (2021). Modern approaches to the preparation system of masters in esports. *Sport Mont, 19*(S2), 69–74. https://doi.org/10.26773/smj.210912

Stambulova, N. B., & Schinke, R. J. (2017). Experts focus on the context: Postulates derived from the authors' shared experiences and wisdom. *Journal of Sport Psychology in Action, 8*(2), 131–134. https://doi.org/10.1080/21520704.2017.1308715

Swettenham, L., & Whitehead, A. E. (2022). Working in esports: Developing team cohesion. *Case Studies in Sport and Exercise Psychology, 6*(1), 36–44. https://doi.org/10.1123/cssep.2021-0023

Watson, M., Abbott, C., & Pedraza-Ramirez, I. (2021). A parallel approach to performance and sport psychology work in esports teams. *International Journal of Esports, 1*(1). https://www.ijesports.org/article/52/html

Weinberg, R. S., & Gould, D. (2024). *Foundations of sport and exercise psychology* (8th ed.). Human Kinetics.

Zentgraf, K., Musculus, L., Reichert, L., Will, L., Roffler, A., Hacker, S., … Krüger, K. (2024). Advocating individual-based profiles of elite athletes to capture the multifactorial nature of elite sports performance. *Scientific Reports, 14*, 76977. https://doi.org/10.1038/s41598-024-76977-8

8 Working with Military & Tactical Professionals

For students graduating from their sport, exercise, and performance psychology (SEPP) degree programs, the U.S. military has long provided prime employment opportunities. Many recent graduates start their career within this performance realm, finding employment in the various SEPP programs the U.S. military has established at bases around the country as well as in others. Globally, however, not many countries may provide similar employment opportunities for SEPP professionals. Still, providing mental performance work for military populations remains a relevant career path in the field of SEPP. A path less traveled, however, is service provision to emergency first responder populations such as firefighters, police officers, and emergency medical technicians. Our global group of authors will shed some light on what a scientist-practitioner's work can look like when consulting with these various tactical population performers.

SPORT AND PERFORMANCE PSYCHOLOGY FOR FIRST RESPONDERS: FROM THEORY TO PRACTICE

Robert E. Owens & Charlie Frost

There is an increasing prevalence of occupationally related health issues associated with law enforcement, firefighting, and emergency management services, including obesity and heart disease (Mumford et al., 2015), trauma and post-traumatic stress (Bonumwezi et al., 2022), moral injury (Papazoglou et al., 2020), and suicidality (Violanti, 2022). The U.S. Department of Justice published a 2015 report highlighting officer safety and wellness as one of six pillars critical for successful policing in the 21st century (Kuhns et al., 2015). As a result, helping professionals are challenged to design effective interventions to mitigate stress and foster resilience in public safety personnel. Sport psychology practitioners who are often trained in sports performance, exercise adherence, decision-making, and behavior change have a unique skillset to address and mitigate the wellness and performance concerns facing today's first responders.

Before working with first responders, practitioners should understand the role of today's first responder as protector and enforcer (Heil et al., 2023). Protectors in the sense that first responders are expected to provide services "within a context of compassion" (Heil et al., 2023, p. 93), and enforcers because "their duties within these high-risk occupations require courage, determination, and effective communication" (Magaletta et al., 2020, p. 127). First responders put themselves at risk for physical and emotional harm every day. While this is potentially true for traditional athletes, competitive sport is a highly structured activity where competitors have a mutually agreed-upon set of rules. The law enforcement officer (LEO)

DOI: 10.4324/9781003781486-8

is tasked with protecting the lives of civilians, which requires making tactical decisions about the appropriate use of force. Even athletes who compete in combat sports like boxing or mixed martial arts rarely experience the types of aggression meant to maim or kill. Despite this, there are some similarities between enforcing the law and competing in an athletic competition, as each requires an athlete to meet the physical and mental demands of the performance environment and make decisions under pressure.

Practitioners can and should provide services outside of traditional performance domains of sport and exercise (Hays, 2006). Although many practitioners have academic training in kinesiology or clinical psychology, they do not typically have formal training (e.g., domain-specific knowledge) for consulting with performers in business, healthcare, the performing arts, or tactical settings like policing, firefighting, or the military. Some graduate-level training programs in sport psychology might include coursework in consulting with non-sport populations, but this training may not be part of a standard core curriculum. For this reason, practitioners who work with tactical athletes are faced with finding training and experiential opportunities outside of sport psychology to develop competence. As demands for the provisioning of sport psychology services to non-sport populations continue to grow, the professional development of practitioners with the identification and cultivation of credit, non-credit, and fieldwork opportunities to support the dynamic nature of change within the field is tantamount to the field's ultimate success and survival.

Navigating First Responder Culture

First responders may question the efficacy of applying sport psychology principles within public safety settings. After all, policing, firefighting, and emergency management are not sports. First responders, particularly those who work in law enforcement, are highly skeptical of perceived outsiders (Gilmartin, 2021) and might question a practitioner's motives. To effectively provide services to first responders, practitioners (who do not have direct work experience in public safety settings) should develop contextual intelligence (Brown et al., 2005) by participating in civilian programs like ride-a-longs and citizen academies, or volunteering with sports leagues or competitions explicitly tailored to first responders like Police Athletic Leagues or the World Police and Fire Games. In contrast to other athletic contexts, tactical settings offer a variety of different challenges to the implementation of mental skills enhancement programs. For instance, practitioners might help a baseball player develop a hitting routine where they may have them step out of the batter's box to distance themselves metaphorically and physically from a bad swing at a pitch. In comparison, during firearms training, an officer who fires a bad round during required annual qualifications cannot step away from the mistake because in doing so, it might create a safety hazard to others on the firing line. Therefore, contextual intelligence and domain-specific knowledge (Hays, 2006) are critical for applying mental skills training to tactical settings.

Are You Fit for Duty? Considering First Responder Performance and Well-being

One of the barriers to implementing sport psychology principles within law enforcement departments and other public safety settings is the conflation of police psychology and military psychology with sport psychology, particularly as it pertains to performance enhancement and personal well-being. Historically, police psychologists have drawn insights from military psychology to apply mental resilience techniques to enhance performance in law enforcement. For example, David Grossman's (1995) book *On Killing: The Psychological Cost of Learning to Kill in War and Society* is often cited in police psychology manuals. In the book *Warrior Mindset—Mental Toughness Skills for A Nation's Defenders: Performance Psychology Applied to Combat*, the authors, all police psychologists, cited common techniques used in sport psychology, including positive self-talk, concentration, arousal regulation, progressive muscle relaxation, and imagery (Asken et al., 2010). Laurence Miller, another well-known police psychologist, mentions *performance enhancement* throughout the book *METTLE: Mental Toughness Training for Law Enforcement* (Miller, 2009) and cites the work of prominent sports psychologists, like Kate Hays, Ken Ravizza, Richard Thelwell, and others. While these works written by police psychologists may somewhat resonate with "the lived LEO experience" (Heil et al., 2023, p. 92), they might not be fully aligned with current literature on (tactical) athletic performance and well-being (cf. Wise & Trigg, 2020).

From Theory to Practice

Sport psychology principles and concepts have been misapplied in law enforcement contexts. A prime example is the uncritical deployment of the concept of "flow" in the police psychology literature. Little scholarly work has been done to inquire how flow experiences occur in law enforcement and how flow states differ from clutch states within tactical settings. In addition, the efficacy of psychological skills interventions when deployed in first responder settings is nuanced. Although visual imagery might positively impact firefighter operations, it may also increase stress levels and induce cognitive overload (Marquardt et al., 2019). Accordingly, practitioners should rely on evidence-based interventions. For example, when implemented as part of a wellness intervention, psychological models like Anshel's (2019) disconnected values model showed significant increases in the officers' adherence to physical training programs. Moreover, Land and colleagues (2022), when developing the psychological skills inventory for law enforcement (PSI-LE), found that combat breathing, muscle control, self-talk, mental practice, attention management, physical recharge, and a winning mindset were the essential psychological skills needed in law enforcement. The PSI-LE was initially designed based on the curriculum from the San Antonio Police Department's *Performance, Recovery, and Optimization* program.

As the performance demands on law enforcement grow more complex, so must the methods used to optimize performance and well-being. Sport and performance psychology offers underutilized frameworks for addressing the mental, physical, and emotional challenges LEOs and other first responders face. However, for practitioners to effectively apply these techniques requires more than theoretical knowledge—it necessitates a deep understanding of the distinct culture, environment, and stressors inherent to public safety professions. By developing contextual intelligence and adapting evidence-based practices to the realities of tactical performance, practitioners can play a pivotal role in helping first responders thrive under pressure.

PERFORMANCE PSYCHOLOGY PROVIDING VALUE TO MILITARY POPULATIONS

Nick Powell & Eric Biener

The U.S. military is one of the largest employers of mental performance consultants (MPCs) in the world, with several hundred MPCs drawn to the higher cause of serving those who dedicate their lives to serving their country. There are many similarities to consulting in sport, performing arts, and business domains, but also unique differences in working with military service members (SMs).

The delivery of mental skills training to military populations will differ by nationality, military branch, and the specific unit's mission, and the MPC must therefore tailor their approach to the specific context. The authors' intent, based on their experience working with the U.S. Army, is to give an overview of the most common services required of a broad array of military occupational specialties and insight into how MPCs can effectively consult with SMs.

Common Services Required of MPCs

MPCs serving military populations provide training to enhance mental performance, increase resilience and emotional intelligence, and strengthen unit culture and leadership. MPCs can support basic SM tasks like shooting, navigating, communicating, or saving lives by training mental skills such as attentional focus, motivation, and arousal regulation (Holt, 2014; Sackett et al., 2022). Marksmanship, for example, is an essential skill for SMs. While at the firing range, a missed target has the potential to snowball into a series of misses due to strong thoughts about the future impact of that miss or a physiological change like increased muscle tension. MPCs can train skills such as cognitive defusion to help the SM understand that they can still hit the remaining targets despite anxiety from the previous miss, mental cues to shift the SM's attention back to target identification, or diaphragmatic breathing to lower physiological arousal and enter their individual zone of optimal functioning (Robazza et al., 2004).

In addition to mental performance training, MPCs also train resilience and emotional intelligence skills that can benefit all SMs in both their professional and personal lives, such as self-awareness, self-regulation, and empathy. For example, MPCs can help deployed SMs getting into arguments with loved ones back home better self-regulate by understanding how their thoughts impact their emotions and reactions. MPCs can also equip SMs with more effective response strategies, enabling SMs to maintain strong relationships with important people in their lives. By helping SMs better respond to challenges with increased emotional intelligence, MPCs support SMs' ability to navigate their professional and personal lives more effectively.

Another common area of impact for MPCs is organizational culture, and how leadership behaviors impact this culture. With varying amounts of prior leadership experience and know-how, some military leaders might not be equipped with a complete skill set to balance "mission first, people always" (a common leadership principle in the U.S. military). Because of this, MPCs can support military leadership training by providing supplemental leadership and culture development in topics such as motivational climates, mindset development, psychological safety, and effective feedback. For example, MPCs can assist junior leaders in honing their own leadership philosophy to navigate difficult or ambiguous situations arising during their first formal leadership responsibilities. Additionally, MPCs can help more seasoned leaders navigate generational differences that may underlie conflicting beliefs about how to best accomplish tasks and treat people. Leaders may (even if unintentionally) create environments where SMs are not willing to offer new ideas, provide criticism, or ask clarifying questions. Since many military contexts require shared information and interconnected efforts, MPCs can help these units develop a culture of free-flowing information (Edmondson, 2019). By supporting strong cultures and effective leadership, MPCs can help military units be more than the sum of their parts.

Considerations for Consulting with Military Populations

Ascertaining certain background information helps to inform the types of services that will be most impactful. One of the most important pieces of information is the SMs' level of motivation to become elite. Some MPCs work in environments where every SM is driven to be the best they can be, but many will work with SMs who are content with doing their jobs well, satisfied with "good enough," or just counting the days until they get out of the military. The most elite may be more interested in mental skills training to optimize their performance, whereas those lower down the motivational spectrum may benefit more from sleep hygiene or resilience training. Factors such as cultural upbringing, socioeconomic background, and education level may also impact interest levels in mental skills training. For example, commissioned officers are required to have a college education, whereas enlisted SMs do not have this requirement; this might impact the extent to which they have engaged in skills like metacognition or visualization.

Many misconceptions exist within military populations about what mental performance is and the training methods used, which can inhibit the effectiveness of mental skills training unless MPCs clarify the true intent. One of the most common myths regarding mental performance is that one should *only* experience positive emotions all the time, and that resilience is simply "finding the good" in bad things that happen. While this strategy may work in some contexts for some individuals, it often results in frustration when others (understandably) cannot convince themselves that bad events are actually good. Such misunderstandings often lead to broad skepticism with the entirety of mental skills training. Explaining that "negative" emotions are natural often lifts a weight off SMs' shoulders and helps the MPC gain buy-in for further lessons. For example, the MPC can say, "Sometimes, you won't be thrilled about doing a ruck march on a cold, wet, dark morning. That's normal! The question is how you persist with your physical training in spite of that lack of excitement."

Gaining buy-in requires an appreciation of the wide variety of SM jobs and tasks, understanding the organizational structure of various units, and grasping the unit's jargon in order to effectively tailor trainings to SMs' work and experiences. MPCs can best gain this understanding by building relationships with SMs in different units, jobs, and levels in the branch hierarchy, posing open-ended questions about SMs' tasks and organizational structure, and observing their daily tasks whenever possible.

A challenge to gaining buy-in can be introducing a psychological theory before addressing how it can aid the unit or SM, or using examples from non-military domains. While citing the effectiveness of performance psychology topics from the realms of business or sports can sometimes create buy-in, these examples may close SMs off to the idea because of their perception that the military functions differently than these domains. A more effective approach can be to first elicit a specific problem or need the unit or individual has, and then offer solutions to those problems through specific performance psychology actions. For example, motor vehicle accidents are the second-highest cause of death in the U.S. Army (Kaplansky & Toussaint, 2024); an MPC could have SMs brainstorm times when they perceived an inability to speak up about safety hazards that contributed directly to a motor vehicle accident. This approach clearly demonstrates the usefulness of actions that increase unit psychological safety and creates open-mindedness for teaching leader behaviors, resulting not only in reduced safety hazards, but also other benefits to the unit (e.g., bottom-up innovation).

Units and leadership will often seek out MPCs' services without a comprehensive understanding of how they can help, often vaguely requesting "team building," "resilience," or "mental toughness" training. MPCs should therefore conduct a needs analysis with their point of contact in order to design a training plan that will meet unit needs. A productive way to begin is by discussing current issues or priorities within the unit, the unit's training calendar in the next few months, and whether there are opportunities to observe already-scheduled unit activities. In the authors' experience, training the same SMs consistently over time is much more effective than one-off sessions. In addition, it can be beneficial to utilize a periodized, "LMA" approach—Learning Stage, Modification Stage, Application Stage—combining classroom mental skills education with real-world application of the skills, for example, during training exercises or on the firing range (Bompa et al., 2019).

MPCs can be a valuable resource in support of military populations, benefiting individuals, units, and organizations. When MPCs work with SMs to clarify desired outcomes and processes, they can customize interventions that enhance performance, resilience, and readiness.

PERFORMANCE PSYCHOLOGY INTERVENTIONS FOR TACTICAL POPULATIONS: FOCUS ON MENTAL TRAINING, ATTENTIONAL CONTROL, AND DEBRIEFING

Nicki Marquardt

Work Characteristics and Performance—Critical Phases of Tactical Populations

Tactical populations (e.g., firefighters, emergency medical technicians, police officers, first responders, and soldiers) operate in environments that demand exceptional mental and physical performance under challenging conditions. The main work characteristics for these groups (Raabe et al., 2021; Rasteiro et al., 2023) include *stress* (they operate under severe time constraints), *high responsibility* (their actions directly impact public safety, health, and security), *situational dynamics* (their environment changes rapidly and unpredictably), and *risks* (they handle potentially hazardous situations). Hence, whether it's extinguishing a fire, providing medical care, or responding to a security threat, performance psychology interventions can support those people in developing and maintaining peak performance when every second counts. For each of those scenarios, performance psychology interventions can be applied across three performance-critical phases of a task: *Pre-operational, Operational, and Post-operational* (Marquardt et al., 2024). Each phase requires distinct mental skills to ensure successful task execution. Specifically, the pre-operational phase occurs before task execution and involves extensive mental preparation to ensure mental readiness for the upcoming task (Behnke et al., 2019; Marquardt et al., 2023). The operational phase is the actual performance episode during task execution, which is characterized by the implementation of strategies developed during the pre-operational phase. Tactical professionals must remain focused and execute their tasks with high precision while handling stress and maintaining a shared situational awareness through communication and cooperation to warrant the success of operations (Marquardt, 2019). Finally, the post-operational phase follows after task execution, where the operation's success is being evaluated and lessons learned are identified to improve future performance (Allen et al., 2018; Marquardt et al., 2024). The next three sections introduce one exemplary evidence-based performance psychology intervention for each performance-critical phase of tactical populations.

Pre-Operational Phase: Mental Training

In the pre-operational phase, mental training can be used to prepare tactical personnel for upcoming challenges during an operation. Mental training is based on the premise that psychological factors can either enhance or inhibit individual and team performance. Thus, mental training is highly beneficial for tactical populations because it enhances task focus, resilience, and decision-making under pressure (Marquardt et al., 2023). It helps individuals to improve emotional regulation and situational awareness, leading to better performance in high-stakes situations, which can be critical for mission success and safety (Marquardt, 2019).

Several components of mental training have been identified, such as mental imagery techniques, self-talk techniques, and pre-performance routines (Behnke et al., 2019). Among these, mental imagery has proven to be one of the most crucial skills for achieving performance excellence in diverse task domains (Marquardt et al., 2023). Specifically, mental imagery involves using all senses to vividly visualize and simulate a course of action in one's mind (Behnke et al., 2019). Research has shown that imagery enhances both stress reduction and the success of tactical personnel operations (Marquardt et al., 2023). These results can be explained by the similar activation of neuronal patterns that occur during imagery and actual execution, increasing the likelihood of successful performance (Batula et al., 2017). For instance, in case of a resuscitation in a mass casualty accident it would mean to mentally rehearse the procedural health-critical task steps such as securing the accident site, identifying the injuries and assessing their severity, treating the injuries and engaging in the resuscitation, and finally organizing evacuation.

Operational Phase: Attentional Control

Within the operational phase, the actions which were planned in the pre-operational phase are executed. Tactical professionals must remain focused while handling stress (Rasteiro et al., 2023) therefore attentional control techniques are crucial. Attentional control involves directing one's focus to one or more primary task stimuli while simultaneously controlling distractions (Marquardt et al., 2023). Under pressure, especially in situations where primary tasks require critical decisions (e.g., to fire or not to fire in a combat situation), it is vital to focus attention and manage distractions by using attention-directing self-instructions (e.g., "Focus the target"; "Ignore the loud background noise"; "Anticipate what might happen next"). The positive contribution of attentional control techniques to performance is particularly evident in highly stressful situations, where performance can depend entirely on the ability to maintain full task focus (Raabe et al., 2021). For example, in Marquardt et al.'s (2023) study, attentional control was the best predictor for stress reduction in a tactical population sample. Since high levels of situational stress are associated with misperception and attention deficits, leading to limited information intake, attentional control is crucial for tactical professionals, where every second counts and any additional information can be life-saving.

Post-Operational Phase: Debriefing

The primary purpose of the post-operational phase is to debrief and facilitate learning loops. After the execution of actions, it is crucial to compare performance outcomes against intended goals and assumptions. When discrepancies between goals and outcomes arise, adjustments must be made for future actions and their underlying assumptions (Marquardt, 2019). Debriefing is one of the most effective strategies for facilitating learning after task completion (Keiser & Arthur, 2021). In a debriefing, "teams discuss, interpret, and learn from recent events during which they collaborated" (Allen et al., 2018, p. 504). This technique transforms a recent experience into a learning opportunity through systematic review (Keiser & Arthur, 2021). Originally rooted in the military, debriefings have become widely used in different tactical population contexts such as firefighters, law enforcement, and other emergency response teams (Allen et al., 2018; Keiser & Arthur, 2021). Moreover, debriefings for tactical populations carry a deep emotional weight. Therefore, these team reflection sessions can provide a structured and psychologically safe space to process intense experiences, often marked by trauma, high-stress decisions, or life-threatening situations (Ancarani et al., 2025). Participants may experience relief, vulnerability, or even resistance, depending on their personal coping mechanisms and respective team culture. Sharing these experiences can strengthen team cohesion and reduce feelings of isolation, but it also requires a high level of mutual trust, psychological safety, and willingness to open up (Edmondson, 1996). For some, revisiting events can trigger buried emotions, making it vital that facilitators approach the process with empathy and care.

There are numerous forms of debriefings such as the after-action review (AAR). In particular, an AAR is a professional reflection tool focused on performance standards, allowing individuals and teams to address central questions for improving task performance (see Table 8.1; Marquardt et al., 2024).

To summarize, performance psychology interventions can support tactical populations across three critical phases: (1) the pre-operational phase, where mental training prepares them for upcoming challenges; (2) the operational phase, where attentional control techniques help maintain focus and manage stress during task execution; and (3) the post-operational phase, where debriefing facilitates learning and performance improvement through systematic review and reflection on recent events.

Table 8.1 Stages in an AAR Following the GOAL-protocol for a Firefighter Example

After-Action Review Stage	*Firefighting Operation Example*
Stage 1: **G**oal review: What was supposed to happen?	Review intended goals: "We wanted to extinguish the fire in a warehouse with a minimum risk for human lives."
Stage 2: **O**utcome review: What actually happened?	Review actual outcomes: "We put out the fire, but were almost buried under the collapsing warehouse."
Stage 3: **A**ction & error review: Why was there a difference?	Review committed actions and errors stepwise: "We started to extinguish the fire quickly." "Because of the intense smoke, we were a bit nervous and worried to overlook dangers during the mission." "Due to the smoke inside the warehouse, we have overlooked that its ceiling beams were deformed entirely by the heat of the fire."
Stage 4: **L**essons learned review: What can we learn from this?	Review lessons learned: "Next time we will first check whether the critical parts of the building are intact." "In addition, to counteract negative effects of nervousness, we will speak up concerns before we are going to enter a burning building."

EDITORS' TAKEAWAYS

A conversation still underdeveloped in the SEPP literature—and which Owens and Frost briefly note—is the potential misalignment between traditional sport psychology principles and tactical populations. While many argue that sport performance skills transfer easily, there is an important nuance that requires more empirical attention. We need research that goes beyond assumptions and provides clear guidance for practitioners working in these unique, high-stakes environments. Powell and Biener also prompted us to reconsider motivation in the military. We had assumed SMs would always seek maximum performance given the "life or death" framing we often hear. Their contribution reminded us that motivation varies, and that effective support requires understanding each individual's needs and goals rather than relying on broad narratives. Finally, Marquardt highlights how structured team debriefs can help manage emotional responses within tactical groups. By creating space to share perspectives and validate reactions after challenging situations, debriefing normalizes emotional experience and reduces stigma. In turn, it strengthens trust, cohesion, and camaraderie—core elements for teams operating under intense pressure.

RECOMMENDED EXERCISES

1 First responder communities are close-knit and often cautious of outsiders, with a distinct culture that can be hard to understand. How could you use Brown et al.'s (2005) SPAM model (Structure, Patterns, Attitudes, Means of Influence) to build contextual intelligence, gain entry, and develop rapport and trust?
2 What skills are uniquely required when working with military and tactical populations, and how would you develop them?
3 As a mental performance consultant joining a new unit, what key information would you need to effectively support individual members and the group as a whole?
4 As with any venue for consulting, client confidentiality is vital to the working relationship. In working with first responders and law enforcement, you may find yourself in a position where you may learn privileged or confidential information about individual citizens or operations occurring in the community. What ethical concerns might arise for you in this situation? How would you manage any ethical conflicts?
5 You are asked to assist a unit in which many SMs are struggling with their physical training test, six weeks away. How would you design a mental skills training program to help them prepare?
6 You are working with a unit that often deploys on training exercises. The SMs report being exhausted and burned out, being frustrated with others in the unit, and often reacting angrily to perceived slights. How would you begin working to help them solve these issues? How do you think this may be affecting the SMs' personal lives?
7 Stress, critical incidents, and life-threatening situations are commonplace in first responder environments. Despite these traumatic events, first responders must perform their best to help others and keep themselves safe. Working on resilience with first responders must account for repeated exposure to critical incidents, not just surviving the immediate incident. How could you create a holistic resilience program that supports all aspects of their lives?

8 You are called in to help a leader who just joined a new unit in which morale is low, communication is poor, and trust is lacking. They want your help to strengthen the unit's culture. What further information would you want to know to help you better design this training? How would you design your training plan to help the unit?

REFERENCES

Allen, J. A., Reiter-Palmon, R., Crowe, J., & Scott, C. (2018). Debriefs: Teams learning from doing in context. *American Psychologist, 73*(4), 504–516. https://doi.org/10.1037/amp0000246

Ancarani, F., Garijo Añaños, P., Gutiérrez, B., Pérez-Nievas, J., Vicente-Rodríguez, G., & Gimeno Marco, F. (2025). The effectiveness of debriefing on the mental health of rescue teams: A systematic review. *International Journal of Environmental Research and Public Health, 22*(1), 590. https://doi.org/10.3390/ijerph22040590

Anshel, M. H. (2019). The disconnected values model: A brief intervention for improving healthy habits and coping with stress in law enforcement. In J. T. Reese, E. Scrivner, & T. A. Cacioppo (Eds.), *Handbook of police psychology* (pp. 598–614). Routledge.

Asken, M. J., Christensen, L. W., & Grossman, D. (2010). *Warrior mindset: Mental toughness skills for a nation's defenders: Performance psychology applied to combat.* Human Factor Research Group.

Batula, A. M., Mark, J. A., Kim, Y. E., & Ayaz, H. (2017). Comparison of brain activation during motor imagery and motor movement using fNIRS. *Computational Intelligence and Neuroscience, 2017,* 1–12. https://doi.org/10.1155/2017/5491296

Behnke, M., Tomczak, M., Kaczmarek, L. D., Komar, M., & Gracz, J. (2019). The sport mental training questionnaire: Development and validation. *Current Psychology, 38*(2), 504–516. https://doi.org/10.1007/s12144-017-9629-1

Bompa, T., Blumenstein, B., Hoffmann, J., Howell, S., & Orbach, I. (2019). *Integrated periodization in sports training & athletic development: Combining training methodology, sports psychology, and nutrition to optimize performance.* Meyer & Meyer Sport.

Bonumwezi, J. L., Tramutola, D., Lawrence, J., Kobezak, H. M., & Lowe, S. R. (2022). Posttraumatic stress disorder symptoms, work-related trauma exposure, and substance use in first responders. *Drug and Alcohol Dependence, 237,* 109439. https://doi.org/10.1016/j.drugalcdep.2022.109439

Brown, C. H., Gould, D., & Foster, S. (2005). A framework for developing contextual intelligence (CI). *The Sport Psychologist, 19*(1), 51–62. https://doi.org/10.1123/tsp.19.1.51

Edmondson, A. C. (1996). Learning from mistakes is easier said than done: Group and organizational influences on the detection and correction of human error. *Journal of Applied Behavioral Science, 32*(1), 5–28. https://doi.org/10.1177/0021886396321001

Edmondson, A. C. (2019). *The fearless organization: Creating psychological safety in the workplace for learning, innovation, and growth.* John Wiley & Sons.

Gilmartin, K. M. (2021). *Emotional survival for law enforcement: A guide for officers and their families* (Rev. ed.). E-S Press.

Grossman, D. (1995). *On killing: The psychological cost of learning to kill in war and society.* Little, Brown.

Hays, K. F. (2006). Being fit: The ethics of practice diversification in performance psychology. *Professional Psychology: Research and Practice, 37*(3), 223–232. https://doi.org/10.1037/0735-7028.37.3.223

Heil, J., Owens, R., & McDaniel, T. (2023). Sport psychology applied to the tactical training of law enforcement officers. In K. Papazoglou & D. M. Blumberg (Eds.), *Police conflict management, volume II* (pp. 87–112). Springer. https://doi.org/10.1007/978-3-031-41100-7_5

Holt, T. (2014). Training the tactical soldier-athlete. In J. G. Cremades & L. S. Tashman (Eds.), *Becoming a sport, exercise, and performance psychology professional: A global perspective* (pp. 119–126). Psychology Press.

Kaplansky, G. F., & Toussaint, M. (2024). U.S. Army mortality surveillance in active duty soldiers, 2014–2019. *Medical Surveillance Monthly Report, 31*(5), 2–8.

Keiser, N. L., & Arthur, W. (2021). A meta-analysis of the effectiveness of the after-action review (or debrief) and factors that influence its effectiveness. *Journal of Applied Psychology, 106*(7), 1007–1032. https://doi.org/10.1037/apl0000821

Kuhns, J. B., Maguire, E. R., & Leach, N. R. (2015). *Health, safety, and wellness program case studies in law enforcement.* Office of Community Oriented Policing Services.

Land, W. M., Guan, J., Smith, P., & Burque, B. (2022). Psychological skills inventory for law enforcement (PSI-LE): Development and validation of a multidimensional measure of psychological skill use for law enforcement. *Police Practice and Research, 23*(6), 757–774. https://doi.org/10.1080/15614263.2022.2056036

Magaletta, P. R., Hom, M. A., Stanley, I. H., & Joiner, T. E. (2020). Strategies and solutions to address the mental health needs of protective service workers: An introduction. *Psychological Services, 17*(2), 127–129. https://doi.org/10.1037/ser0000410

Marquardt, N. (2019). Situation awareness, human error, and organizational learning in sociotechnical systems. *Human Factors and Ergonomics in Manufacturing & Service Industries, 29*(4), 327–339. https://doi.org/10.1002/hfm.20800

Marquardt, N., Gades-Büttrich, R., Brandenberg, T., & Schürmann, V. (2024). A model of adaptive error management practices addressing the higher-order factors of the Dirty Dozen error classification: Implications for organizational resilience in sociotechnical systems. *Safety, 10*(3), 64. https://doi.org/10.3390/safety10030064

Marquardt, N., Krämer, L., & Schürmann, V. (2019). Mental preparation strategies and firefighters' performance under stress. *International Journal of Safety and Security Engineering, 9*(4), 332–343. https://doi.org/10.2495/SAFE-V9-N4-332-343

Marquardt, N., Stierle, K. E., van der Velden, E.-M., & Schürmann, V. (2023). Mental readiness in emergency response tasks. *Performance Improvement Quarterly, 36*(2), 111–123. https://doi.org/10.56811/PIQ-21-0011

Miller, L. (2009). *M.E.T.T.L.E.: Mental toughness training for law enforcement.* Looseleaf Law Publications, Inc.

Mumford, E. A., Taylor, B. G., & Kubu, B. (2015). Law enforcement officer safety and wellness. *Police Quarterly, 18*(2), 111–133. https://doi.org/10.1177/1098611114559037

Papazoglou, K., Blumberg, D. M., Chiongbian, V. B., Tuttle, B. M., Kamkar, K., Chopko, B., Koskelainen, M., & Lumley, M. (2020). The role of moral injury in PTSD among law enforcement officers: A brief report. *Frontiers in Psychology, 11,* 507803. https://doi.org/10.3389/fpsyg.2020.00310

Raabe, J., Castillo, E. A., & Carl, J. (2021). Mental qualities and techniques in tactical populations: A systematic review. *The Sport Psychologist, 35*(3), 223–239. https://doi.org/10.1123/tsp.2020-0096

Rasteiro, A., Santos, V., & Massuça, L. M. (2023). Physical training programs for tactical populations: Brief systematic review. *Healthcare, 11*(7), 967. https://doi.org/10.3390/healthcare11070967

Robazza, C., Pellizzari, M., & Hanin, Y. (2004). Emotion self-regulation and athletic performance: An application of the IZOF model. *Psychology of Sport and Exercise, 5*(4), 379–404. https://doi.org/10.1016/S1469-0292(03)00034-7

Sackett, S. C., Durand-Bush, N., & Tashman, L. S. (Eds.). (2022). *Essential guide for mental performance consultants.* Human Kinetics.

Violanti, J. M. (2022). Suicide clusters in law enforcement: A descriptive analysis. *Policing: An International Journal, 45*(5), 757–775. https://doi.org/10.1108/PIJPSM-01-2022-0006

Wise, S. R., & Trigg, S. D. (2020). Optimizing health, wellness, and performance of the tactical athlete. *Current Sports Medicine Reports, 19*(2), 70–75. https://doi.org/10.1249/JSR.0000000000000689

9 Working in the Corporate World

Increasingly, sport, exercise, and performance psychology professionals (SEPPPs) have ventured into offering their services to corporate clients. Notably, the COVID-19 pandemic led to a spur in client interest in coaching, making it also more accessible as online service delivery became a common form of practice. I (Sebastian) have branched into business consulting and leadership coaching with corporate clients, building my client base when starting my private practice full-time during the pandemic. The journey has certainly been an interesting and rewarding experience that helped me sharpen my skills, expand my toolbox, and build my expertise. In this chapter, we provide a very hands-on, real-life approach to working in the corporate world as a SEPPP sharing personal narratives as well as case study examples.

THE TRANSITION FROM SPORT PSYCHOLOGY TO BUSINESS CONSULTING

Paul Ashbrook, Grayson Kimball, & Greg Cartin

While the world of sport and business are entirely different domains, they do often share a "bottom-line" focus on performance. As Jones (2002) noted, having this understanding can be valuable for sport psychology practitioners looking to transition into performance psychology in business. However, as each of our experiences illustrates, self-doubt and imposter syndrome are normal parts of the transition process. This seems to be in line with the research of Hings et al. (2020) who found that despite having gained theoretical knowledge in performance psychology, a lack of experience within a specific domain led practitioners to experience discomfort when consulting, with many noting a need to act like they were someone else. To mitigate these concerns, it has been suggested that practitioners utilize reflective practice, which appears to positively impact service delivery, and helps practitioners become more self-aware and client-centered (Cropley et al., 2016; Tod & Bond, 2010). We invite you to consider our shared narratives as a form of reflective practice.

Dr. Paul Ashbrook

As a practitioner, the transition between traditional sport psychology work and performance psychology in the business sector can feel quite daunting. When I decided to pursue sport psychology, there was never a doubt that I would work with athletes. Throughout my life,

DOI: 10.4324/9781003781486-9

sport has been an integral part of my identity, both as a fan, and as a competitor. As such, I was confident in my contextual knowledge around sport. I could talk the talk, but more importantly, walk the walk. In my mind, I had credibility before even stepping foot in front of a client.

When entering the business environment, that self-assuredness wasn't present. While I did have "work experience," much of it revolved around the sport and education sectors, which are not typically what you associate with performance psychology in business. Considering this lack of corporate experience, I was understandably insecure about my ability to help these new types of clients. Would I be able to communicate effectively? Would my understanding of performance psychology translate beyond athletics?

In addition to concerns about my contextual knowledge, I also felt a great deal of insecurity regarding my age and perceived competence. I remember early in my career, an older, well-established friend of mine remarked that I wouldn't be taken seriously until I "got older and developed some gray hairs." While I initially brushed that comment aside, my transition into the business world during my early thirties certainly played on that insecurity. I remember meeting with individuals 20 years my senior and questioning how much value I could offer them.

Funny enough though, the thing that allowed me to ultimately shine in the business world was my background in athletics! See, lots of people in the business world either have played sports or enjoy sports. As a result, sport becomes a natural connection point between individuals. Clients would regularly ask me about my athletic background, the traits of successful athletes, or even big games that had just occurred. Instead of shying away from my expertise, I was able to lean in and be my authentic self. This was great for building rapport and ultimately a strong working alliance.

Dr. Grayson Kimball

Reflecting on my own experiences as a mental performance coach, I remember questioning my worth as a professional in the field. The first two clients I ever worked with participated in sports I had never participated in—marathon running and tennis. I would be lying if I said I didn't question my ability to help these clients after the first few sessions! However, once I learned more about one of the sports (tennis), and started participating in the other (running marathons), I not only felt more competent in my ability to help those clients, but I was feeling capable and confident with all types of athletes.

When I transitioned from sport performance coaching to executive business coaching, I was very much unsure of how I would be able to relate to my clients who were performing in an area in which I had little to no experience. What I quickly realized was that I was falling into a cognitive trap, questioning my expertise in the services I was providing. I had to remind myself that it wasn't my job to make my clients "better or more skilled" physicians, sales reps, or marketing experts. That is the role of their mentors, bosses, and supervisors. This is similar to working with athletes—it's not our job to help a client become more "skilled" as a football player or soccer player—it's to make them a mentally stronger and more disciplined athlete. So, as I began working in the corporate world, I took the time to learn more about their roles and responsibilities so I could help them think differently, control their performance to the extent they can, and perform as effectively and consistently as possible.

Some clients were brand new to their company, some were recently promoted to a managerial position, and some were thinking about leaving their current company for new opportunities. In all cases, they questioned their own worth and ability to succeed in new environments. Having casual conversations that focused them to identify professional strengths and weaknesses has been an effective strategy to help them overcome the imposter mindset.

One specific strategy that has helped me reduce my own imposter mindset and feel more effective and confident with my business clients is by building rapport and trust. Many of my clients have either played organized sports growing up, have kids who are currently playing sports, or still compete athletically at some level. When they see that my background is in sport and performance psychology, they quickly feel a connection and this helps set a positive tone for our coaching relationship. For many of my clients, starting each session with a general discussion on the world of sports allows us to ease into deeper conversations about their work.

Dr. Greg Cartin

While I had logged many hours with clients in sport over the years, it was hard not to feel a sense of imposter syndrome as I began the journey helping those in the corporate world. My experience would no longer be an entry to building rapport as I had no background in working with clients from fields outside the world of sports. Yet, almost immediately, I found that with a majority of my clients my background in sport coaching provided the instant rapport I was originally concerned would be lacking. Prior to each initial session I did my homework, researching the companies as well as the specific job descriptions listed by my new clients. I developed an interview guide for the initial conversation as I had done with my sport clients and did the best I could to prepare myself for this new, exciting work. Doing research and finding connections was a technique I found to be helpful in battling the imposter syndrome that existed early on.

The most important piece of information I took from those early meetings was the reminder that all of us at some point in our careers had taken on clients from sports or backgrounds we were unfamiliar with. I reflected back on those experiences and remembered how important it was to be a good listener. Active listening, repeating what my clients were saying, and reconfirming their own words and concerns, helped to ease the feelings I had that I wasn't providing them enough. As I gained confidence in working with this new population, it was apparent that regardless of the job, the work was very similar. Incorporating the skills I had previously used with athletes from unfamiliar sports helped me to make a smooth transition and gain the confidence to work with clients in the corporate world.

Not only did I draw on prior experiences with different backgrounds to gain confidence, but I also started to realize the power that the techniques used to develop and sustain excellence in athletes were also beneficial to those in the corporate world. Clients were looking for ways to stay cool under pressure, make good decisions, avoid burnout, and overall find enjoyment and fulfillment in their jobs. No different than the issues presented by my athlete clients! Staying true to who I was and what I believed in proved valuable. Too often we get focused on goals (making teams, winning championships, making quota, etc.), and at times what it takes to achieve our goals may not align with what it is we value. Burnout in the corporate world is a major issue, and from experience in the field I can safely say it stems from a lack of fulfillment and enjoyment. Helping clients in both sport and the corporate world cultivate fulfillment by aligning their goals with what they value can have a dramatic effect on burnout avoidance as well as performance.

Conclusion

To conclude, when making the jump to working with clients in a new environment, do your research, leverage your experience, be a good listener, and be true to yourself. Altering the approach based on what you "think" the client may want or need will only make the transition more confusing. As Petitpas et al. (1999) noted, the relationship between athlete and practitioner may actually be more important than the specific interventions used. Connecting on a mutual sports interest may help build that relationship. Lastly, learn to overcome an imposter mindset by adopting an optimistic perspective of your experiences and achievements, choosing to feel good about yourself, and striving for consistency in your approach to high-performance coaching.

THE ECONOMY OF BEHAVIOR: THE ROAD TO UNLOCKING OPTIMAL HUMAN PERFORMANCE

Shruti Nair & Nimrod Mon Brokman

The business world mirrors the high-stakes intensity of elite sports. Just as athletes push their limits on the field, CEOs and entrepreneurs navigate a landscape marked by ambitious goals, targets, and high stakes. The relentless pressure and multifaceted challenges they face demand not just skill, but a dynamic mindset capable of juggling decision-making, problem-solving, and a myriad of roles. To truly excel in this demanding environment, sport, exercise, and performance psychology (SEPP) practitioners should delve into the psychological intricacies that underpin effective leadership—the first step toward thriving in the high-stakes arena of business.

Identifying Stressors of a High-Performer in Business

We have observed common personal and professional stressors in practice across the business and entrepreneurship worlds (see Table 9.1).

The natural physiological, emotional, and cognitive responses to stress can gradually accumulate, affecting the mind-body connection, ultimately impacting our overall health and performance (Carmichael et al., 2023). A consolidated graph below (see Figure 9.1; Cohen et al., 2007) illustrates the rising prevalence of health issues among business executives in Asia over a 12-year period (Kim & Lee, 2018; Park & Choi, 2017; Singh & Patel, 2019). Business executives face a daunting paradox - despite advances in technology and medicine, their quality of health and quality of life are steadily declining.

Solving the Paradox: The Economy of Behavior Mindset

"Imagine yourself as the CEO of the world's greatest bank—except that this bank does not handle money. It deals in something far more valuable and precious, your Psychological Capital." This is how we bring the concept to life—so clients don't just understand it, they connect with it deeply and begin to shift from insight to transformation. The "Economy of Behavior" (EoB) mindset (for an explanation, see Behavioural Foresight, 2023), a concept invented by Nimrod Mon Brokman, blending performance psychology with behavioral economics and ancient philosophies is not just about surviving in the

Table 9.1 Common Stressors Faced by Business Professionals

	Personal Stressors	*Professional Stressors*
Internal	High self-expectations Perfectionism and feelings of inadequacy Emotional strain from balancing work and home resulting in guilt Struggling to maintain good health	Fear of failure Relentless drive for excellence leading to burnout High-stakes decision-making pressure
External	Family responsibilities Supporting a career-focused partner Maintaining social connections	Heavy workload Inadequate rest and recovery Constant pressure from investors to deliver results and maintain growth Dealing with conflict within teams

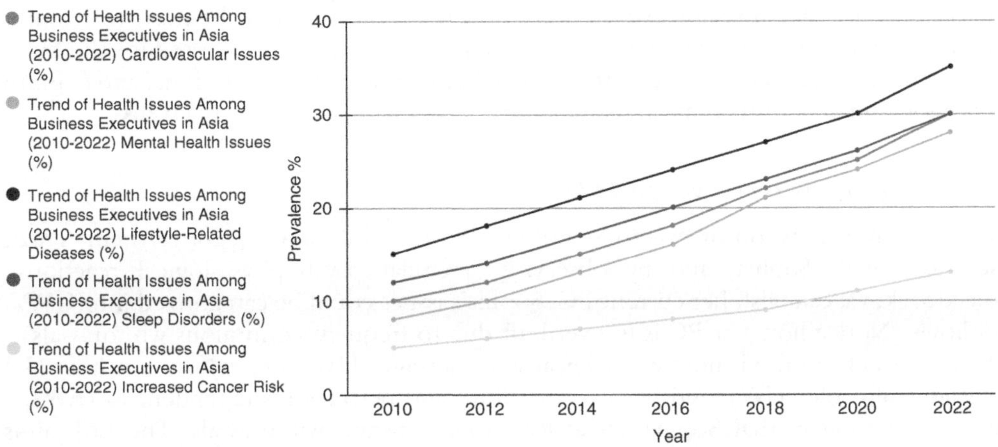

Figure 9.1 Trendline of health issues among business executives in Asia (2010–2022).

fast-paced world of business—it's about thriving. This framework offers a powerful lens through which clients can take ownership of their mental resources much like managing financial assets. Within the EoB lens, by fostering awareness and mastery of the stress response (particularly through nervous system regulation), the practitioner helps the client to identify their energy-consuming activities and draining behaviours directing them toward the optimization of their psychological bank, thereby enabling the free flow of psychological capital.

In this framework, we use the following key terms:

- Psychological capital (PC): The client's overall mental resources.
- Current PC: The client's current mental resources are determined by the practitioner and informed by the client's perception of their current mental skills.
- Withdrawals (W): The mental energy expended by the client (i.e., the loss of PC).
- Avoidable Withdrawals (AW): The stressors, activities, and mindsets the client is choosing that overextend their PC.

- Unavoidable Withdrawals (UW): The stressors and activities that are part of their personal and professional roles and responsibilities.
- Discounts & Savings (DS): The goal is to minimize AW and create savings on UW behaviours by teaching clients tools and techniques to economize withdrawals and save PC.
- Mental Investment (MI): Investing in crediting more PC by teaching clients tools and techniques to expand it.
- Mental Deposits (MD): As with MI aimed at building clients' PC.
- Optimized PC: This is the goal of the work with the client—continuously developing and expanding their PC by suggesting interventions that transition W to DS or MD.

EoB Mindset in Business: Case study of Sophia

Sophia is a 38-year-old tech executive and mother of two girls, juggling a demanding leadership role. She struggles with fear of failure, certain perfectionist tendencies accompanied by external stressors like investor expectations, a heavy workload, and the need to relentlessly excel in a competitive, evolving industry. She approached us in order to reduce the burnout feelings she was experiencing and better handle her mental energy (emotional and cognitive). We are looking at an intervention plan of 6–10 weeks with 1–2 sessions a week.

Step 1: Identifying the Issues Through the EoB Lens

Usually, it takes a session or two to identify the withdrawals and categorize them. Through discussions with Sophia, and by observing irregular psychophysiological reactions via biofeedback, we establish her current PC. Sophia's issues could be categorized into UW/AW as follows (Notice how her PC is in overdraft due to frequent continuous withdrawals): she felt she was getting tired more easily because of her age (UW), her role as a mother (UW), her leadership role (UW), and her fear of failure and perfectionistic tendencies (AW). The equation symbolizes that Sophia has at least four constant withdrawals. The EoB aims to convert this into DSs and MDs to optimize the PC (Figure 9.2).

$$\textit{Current PC} = AW + 3UW + ?W$$

Figure 9.2 EoB equation mapping the client's current PC based on types of Withdrawals (Behavioural Foresight, 2023).

Step 2: Identifying DS Within the UW Behaviors

In the EoB method, it's about converting UWs into DS behaviors. For Sophia, we were looking to convert the motherhood role (UW) into a beneficial mindset by creating a new attitude (DS). Over the next two weeks, we focused on this conversion process, using HRV biofeedback training alongside guided visualizations of a typical morning routine. During these sessions, Sophia reached a point where her HRV remained elevated even while recalling several of her usual morning stressors. To support sustainable progress, we recommended that Sophia practice the same HRV breathing exercise immediately after her morning alarm or just before waking her kids. This would help her initiate the DS mindset from the start of the day, enabling her to manage daily challenges more effectively and move toward mobilizing her Optimal PC.

$$\textbf{OPC} = \textbf{MD} + \textbf{DS} + \textbf{?}$$

Figure 9.3 EoB equation showing how Withdrawals can be converted into DS and MD to move toward Optimized Psychological Capital (OPC) (Behavioural Foresight, 2023).

Step 3: Building Mental Deposits Out of the AWs

The next step of the process is converting AWs to MDs. We intentionally exposed Sophia to her fear of failure (AW) through biofeedback-based gamification (a version of Temple Run where the practitioner controls the speed of the game and the system reacts to the client's physiology), setting both high expectations as well as increasing the game's difficulty level. As she encountered and expressed failure (AW), the game was paused, and a targeted intervention was introduced—reframing the experience as a growth opportunity (MD). At that point, a classic biofeedback technique—extended exhalation to lower heart rate—was used to support this shift. Through this, Sophia began to convert the AW into an MD in real time. Over the next three weeks, she trained to reduce psychophysiological reactivity to failure, maintaining composure and ensuring smooth performance even when facing setbacks. After each session, we revisited her daily triggers (AW), actively reframing them using the new mindset tools (MD). This consistent practice built her confidence in applying the approach, bringing her closer to an Optimized (PC). For the remainder of the training period, we continued working with identified withdrawals, transforming them into DS and MD. This equation symbolizes the conversion of 1 UW into a DS and 1 AW into an MD as explained above (Figure 9.3).

Outcome after 10 Weeks and Summary

Sophia integrated the EoB mindset into her work and personal life, viewing daily activities as transactions in her psychological bank. She consciously made more "deposits" than "withdrawals" by identifying and converting AWs into MDs and creating DS behaviors. This led to reduced stress symptoms as measured by the biofeedback system throughout the process. Moreover, Sophia reported improved quality of sleep as she started waking up more energized. As a result, she experienced an enhanced work-life balance. Interestingly, by managing her mental resources strategically, Sophia maintained the required high-performance while maintaining an Optimal PC. Using the EoB lens helps to accelerate behavioral changes and sustain them over time. Blending the wisdom of ancient philosophies with the precision of modern technology and the richness of real-life experiences, the EoB mindset becomes a powerful, sustainable tool to utilize anywhere at any time. The impact is a significant boost in daily energy, sharper cognitive clarity, and a stronger grip on emotional challenges, empowering clients to navigate life's demands with greater resilience and finesse.

WORKING ON STRENGTHS WITH HIGH PERFORMERS IN BUSINESS

Sandy Gordon

High-performing leaders in all work environments are attracted to and benefit from strengths-based coaching approaches. They understand that leadership development starts with self-awareness and how they can use their uniqueness to further develop their career success. In this chapter, a brief history of strengths-based approaches to high-performance coaching—and the research supporting them—precedes an explanation of the *Leader Strengths Profile,* which addresses how strengths can be applied to leading yourself, leading others, and leading an organization. A case study of a CEO choosing to complete the assessment is described and to illustrate the strengths-based coaching approach in business, some examples of coaching questions for realized and unrealized strengths, learned behaviors, and weaknesses are provided.

Strengths-Based Approaches: A Brief History

Over the last decade the strengths movement, and positive psychology in particular, has flourished; however, the study of positive psychology has a long past and readers are directed to full histories and philosophical perspectives of strengths approaches, positive psychology, coaching psychology, and their applications elsewhere (e.g., Gordon, 2024; Lopez & Snyder, 2009; Peterson, 2006).

Research directions have also quickly developed including measuring well-being and mapping human strengths spawning several strengths identification assessment tools such as the *VIA Inventory of Strengths* (Peterson & Seligman, 2004), *StrengthsFinder* (Rath, 2007), and *Realise2 Strengths* (Linley et al., 2010). Mike Pegg (2008) and Sir Ken Robinson (2009) claim we are in our "element" when our natural aptitude and personal passions meet, like characteristics of "flow" experiences. Most recently, Alex Linley and Trudy Bateman, and their colleagues at the Center of Applied Positive Psychology (Linley & Bateman, 2018) distinguished both unrealized and realized strengths from learned behaviors and weaknesses.

Strengths-Based Coaching: Applied Research

As alluded to by Maslow (1954) and Seligman (1999, 2011), historically human endeavors have been characterized as "fixing weaknesses" and the coaching process in business is no exception. Currently, deficit-based coaching typically focuses on identifying weaknesses and fixing them. Strengths-based coaching, on the other hand, is about spotting and exploiting strengths. During strengths coaching the focus is on what is already working, and because strengths are part of basic human nature, our areas of greatest potential are in the areas of our greatest strengths.

Considerable research evidence shows that, in addition to being more confident, having higher levels of energy and vitality (Govindji & Linley, 2007), and being more likely to achieve their goals, people who use their strengths are more effective at developing themselves and growing as individuals than individuals who do not (Sheldon et al., 2002). Linley et al. (2010) have demonstrated that people who use their strengths more are happier, have higher self-esteem, experience less stress, are more resilient, perform better at work, and are more engaged at work. Losada and Heaphy (2004) found that in high-performing business team meetings there was a 6:1 ratio of appreciation to criticism, while in medium-performing and low-performing teams, it was 2:1 and well below 1:1, respectively. Roarty and Toogood (2014) have reported research with executive coaches who have adopted a strengths approach and the following desirable coaching outcomes were evident: easier and more enjoyable goal achievement; improved team performance and faster and better results; more energy for doing what coachees want to do; a wider perspective and more clarity about choices; increased confidence, self-belief, and a stronger sense of identity; and greater satisfaction, fulfilment, and engagement.

Case Study

When I first met my coachee, he was in an acting CEO role (aviation industry) and eagerly anticipating promotion to the actual role, which happened a few months later. He was interested in understanding and applying a strengths-based lens to his leadership of others, the organization, as well as to himself mainly because this approach was a completely new experience for him and one which we both agreed seemed timely and appropriate. He was excited to be part of the strengths-based assessment process, for which I facilitated over five coaching sessions.

Briefly, the *Leader Strengths Profile* assesses 60 strengths and reveals, in rank order and four quadrants, up to seven realized strengths (RS; strengths you frequently use, are good at and enjoy doing, so you ***should use them wisely***), seven unrealized strengths (URS; strengths you don't use as often so you ***should use them more)***, four learned behaviors (LB; strengths you have learned to do well but might not enjoy so you ***should use them only when needed***) and up to three weaknesses (W; things you find hard and don't enjoy so you ***should use them less***).

During our debrief and coaching sessions, we discussed the impact of all identified strengths in each quadrant on his personal leadership development, leading others, and leading the organization. He understood immediately the ***hidden risks*** behind overplaying his RS and how his LBs were negatively impacting his current leadership. For example, his number one RS *Incubator* (thinking deeply about things to arrive at the best conclusion for all concerned) particularly fascinated him as he saw himself as more of an action man. So, in the future, to avoid being slow to make decisions and frustrate others by "sleeping on it" before making decisions, he endeavored to "read his audience" and determine when his staff might prefer to take action and thereby use this strength more wisely. His number one LB *Competitive* (being motivated by competing against others, winning is important) made sense to him having previously played professional sport. So, in the future to avoid feeling drained by pushing himself to be "the winner" in areas that don't really matter to him, he committed to finding what success looks like for others so a shared approach could work and thereby use this strength only when needed. The biggest impact for him seemed to be responding to how his strengths would serve the organization's goals and vision and would benefit the organization further. He wrote on his profile a reminder-to-self to think how he could personally role model his RS and URS (e.g., humility, gratitude, equality) more often. He had never previously been obliged to think about "leading others" or "leading the organization." See Table 9.2 for example, coaching questions you can use to explore the four different areas of the profile.

For this client, I think identifying his LBs and differentiating between URS and RS were the most impactful and valuable outcomes from his assessment. I am impressed with the *Leader Strengths Profile* and anticipate using it often. Because my coachee told me he benefited from reading my copy of *The Strengths Profile Book* (Linley & Bateman, 2018), wherein all strengths are described in greater detail, I strongly recommend that coaches consider obliging coachees to consult a copy after they have completed their profile and prior to a debrief.

Table 9.2 Sample of *Leader Strengths Profile* Coaching Questions

Realized Strengths	• Which strengths would benefit your career goals if used more? How? • Which strengths do you rely on when it comes to leading others? How? • Which strengths would benefit the organization to role model further? How? • Do you recognize any overplayed strengths and hidden risks?
Unrealized Strengths	• How can your unrealized strengths support your future career goals? • What could you do to support others further using your unrealized strengths? • How could your unrealized strengths support the organization's vision and strategy? • Where does the organization have gaps that you could support with using your unrealized strengths?
Learned Behaviors	• Which learned behaviors drain you the most? Why is this and what could you do? • Which learned behaviors do others rely on you for? Could you delegate further in this area? • Do any learned behaviors limit your ability to lead others effectively? • How could your strengths support the impact of your learned behaviors?
Weaknesses	• Which strengths are you known for and how can they help you compensate for any weaknesses? • Could any weaknesses be performance critical and have a future impact on your career goals? • Which realized or unrealized strengths could support you further in these areas? • How could you delegate any weaknesses to others?

EDITORS' TAKEAWAYS

This chapter is a great read for anyone in SEPP considering working in the corporate context. The first contribution is really helpful in illuminating the common experiences of transitioning from sport to business. Personally (Lauren), as someone who has also navigated this transition, it was one that I felt like there was no map to really follow. One of my greatest reflections has been that as a field we too flippantly make it sound like you can just take your sport psychology knowledge and experience and go apply it in other performance domains. That doesn't do a service to any of us—nor the clients or the field at large and our credibility. There is definitely a place for, and immense value of, bringing sport psychology into the corporate context, but it is a very crowded space (even more so than sport!) and it takes some work to become competent, confident, and credible in providing services in this performance domain. Nair and Brokman's model provides a great example of this—I can see how it would be a valuable framework not only for us as practitioners to follow, but also one that would really resonate in the corporate context. It was also really valuable to see how they incorporate biofeedback with this population. The last contribution is a useful practical example of using an assessment as part of applied practice in addition to highlighting the value of taking a strengths-based approach in business or in other contexts. My experience in the corporate space has been that they are very keenly interested in the use of assessments, but vary in their understanding and concern about the psychometrics behind many of the ones on the market or in use by the many professionals they contract to support achievement of their objectives!

RECOMMENDED EXERCISES

1 Think about your own perceptions of corporate environments—your experiences, cultural impressions, or assumptions.

  a What words or feelings come to mind when you think of "corporate clients"?
  b How might these impressions influence your openness, empathy, or communication style?
  c What parts of corporate culture are easiest for you to relate to? Which feels unfamiliar?
  d What similarities do you see between business performance and athletic performance?
  e What differences might require you to adapt your approach?
  f Which aspects of workplace performance do you feel more and less confident navigating?

2 It is important that you are able to explain the foundation of your performance work to corporate professionals. How do you understand human performance, and what are its non-negotiables? Which mental performance skills would you emphasize with corporate clients, and how would you present your value to them?

3 Identify three sport psychology concepts or techniques you could translate to corporate settings. How are they used with athletes, and how might you adapt them for corporate clients?

4 Choose a business sector (e.g., tech, finance, retail). Identify three to five aspects you would need to research to understand that sector's culture and be prepared to offer effective services.

5 Identify your top three to five stressors.

  a How much "mental currency" do they consume daily or weekly? Map your deposits and withdrawals. For each stressor identified, ask yourself: Is this stressor truly necessary or can it be eliminated? What patterns emerge?
  b Design your personalized pyramid structure: Start by listing your stressors at the base. In the middle, jot down the neutralization strategies you plan to implement. At the top, choose micro-interventions that you can use to manage your stressors. Where and when will you use these interventions to maintain balance?
  c Based on your own experience of trying this framework for consultation, how would you use it with clients in the corporate context?

6 Choose a business professional of interest (e.g., founder, salesperson). Research their key stressors. How could you use Nair & Brokman's framework or Gordon's strengths-based approach to consult effectively with someone in that role?

7 Utilize a strengths-based approach to analyze your strengths relative to your career goals.

  a What are your Realized Strengths (i.e., strengths you use a lot, are good at, and enjoy)? How do they benefit your current role and career goals? Do you recognize any overplayed strengths and hidden risks?
  b What are your Unrealized Strengths (i.e., strengths you don't get to use as often as you would like to)? How can they support your current role and career goals? What barriers are there to using these strengths more and how could you overcome them?
  c What are your Learned Behaviors (i.e., things you've learned to do well but may not enjoy and drain you)? Which drain you the most, and why? Which do others rely on you for? How could your strengths support the impact of your learned behaviors?

   d What are your Weaknesses (i.e., things you find hard to do and don't enjoy)? Could any weaknesses be performance critical and have a future impact on your career goals? Which realized or unrealized strengths could support you further in these areas? Could you delegate any weaknesses to others?

8 Reflect on a current corporate client, or one you would like to work with in the future. Based on what you read in this chapter, design a strengths-based intervention to use with this client.

   a What would be the benefits and desired outcomes of taking such an approach?
   b Who and what influences their mindset and performance?
   c What pressures do they face from above, below, and within their team?
   d How would you design the intervention?

REFERENCES

Behavioural Foresight. (2023, October 11). *Economy of behaviour* [Video]. YouTube. https://youtu.be/J1PjWC4yPK0?si=euCekvJ0f7IOCOXR

Carmichael, A., Coe, E. H., & Dewhurst, M. (2023). *Employee mental health and burnout in Asia: A time to act.* McKinsey & Company. https://www.mckinsey.com/featured-insights/future-of-asia/employee-mental-health-and-burnout-in-asia-a-time-to-act

Cohen, S., Janicki-Deverts, D., & Miller, G. E. (2007). Psychological stress and disease. *JAMA, 298*(14), 1685–1687. https://doi.org/10.1001/jama.298.14.1685

Cropley, B., Baldock, L., Mellalieu, S. D., Neil, R., Wagstaff, C. R. D., & Wadey, R. (2016). Coping with the demands of professional practice: Sport psychology consultants' perspectives. *The Sport Psychologist, 30*(3), 290–302. https://doi.org/10.1123/tsp.2015-0125

Gordon, S. (2024). Positive psychology. In D. Tod, K. Hodge, & V. Krane (Eds.), *Routledge handbook of applied sport psychology* (2nd ed., pp. 174–183). Routledge.

Govindji, R., & Linley, P. A. (2007). Strengths use, self-concordance and well-being: Implications for strengths coaching and coaching psychologists. *International Coaching Psychology Review, 2*(2), 143–153.

Hings, R. F., Wagstaff, C. R. D., Anderson, V., Gilmore, S., & Thelwell, R. C. (2020). Better preparing sport psychologists for the demands of applied practice: The emotional labor training gap. *Journal of Applied Sport Psychology, 32*(4), 335–356. https://doi.org/10.1080/10413200.2018.1560373

Jones, G. (2002). Performance excellence: A personal perspective on the link between sport and business. *Journal of Applied Sport Psychology, 14*(4), 268–281. https://doi.org/10.1080/10413200290103554

Kim, S., & Lee, J. (2018). Depression and anxiety among business leaders in South Korea: A cross-sectional study. *Asian Journal of Psychiatry, 32,* 120–127. https://doi.org/10.1016/j.ajp.2018.03.012

Linley, A., Willars, J., & Biswas-Diener, R. (2010). *The strengths book: Be confident, be successful, and enjoy better relationships by realising the best of you.* CAPP Press.

Linley, P. A., & Bateman, T. (2018). *The strengths book.* CAPP Press.

Lopez, S. J., & Snyder, C. R. (Eds.). (2009). *Oxford handbook of positive psychology* (2nd ed.). Oxford University Press.

Losada, M., & Heaphy, E. (2004). The role of positivity and connectivity in the performance of business teams: A nonlinear dynamics model. *American Behavioral Scientist, 47*(6), 740–765. https://doi.org/10.1177/0002764203260208

Maslow, A. H. (1954). *Motivation and personality.* Harper.

Park, J., & Choi, M. (2017). Prevalence of sleep disorders among executives in South Korea. *Sleep Medicine, 42,* 72–80. https://doi.org/10.1016/j.sleep.2017.08.005

Pegg, M. (2008). *The strengths toolbox: All the tools you need to build and develop strengths in the workplace.* Management Books 2000 Ltd.

Peterson, C. (2006). *A primer in positive psychology.* Oxford University Press.
Peterson, C., & Seligman, M. E. P. (2004). *Character strengths and virtues: A handbook and classification.* American Psychological Association; Oxford University Press.
Petitpas, A. J., Giges, B., & Danish, S. J. (1999). The sport psychologist–athlete relationship: Implications for training. *The Sport Psychologist, 13*(3), 344–357. https://doi.org/10.1123/tsp.13.3.344
Rath, T. (2007). *Strengths finder 2.0.* Gallup Press.
Roarty, M., & Toogood, K. (2014). *The strengths-focused guide to leadership.* Pearson.
Robinson, K. (2009). *The element: How finding your passion changes everything.* Penguin Group.
Seligman, M. E. P. (1999). The president's address. *American Psychologist, 54*(8), 559–562. https://doi.org/10.1037/h0088184
Seligman, M. E. P. (2011). *Flourish.* Heinemann.
Sheldon, K. M., Kasser, T., Smith, K., & Share, T. (2002). Personal goals and psychological growth: Testing an intervention to enhance goal-attainment and personality integration. *Journal of Personality, 70*(1), 5–31. https://doi.org/10.1111/1467-6494.00176
Singh, R., & Patel, K. (2019). Obesity and diabetes prevalence among executives in India: A growing concern. *Indian Journal of Endocrinology and Metabolism, 23*(4), 487–493. https://doi.org/10.4103/ijem.IJEM_56_19
Tod, D., & Bond, K. (2010). A longitudinal examination of a British neophyte sport psychologist's development. *The Sport Psychologist, 24*(1), 35–51. https://doi.org/10.1123/tsp.24.1.35

10 Working with Performing Artists

I (Sebastian) vividly remember a conversation with a sport, exercise, and performance psychology professional (SEPPP) sharing about his work with circus professionals... and one challenge he often helped circus performers with: Those who had been competitive athletes prior to joining the circus needed to embrace a different performance mindset. It needed to change from performing 100% and aiming for personal bests or winning at spread out competition events—to one where optimal performance required being on stage sometimes twice a day for almost every day of the year... and performance excellence was characterized more by connecting with the audience emotionally rather than pushing physical limits. Such a shift in mindset for performers one might work with, of course, also requires a change in SEPPP mindset and approach. Our author groups dive deeper into the required mindset shift and cultural humility required when working with artists across the gamut of artistic performance: from circus to music and dance—in all their varieties.

CONSULTATION IN THE PERFORMING ARTS: CULTURE, PERSPECTIVE, AND COMMON THEMES

Mitchell DeSimone, Chelsea Butters Wooding, & Leigh Skvarla

Sport psychology began with an interest in athletes, but over the last 20 years, it has expanded to broader performance domains. The performing arts are an emerging area of service delivery, with a focus on domains in which people perform for an audience, often including dance, acting, and music. It is crucial to recognize the vast differences that exist within performing arts domains (e.g., singing encompasses opera, acapella, rap, and others) as well as between them. Therefore, as in sport, it is essential to know the culture and context of each subgroup with which you work.

Some artists train for competitions; others focus on non-competitive performances. Instead of winning, these artists hone their craft to please critics and the audience. Globally, it is important to consider how a person's country of origin, culture, values, belief systems, and related factors can impact their relationship and interaction with the performing arts. In this chapter, we present five common psychological themes throughout the performing arts.

Theme 1: Subjective Nature of Performing Arts

Defining success can be uniquely complicated in the performing arts. In the absence of clear wins and losses, "good enough to win" rarely exists. Further, musicals, concerts, and movies

DOI: 10.4324/9781003781486-10

do not easily produce statistics that can be analyzed and compared. Even in competitive subdomains where judges provide scores and rank performers, scores are often arbitrary and may vary greatly between judges (Bouwens et al., 2022). Objective data in the performing arts is rare, if it even truly exists. While there is value in the subjectivity of the performing arts (Arnold, 1995), the challenges it presents to the artist's performance and well-being are significant. At the individual level, the subjectivity of this domain makes it difficult to get quality constructive feedback. It is common to receive conflicting feedback from a director and choreographer, for example. Even when feedback from superiors aligns, it might conflict with the performer's view. The origin of this conflict may be conscious (technical) or subconscious (self-preservation) but in either case feedback might be viewed as inaccurate, unhelpful, or offensive (Tohver, 2023), leading to deteriorated relationships and diminished self-confidence.

Subjectivity in the performing arts creates an environment that easily and often allows for disagreement around what constitutes success and whether it was achieved. Therefore, a consultant should find a way to help the performer determine whether and how to integrate difficult or ambiguous feedback, perhaps using "filtering" to select components that are helpful for the performer to focus on. Further, consultants using an acceptance and commitment therapy-based approach (Harris, 2019) might help performers use values-aligned action and acceptance to determine the feedback they hold onto versus what they set down.

Theme 2: Comparison to Others

In the absence of objective outcomes, success in the performing arts is very often determined by subjective comparison to others at organizational and individual levels. Performers are compared to their peers to determine who will perform lead roles, solos, and positions from night to night. It is not uncommon for roles to be lost to performers with similar, or occasionally, worse execution who are less expensive, or have a preferred look and physique. In the absence of objective statistics, subjective comparison often informs these decisions. If artistic decisions are not based on merit, subjectivity can easily justify them.

Social comparison is a major distractor for artists, and its impact on well-being and performance is well documented. Gerber et al. (2018) noted that individuals typically only compare themselves to those with higher ability, focusing on differences in performance ability (e.g., what they do better) rather than on similarities (i.e., where we are equal), leading to a strong likelihood of self-deflating thoughts. Social comparison has been negatively correlated with well-being (Fujita, 2008) and performance, particularly when comparing oneself to an individual of higher ability (Suls & Wheeler, 2012). Consultants should expect to encounter social comparison throughout an artist's career and recommend strategies to direct their attention to controllables fostering individual development, such as developing process goals aimed at improved execution, or building more stable sources of confidence.

Theme 3: The Role of Perfectionism

Like elite sport, flawless performances are expected throughout the performing arts (Hill et al., 2015). Dancers are expected to hit every count and line, musicians every note and key, and actors every mark and cue. A single mistake negatively impacts the performance of both the artist and those around them; continued mistakes often cost performers their jobs. Feedback is intensely focused on failures in performance as they are much easier to notice, and therefore conversations with superiors often take an overwhelmingly critical form. If a consultant working with a performing artist tries to minimize the reality of perfectionism, the client is likely to feel misunderstood or as though the consultant does not understand the realities of the environment.

Perfectionism can be broken down into two dimensions: perfectionistic strivings (setting high standards for performance) and perfectionistic concerns (focus on negative outcomes of failing to achieve perfection; Gotwals et al., 2012). The impact of perfectionism is complex, but even its most helpful applications have negative consequences (Hill et al., 2015). Given that perfectionism is inherent in the performing arts, Gaudreau (2019) argues that focusing on "excellencism" can help performers achieve many of perfectionism's benefits while minimizing consequences. Excellencism is simply the pursuit of excellence rather than a relentless pursuit of perfection (Hays, 2012). Overall, emphasizing excellencism could help performing artists focus more on prioritizing quality, not quantity, of rehearsal and performance (Ericsson et al., 1993).

Theme 4: Reality and Fear of Failure

With such high standards prevalent in performing arts contexts, failure becomes simultaneously unacceptable and unavoidable. Performers, aware of how easily they can be replaced, often allow perfectionistic tendencies to feed fear of failure. This fear is often tied to concerns around being judged by superiors, peers, and the audience (Kokotsaki & Davidson, 2003). Rumination over a minor or uncharacteristic mistake, especially if paired with fear of failure, amplifies stress regardless of the actual magnitude of the mistake (Kenny et al., 2004). Uncertain they will be able to succeed at the next opportunity, fear of the next mistake and its potential consequences clouds the performer's mind and further prevents success (Hays, 2009).

While many performance fears are present in the performing arts, fear of failure is likely to be the most influential. Consultants in this domain should acknowledge the actual consequences of failure while helping performers accept the inevitability of mistakes. It will likely be helpful to build perceptions of competence both in technical ability and in the performer's ability to quickly recover from minor errors before they are amplified.

Theme 5: Identity of Performer versus Self

Similar to athletes, elite artists often integrate success and ability into their personal identity. Although compartmentalization can be a useful tool, the subjective nature of performance leads to challenges. Additionally, while athletes can attribute failure to diverse situational and environmental factors, a performing artist has only themself and their instrument (e.g., voice, lines, movement, musical instrument) during an audition. While this pressure can be motivating, it can also lead to increased anxiousness, self-doubt, blame, and shame that may debilitate not only the performance, but also the ongoing mental well-being of the person outside of the performance context (Kausar & Ahmad, 2021). Imbalance between personal values and professional demands is common, often contributing to mental health challenges (Lim et al., 2019). Feedback that emphasizes minor missteps as failures and ignores successes can exacerbate this issue, even when mistakes are minor or infrequent. If a performer has high identity foreclosure, then that negative feedback combined with an imbalance between values and demands can lead to questions about their belonging within a performance space.

This struggle can be further complicated because performing artists often embody a distinctive character or set of character traits for each performance. Concerns may stem from struggling to delineate between the true self and either their character or a "performing artist ideal" (Alačovska & Kärreman, 2022). Artists might also feel less vulnerable while in character. Consultants, then, can help clients find and separate personal and professional values, identify meaningful components of the self beyond the performance context, and, leading into particularly challenging roles, identify where and how personal and character traits diverge. Performance routines can also help establish boundaries for when the performer is in character, and when they return to themselves.

Conclusion

While the performing arts are made up of complex domains and subdomains, each with a unique culture, several key trends persist. Subjectivity complicates the determination of outcomes and feeds comparison to others individually and organizationally. Social comparison fuels perfectionism, leading to performance fears including fear of failure. Additionally, identity challenges arise alongside excessive internalization of performance errors or challenges in differentiating artists from their roles. Applying performance psychology in the performing arts can be greatly rewarding but requires competence with these and other challenges as they apply to the client's unique environment.

LET'S MOVE INTO DANCE: KEY CONSIDERATIONS FOR PROVIDING SPORT PSYCHOLOGY SERVICES TO DANCERS

Sanna M. Nordin-Bates, Carrie Taylor Johnson, & Jennifer Cumming

In this chapter, we will introduce three key considerations for sport psychology practitioners to work positively and productively with dancers. We discuss the nature of dance training and dance work, typical dancer characteristics, and suggestions on making sport psychology consultations effective and meaningful in dance. We all have extensive experience with dance as an art form and of working with dancers through research and practice, and hope that some of our passion for this domain will shine through as you read and inspire you to get involved!

Although this chapter promises information on "dancers," an important caveat is that there is a huge range of dance styles that vary substantially in their subcultures and expectations. Therefore, we should be clear that our experiences—as consultants, researchers, teachers, and dancers—are mostly based in high-level Western theatrical dance forms such as classical ballet and modern and contemporary dance. We recommend the reader to keep this delimitation in mind both when reading the chapter and when starting to work in dance.

The Nature of Dance Training and Dance Work

The norm is to begin dance training early, with classes often being available for children as young as two or three years old. It is also common, at least in ballet, to intensify engagement around age ten by taking numerous weekly classes or even auditioning for full-time training. Whether this constitutes early specialization is less clear, because dancers typically take classes in several styles and with different teachers. Hence, it is important to ask dancers, particularly those 12 years of age or younger (i.e., a typical cut-off for early specialization) whether they perceive their engagement to be *intense*, *exclusive* (i.e., at the expense of other activities), and whether it feels like a *sacrifice* or not (Downing et al., 2025).

Dance places high value on dedication, hard work, and high standards. For those skilled and lucky enough to become professionals, contracts are often short term and insecure, with relatively low levels of pay and short career spans. Notably, the high standards are typically subjective and can vary between styles, syllabi within styles (e.g., Vaganova versus Cecchetti styles of ballet), schools, and even individuals. There is commonly a strong hierarchy, with those in positions of power (e.g., teachers, artistic directors) becoming important role models and gatekeepers. This can lead to disproportionate responsibility for, and impact on, dancers' lives. For example, a director can often choose who will get a solo or job without having to specify any criteria beforehand or give feedback afterwards. Unfortunately, prior success as a dancer tends to trump academic qualifications when employing people for teaching and leadership positions. While we recognize the immense value of experience, we firmly believe there is a need for training in psychology and pedagogy for professionals holding such leadership positions in dance (Cumming et al., 2024). Perhaps you will join us in promoting such training in dance?

The dance styles considered here are not usually considered "sports" as they traditionally focus on preparing for performances and auditions rather than competitions. However, competing is common in some styles and countries and those dancers might more readily consider themselves athletes (versus artists). We recommend using sport terminology sensitively, as those identifying mostly as artists can be offended by the very idea of dance being seen as a sport! Accordingly, the term "performance (over sport) psychology" may be better when offering services.

Typical Dancer Characteristics

Although dancers are just people and not so dissimilar to athletes, the nature of dance training and work means that certain characteristics are relatively typical. We outline them briefly here, along with applied suggestions. For more specific suggestions on working with dancers' identities, passion/motivation, and perfectionism, see Nordin-Bates (2023).

Narrow Identity

Spending a significant portion of childhood and adolescence in intense training puts dancers at elevated risk of developing a narrow (unidimensional, foreclosed) identity (Willard & Lavallee, 2016). Not exploring other possible identities has implications for dancers' mental health, particularly when navigating challenges (e.g., de-selection, injury, retirement). The narrow identity can also be perpetuated by leaders who promote outdated ideals of "living, breathing, eating dance," emphasize that dance inherently involves sacrifices, or try to control dancers' outside lives (e.g., telling them they cannot eat certain things or do certain activities on holiday). Professionals in touring companies or who work unsociable hours (e.g., performing most evenings) might also focus on dance way beyond their working hours—it is easier to have friends and partners who are also dancers, given that they understand the lifestyle.

Overall, we advocate for a balanced view where dedication is seen as valuable—but not at the cost of having a healthy, multifaceted identity. Consultants might help dancers by encouraging interests beyond dance, facilitating work-life balance and career planning, and openly discussing the pros and cons of a specialized lifestyle. Supporting dancers to reflect on how rest and diverse life experiences can enrich and develop artistry might also help foster a more sustainable approach to performance and career longevity.

Strong Passion

Given their narrow identity, it is perhaps unsurprising that dancers are often highly passionate. While harmonious passion (a flexible love of dance) can be very positive, obsessive passion (rigid, controlling engagement) can be problematic. For instance, it can prevent dancers from taking time off when injured or from seeking help (Rip et al., 2006). It might also make dancers vulnerable to exploitation or abuse, such as always agreeing to work overtime, doing projects with inadequate pay, or accepting harassment or maltreatment in the name of success. Consultants may ask clients to describe their passion for dance, before introducing and discussing the concepts of harmonious versus obsessive passion and their implications. For instance, they can ask dancers what (dis)advantages they can see in being strongly passionate.

Perfectionism

Alongside passion, it is also fairly typical for dancers to be perfectionistic (see Nordin-Bates, 2023). In some environments this is seen as a good thing, and so caution is warranted. For example, a consultant might ask what a dancer means by "pursuing perfection." If it is about setting ambitious goals and hard work, this may be a recipe for success; if it means unrealistic goals, overwork, and constant self-criticism then it clearly is not. Unfortunately, it is not unusual for dancers to struggle with their body image as well as with perfectionism, making clinical problems such as disordered eating more likely (e.g., Goodwin et al., 2014).

Consultants can support perfectionistic dancers by helping them to distinguish ambitious from unrealistic goals, and encouraging self-compassion when expectations aren't met. Reinforcing the value of flexibility with regard to how dancers evaluate goal achievement, adapt their schedules, and assess artistry can also be beneficial. Reflective questions such as, "is there such a thing as a perfect performance?" can help build awareness. Importantly, a clinical referral should be made if perfectionism appears highly rigid or causes impairments to dance activity or everyday life.

Making Sport Psychology Consultations Effective and Meaningful in Dance

We have found that nearly all traditional sport psychology topics are relevant to dance; in addition, it is important to be aware of the value of artistry and creativity. For instance, it is helpful to encourage imagery not only as mental practice but also as a creative, expressive tool (i.e., movement quality-types of imagery, including metaphors; see Nordin-Bates, 2023). Artistic aspects such as movement quality imagery, musicality, and storytelling are also very useful to promote as external foci of attention (Guss-West, 2020). Helping dancers to focus on such aspects can help promote task-involvement and a sense of control, both important considerations in a domain often characterized by subjectivity and uncertainty.

The inherent subjectivity of dance alongside its strongly teacher-led traditions means that dancers can need help to find pockets of autonomy in their daily lives. Again, a focus on meaning-making through artistry can be helpful here, as can a carefully guided goal-setting process (for example, helping dancers find personally meaningful goals that can be pursued within the constraints of having to follow classes and rehearsals (i.e., training schedules) dictated by others.

Finally, we wish to re-emphasize that although we have given examples of typical characteristics of dance and dancers, these are generalizations. Especially if consulting outside our focus area (i.e., high-level ballet and related Western theatrical styles), it is imperative to keep an open mind and avoid assumptions. If you can, spend time learning the context, its norms, and essential terminology, and be honest about what you do and do not know. We hope that you, like us, will enjoy working in, and perhaps also working to change, dance so that it can become as enjoyable, health-promoting, and sustainable as possible.

FEELING THE MUSIC: AN EMBODIED APPROACH TO MENTAL SKILLS TRAINING WITH MUSICIANS

Chantale Lussier & Veronica Allan

Music has long been a captivating force in human lives. Rhythm in music is something we not only hear but feel, and we feel it through our very own primordial instruments, our bodies. A challenge many musicians face pertains to performance standards which have become so high in today's hyper-competitive professional music market that the pursuit for virtuosity and technical prowess has led many artists to experience a disembodied "analysis to paralysis" rooted in a growing lack of somatic connectivity (Lussier, 2013). One of the many ways that Mental Performance Consultants (MPCs) can serve this artistic population is by helping musicians "feel" the music once again, get out of their heads, and reconnect to their natural, embodied experience of music. But what does that mean and how do we do that? These are the questions this chapter aims to answer.

Somatics and Music

Children learn to crawl, stand, walk, and run. They learn many different ways of being in motion. Both physical education and arts education meaningfully contribute to this expanding repertoire of being in, and moving about, the world. Athletes, artists, dancers, and musicians alike continue this process of learning their bodies perhaps longer than others who unconsciously default their experiences of being in motion to predominantly pedestrian, automated daily movements (Lussier, 2013). Somatics is both a philosophical and pedagogical perspective whose emphasis on the body might help deepen our understanding of how to bridge sport and performance psychology, arts education, and physical education pedagogies into a holistic view that can meaningfully inform MPCs wanting to work with musicians.

Somatics value subjective experience as the primary focus via the body, and the body's constant ability to perceive a flow of information by interoceptive, proprioceptive, and kinesthetic ways of sensing the world around and within us. The somatic approach allows us to support and enrich musicians' learning, training, and performing experience by inviting all of their faculties to participate in the phenomenon of music. Somatics recognizes that movement has the potential to regulate emotions as well as shift one's thinking and behavior. This inner and outer experience becomes an integration of one's motion, emotion, intention, attention, intuition, and actions. Musicians create music through the intersection of their bodies in motion along with an instrument, such as a drum, flute, guitar, violin, voice, or orchestra. Practically speaking, the challenge and opportunity for MPCs becomes how to cultivate rich somatic wisdom in ways that support the technical, tactical, physical, and psychological elements of musical performance. One of the ways to do so is by recognizing that musicians' bodies are one of the instruments at play.

Body as Instrument

How we perceive and define "the field of play" as MPCs inevitably informs our approaches to psychological intervention (Kalenska-Rodzaj, 2020). Psychology generally considers musical affect in terms of higher cognition. Thus, it is not surprising that dualistic notions of body and mind are often reinforced, and the embodied nature of musical affect does not receive proper consideration. It is for these reasons that Van der Schyff (2013) argued for the inclusion of an embodied approach to musical affect and meaning. Music is a biologically powerful "transformative technology of the mind" that physically shapes the brain in ways that afford all manner of physical, cognitive, and social benefits to those who participate in it (Patel, 2010, as cited in Van der Schyff, 2013). While some highly trained musicians might struggle to experience music without engaging in some form of analysis, for most, music is first and foremost something felt. As Van der Schyff (2013) explained, music bridges dualistic conceptions, such as inner and outer—mind, body, and world. For MPCs, this understanding may open new ways to consider how embodied action brings the music—and the musician—to life.

The Embodied Mind

Important to understand, especially when addressing various elements of psychological performance, is the complex nuances between how researchers have conceptualized feelings, emotions, and how we *feel* holistically as a lived experience. The work of Damasio (2004) has shed light on the fact that emotions stem from our neurological system and as such are irrefutably part of an embodied, physical cognition. As neuroscience has proven, emotions are a "patterned collection of chemical and neural responses that is produced by the brain when it detects the presence of an emotionally competent stimulus," while feelings are rather the "mental representation of the physiological changes that characterize emotions" (Damasio, 2001, p. 781). However, we do not experientially separate feelings (mental representations) from emotions (physiological experience), but rather phenomenologically *feel* the moment. Damasio's work refutes the Cartesian mind/body dualistic philosophy and invites us to pay close attention to how we feel particularly during creative experiences, like those found in music. Given that mind and body are phenomenologically integrated, it seems important for MPCs to consider the holistic nature of feel in music. The Resonance Performance Model (RPM), as an applied tool, may serve MPCs working with musicians, by inviting awareness, reflection, and qualitative conversation about how it feels to create and play music.

The Resonance Performance Model in Music

The RPM is a framework that describes how high-level performers achieve excellence by aligning their internal selves with their external environment (Newburg et al., 2002). It suggests that *feel* is akin to an experiential bridge across parts of the whole (mind/body, cognition/affect, individual/social), and stipulates that when the internal (e.g., values, beliefs, motivations) and external (e.g., work, relationships, activities) are in alignment, one has achieved a state of resonance. For example, in a study of dancers, group conversation around feel seemed to have the effect of enhancing participants' awareness of feel in their dancing experiences (Lussier-Ley & Durand-Bush, 2009). These findings indicated that both individual and collective feel were meaningful aspects of dancers' creative experiences. Like dance, music is both an individual and group experience. Thus, individual and collective feel might be worth cultivating as part of a well-rounded, mental skills training intervention.

Mental Skills Training for Musicians

While musical skills are necessary for successful musical performances, mental skills play an equally important role. For instance, mental challenges such as low confidence, misplaced focus, and negative self-talk have been found to interfere with musician students' capacity to perform optimally (see Allen, 2016 for a summary of research). Interestingly, in survey-based studies of musician students, over 40% of respondents stated that they did not know how to use mental strategies to improve their performances (Allen, 2016). In contrast, studies have shown that participating in mental skills training can significantly reduce music performance anxiety and improve performance quality (e.g., Cohen & Bodner, 2018). One significant conclusion from this research is that musicians and music programs would be wise to employ MPCs to teach musicians' mental skills to support their growth and development.

Feel can be nurtured and optimized through various self and collective regulatory strategies, including goal-setting, planning, monitoring, reflecting, and adapting. For example, MPCs might consider the following approach to working with musicians based on the RPM:

1 Identify your "dream" or optimal feeling state. For some musicians, this task will be easy. For others, it will take serious thought. It's also possible that the "dream" will change over time. This process can be facilitated through daily journaling and reflection, group discussion, and/or one-on-one conversations with an MPC.
2 Identify the barriers and facilitators of this dream feeling. In other words, what prevents or hinders the musician when it comes to achieving this feeling? What makes it easier or more likely to occur? Consider how these barriers and facilitators are internal and external in nature. An MPC might consider using a worksheet that allows musicians to identify and list internal and external barriers and facilitators.
3 Identify strategies that allow the musician to prepare for, connect with, and revisit the dream feeling when rehearsing and performing. These strategies should focus on overcoming the barriers and leveraging the facilitators identified in Step 2. For example, negative self-talk or pressure from parents may limit a young musician's ability to achieve resonance. Visualizing the dream feeling, talking through negative feelings with a trusted friend, and reframing negative thoughts with positive cue words are ways of connecting with and revisiting the dream.

Thus, it is our recommendation that MPCs embrace an embodied lens while working with musicians. Incorporating an embodied, somatic, and resonance-informed mental skills training intervention can allow MPCs to better support musicians in their quest to listen, to pay attention, to create, to play, and to truly *feel* the music.

EDITORS' TAKEAWAYS

The first contribution paints a great overall picture of working with performing artists and really helps readers understand this performance domain—such as, understanding that when we say, for example, "dance" it's not like saying, for example, "soccer" as we have to learn about and consider the various forms within each subdomain of performing arts as well as the unique cultures and subcultures of this performance domain. The next two contributions provide valuable insight into working with two of these subdomains—dance and music. They made me (Lauren) reflect on my own experience working with performers in these domains. For example, the first time I worked with a pianist, I realized the importance of working on confidence and performance anxiety as you may expect, but also other typical things I work on with athletes, such as performance under pressure and shifting from practicing to performing. However, the first time I worked with a dancer who was doing auditions in order to pursue a career as a touring backup dancer, I realized that we couldn't apply imagery in the same ways I might with an athlete since she didn't often know what she was going to be asked to dance in an audition ahead of time. The final contribution brings both value to learning about working with musicians but also in gaining a better understanding of the RPM framework and how we can use that with many clients across performance domains. How many of us and our clients are not "in our bodies" and could use some help in realigning things and focusing on "feel" again?!

RECOMMENDED EXERCISES

1 What assumptions—positive or negative—do you hold about performing artists or the performing arts? How might these influence or bias your interactions and work with performers?
2 Attend a local performance, ideally in a domain unfamiliar to you, to learn more. To deepen your insight, try the performance yourself (e.g., dance, singing, acting). Note the challenges and emotions you experience, and consider mental skills and strategies you could teach performers.
3 Think about a task you perform at a high level. Now, imagine that as you are doing the task you have multiple sources offering conflicting feedback based on their subjective opinions of your technique; none more or less correct than another. How would this make you feel? Would you approach the task differently? Second-guess yourself? Stay the course? Notice what thoughts, emotions, sensations, or values might come up.
4 Reflect on what you think might be the stressors and challenges that dancers may experience in their pursuit of excellence. How many of these stressors or challenges are unique to dance versus those that would be encountered in everyday life? Next, consider different ways that dancers might cope with these stressors or challenges. How many of these coping strategies are unique to dance versus apply across a number of performance contexts?
5 Find an online video of the dance style you're interested in. How would you describe it? What story or emotion are they conveying, and how could you help performers use imagery to enhance focus, confidence, and performance?
6 Access a biography or documentary about a performing artist. What does their story reveal about life in the field, its culture, and the stressors performers face? Note culturally specific terms and practices to better understand their training and work context.
7 Reflect on an instrument you play or have played. If you have never played an instrument, reach out to a musician to interview them.

   a Dream Feeling(s): When playing feels best to you, when there's a connection or resonance between you, your instrument, and the music, how do you feel? Can you describe what that feels like to you, and in your body? Where in your body do you feel that? If you could pick your optimal dream feelings while you play, what would they be?

b Preparation (Skills, Tools, and Strategies): How do you prepare yourself to play and to feel the way you want to feel when you play? What are the technical, tactical, physical, and psychological things you can do to best prepare yourself to play? How can you support your mind and body to be ready to play and feel the music optimally?
c Obstacles and Challenges: What sometimes gets in the way of you feeling like you want to feel when you are playing? What internal challenges or obstacles (thoughts, feelings, sensations) do you encounter? What external challenges (outside of yourself, be it with your instrument, peers, audience, environment, etc.) sometimes arise? When you're not feeling the way you want to feel, what tends to happen and what are you most paying attention to in these moments?
d Revisit the Dream Feeling(s): What can you do to reconnect with the music, and how you ideally want to feel, while playing it? What internal and/or external skills or strategies can you do now to effectively move you from experiencing obstacles to feeling the way you'd rather be feeling instead?

8 Reflect on a performing arts client you are working with—or a performing arts domain you want to enter. How could you use the RPM to support them?

REFERENCES

Alačovska, A., & Kärreman, D. (2022). Tormented selves: The social imaginary of the tortured artist and the identity work of creative workers. *Organization Studies, 44*(6), 961–985. https://doi.org/10.1177/01708406221089594

Allen, D. (2016). Mental skills training for musicians. *International Journal of Music and Performing Arts, 4*(1), 7–20.

Arnold, P. J. (1995). Objectivity, expression and communication in dance as a performing art. *The Journal of Aesthetic Education, 29*(1), 61–68. https://doi.org/10.2307/3333517

Bouwens, J., Hofmann, C., & Lechner, C. (2022). Transparency and biases in subjective performance evaluation. *TRR 266 Accounting for Transparency Working Paper Series, 72.* https://doi.org/10.2139/ssrn.4012905

Cohen, S., & Bodner, E. (2018). Music performance skills: A two-pronged approach – Facilitating optimal music performance and reducing music performance anxiety. *Psychology of Music, 47*(4), 521–538. https://doi.org/10.1177/0305735618765349

Cumming, J., Nordin-Bates, S. M., Johnson, C., Sanchez, E. N., & Karageanes, S. J. (2024). High time to enhance dancer welfare: A call to action to improve safeguarding and abuse prevention in dance. *BMJ Open Sport & Exercise Medicine, 10*(2), e001811. https://doi.org/10.1136/bmjsem-2023-001811

Damasio, A. R. (2001). Fundamental feelings. *Nature, 413*(6858), 781. https://doi.org/10.1038/35101669

Damasio, A. R. (2004). Emotions and feelings: A neurobiological perspective. In A. S. R. Manstead, N. Frijda, & A. Fischer (Eds.), *Feelings and emotions: The Amsterdam symposium* (pp. 49–57). Cambridge University Press. https://doi.org/10.1017/CBO9780511806582.004

Downing, C., Redelius, K., & Nordin-Bates, S. M. (2025). Aesthetic athletes' reflections on early specialisation: A self-determination theory perspective. *The Sport Psychologist, 39*(3), 153–162. https://doi.org/10.1123/tsp.2023-0090

Ericsson, K. A., Krampe, R. T., & Tesch-Römer, C. (1993). The role of deliberate practice in the acquisition of expert performance. *Psychological Review, 100*(3), 363–406. https://doi.org/10.1037/0033-295X.100.3.363

Fujita, F. (2008). The frequency of social comparison and its relation to subjective well-being. In M. Eid & R. J. Larson (Eds.), *The science of subjective well-being* (pp. 239–257). Guilford Press.

Gaudreau, P. (2019). On the distinction between personal standards perfectionism and excellencism: A theory elaboration and research agenda. *Perspectives on Psychological Science, 14*(2), 197–215. https://doi.org/10.1177/1745691618797940

Gerber, J. P., Wheeler, L., & Suls, J. (2018). A social comparison theory meta-analysis 60+ years on. *Psychological Bulletin, 144*(2), 177–197. https://doi.org/10.1037/bul0000127

Goodwin, H., Arcelus, J., Geach, N., & Meyer, C. (2014). Perfectionism and eating psychopathology among dancers: The role of high standards and self-criticism. *European Eating Disorders Review, 22*(5), 346–351. https://doi.org/10.1002/erv.2282

Gotwals, J. K., Stoeber, J., Dunn, J. G. H., & Stoll, O. (2012). Are perfectionistic strivings in sport adaptive? A systematic review of confirmatory, contradictory, and mixed evidence. *Canadian Psychology, 53*(4), 263–279. https://doi.org/10.1037/a0030288

Guss-West, C. (2020). *Attention and focus in dance: Enhancing power, precision, and artistry.* Human Kinetics.

Harris, R. (2019). *ACT made simple: A quick-start guide to ACT basics and beyond* (2nd ed.). New Harbinger Publications.

Hays, K. (2009). Performance anxiety. In K. Hays (Ed.), *Performance psychology in action: A casebook for working with athletes, performing artists, business leaders, and professionals in high-risk occupations* (pp. 101–120). American Psychological Association. https://doi.org/10.1037/11876-005

Hays, K. F. (2012, July 12). Being an excellentist: From perfectionism to... [Blog post]. *Psychology Today.* https://www.psychologytoday.com/us/blog/the-edge-peak-performance-psychology/201207/being-an-excellentist

Hill, A. P., Witcher, C. S. G., Gotwals, J. K., & Leyland, A. F. (2015). A qualitative study of perfectionism among self-identified perfectionists in sport and the performing arts. *Sport, Exercise, and Performance Psychology, 4*(4), 237–253. https://doi.org/10.1037/spy0000041

Kalenska-Rodzaj, J. (2020). Music performance anxiety and pre-performance emotions in the light of psychology of emotion and emotion regulation. *Psychology of Music, 49*(6), 1553–1568. https://doi.org/10.1177/0305735620961154

Kausar, S., & Ahmad, G. (2021). Perceived stress, self-efficacy and psychological wellbeing among performing arts students. *Academic Journal of Social Sciences, 5*(3), 289–302. https://doi.org/10.54692/ajss.2021.05031509

Kenny, D., Davis, P., & Oates, J. (2004). Music performance anxiety and occupational stress amongst opera chorus artists and their relationship with state and trait anxiety and perfectionism. *Journal of Anxiety Disorders, 18*(6), 757–777. https://doi.org/10.1016/j.janxdis.2003.09.004

Kokotsaki, D., & Davidson, J. (2003). Investigating musical performance anxiety among music college singing students: A quantitative analysis. *Music Education Research, 5*(1), 45–59. https://doi.org/10.1080/14613800307103

Lim, S., Kim, J., Sea-hee, Y., & Yoon, J. (2019). Depressive symptoms among dance artists in South Korea: Balance between self- and social identity on job value. *Annals of Occupational and Environmental Medicine, 31*(1), e14. https://doi.org/10.35371/aoem.2019.31.e14

Lussier, C. (2013). *Towards an enhanced pedagogical understanding of dance education: Aesthetic learning and the creative experience* [Unpublished doctoral thesis]. University of Ottawa.

Lussier-Ley, C., & Durand-Bush, N. (2009). Exploring the role of feel in the creative experience of modern dancers: A realist tale. *Research in Dance Education, 10*(3), 199–216. https://doi.org/10.1080/14647890903324154

Newburg, D., Kimiecik, J., Durand-Bush, N., & Doell, K. (2002). The role of resonance in performance excellence and life engagement. *Journal of Applied Sport Psychology, 14*(4), 249–267. https://doi.org/10.1080/10413200290103545

Nordin-Bates, S. (2023). *Essentials of dance psychology.* Human Kinetics.

Rip, B., Fortin, S., & Vallerand, R. J. (2006). The relationship between passion and injury in dance students. *Journal of Dance Medicine & Science, 10*(1–2), 14–20. https://doi.org/10.1177/1089313X06010001-205

Suls, J., & Wheeler, L. (2012). Social comparison theory. In P. A. M. Van Lange, A. W. Kruglanski, & E. T. Higgins (Eds.), *Handbook of theories of social psychology* (Vol. 1, pp. 460–482). Sage. https://doi.org/10.4135/9781446249215.n23

Tohver, T. (2023). Director's fear and self-cultivation. *Theatre, Dance and Performance Training, 14*(3), 341–346. https://doi.org/10.1080/19443927.2023.2243185

Van der Schyff, D. (2013). Emotion, embodied mind and the therapeutic aspects of musical experience in everyday life. *Approaches: Music Therapy & Special Music Education, 5*(1), 35–45.

Willard, V. C., & Lavallee, D. (2016). Retirement experiences of elite ballet dancers: Impact of self-identity and social support. *Sport, Exercise, and Performance Psychology, 5*(3), 266–279. https://doi.org/10.1037/spy0000057

11 Working in the Healthcare Sector

A shared human experience is that everyone has or at some point will be dependent on receiving some form of medical care throughout their lives. As such, we can all relate to focus, execution, and ultimately also performance of healthcare professionals being critical. Whether these professionals are physicians, nurses, surgeons, or emergency medical personnel—all need to perform, often under pressure, in complex systems and contexts. As such, building performance and mental training strategies into medical training programs and developing support systems for health care professionals to improve patient care by adapting creative solutions from other industries, in this case, sport psychology, is an increasing opportunity within sport, exercise, and performance psychology. Our authors share key aspects for gaining contextual understanding as a sport, exercise, and performance psychology professional (SEPPP) working in health care, discuss the use of pre-performance routines by healthcare professionals, and highlight key psychological effects of the hospital emergency room performance environment SEPPPs need to consider when working with this population and creating mental performance programs.

BEYOND GREY'S ANATOMY: UNDERSTANDING THE HEALTHCARE ENVIRONMENT AND PRACTITIONERS TO OPTIMIZE PERFORMANCE

Eric Bean & Nicholas E. Anton

This chapter will introduce various considerations for working with professionals in healthcare, including a brief contextual roadmap, suggestions for achieving and maintaining programmatic support for mental skills services, and insights on how to develop effective mental skills programs for healthcare providers.

Gaining Contextual Understanding

To develop contextually intelligent and culturally appropriate interventions, mental performance consultants (MPCs) must take time to understand and learn about the nuances facing performers in their respective fields (Brown et al., 2005). Healthcare is a particularly diverse setting because contemporary patients' comorbidities require a multidisciplinary team of specialists and subspecialists to effectively manage their conditions (Tonelli et al., 2018). In Western healthcare settings, providers range in experience from students, trainees (i.e., resident physicians and fellows), and attending physicians. Academic hospital settings require

DOI: 10.4324/9781003781486-11

physicians to balance effort between patient care and the education of students and trainees (Pololi et al., 2015). Physician scientists are doctors who conduct research concurrently with their clinical responsibilities and often find the dual roles stressful (Stoll & Taegtmeyer, 2018). Providers must care for a diverse set of needs, as patients might require emergent care (i.e., preventing and treating unexpected injury and illness), inpatient care (i.e., admission to the hospital), or outpatient care (i.e., consultation or care that does not result in inpatient admission; Schneider et al., 1998). The cognitive demands of each need present unique challenges to providers, which can often contribute to acute and chronic stress, and must be managed effectively to execute technical and non-technical skills in the clinical environment (Kent et al., 2020).

Beyond healthcare providers, there are numerous support staff members who assist with the delivery of healthcare and ensure continuity of patient care including nurses, staff with specific technical proficiencies to assist with healthcare delivery (e.g., pulmonary technologists, scrub technologists, etc.), and administrative personnel. MPCs must understand not only the primary performance context (i.e., what does excellent care look like?), but also the systemic (i.e., academic or community) and environmental factors (e.g., specific discipline, availability of specialists, or specific equipment to manage unforeseen issues) that could influence performance for their clients.

The healthcare system is primarily geared toward optimizing patient outcomes (e.g., patient satisfaction, safety, mortality and morbidity, care efficacy). However, most patient outcomes are self-reported and multivariable, with many factors outside of the physician's control. Controllable performance factors for healthcare providers include the ability to execute complex motor skills, manage pressure, and communicate well. Therefore, it is important for MPCs to consider both outcomes and performance factors.

For physicians and nurses, clinical outcomes are a key metric—how well they diagnose, treat, and care for patients. However, delivering high-performance care includes effective communication, teamwork, and the ability to manage stress while maintaining a high level of professionalism and thorough decision-making under pressure. Performance for support staff might be measured by their consistency, efficiency, and accuracy in ensuring the healthcare environment is conducive to patient care. Finally, surgeons are also measured by clinical outcomes, but excellent performance requires executing intricate techniques flawlessly, maintaining concentration despite environmental distractions, communicating effectively, and navigating stress and pressure (Anton & Bean, 2019).

With an understanding of outcome and performance demands, let's consider some barriers to high performance. Perhaps the most common barrier to high performance in a healthcare setting is burnout. Rotenstein et al. (2023) found that over half of the 43,026 health professionals in their study met the criteria for burnout, with 47.3% of physicians reporting that they felt burned out. Long hours, emotional strain, work overload, and the pressure to perform can lead to burnout and significantly interfere with optimal performance. Interpersonal dynamics can also be a barrier. Miscommunication, conflicts within teams, or a lack of organizational support can create a difficult work environment which can reduce motivation and interfere with performance. Other barriers include hospital politics, remuneration, and healthcare insurance policies but these vary greatly depending on the hospital setting. An understanding of the barriers to performance is critical to achieving buy-in and creating a mental training program that enables practitioners to overcome these barriers and not add to their stress.

Achieving and Maintaining Buy-In

There are several key stakeholders that MPCs must consider when planning to interface with healthcare providers. Medical departments (e.g., surgery) are led by a departmental chair, who oversees all aspects of academic and clinical work. Divisional leaders (i.e., subspecialties within a department) have a closer understanding of the demands of their practicing physician partners and have a better rapport with them, which can create inroads between a consultant and members of a division. Departments may also have a vice-chair of education who oversees all departmental education initiatives for graduate, post-graduate, and continuing education. For post-graduate education specifically, resident physician training programs have a director and associate program directors to control curricula and resident education obligations. These stakeholders are critical to interface with if consultants hope to offer large-scale interventions with providers or trainees.

There are numerous ways consultants can develop rapport with these stakeholders. First, offering an educational presentation, such as a grand rounds or resident education talk, can introduce oneself to a department and discuss services that can be offered. Alternatively, one can reach out to various stakeholders and offer their consultant services on a referral basis. Any presentation must have a strong evidence-based component to it and be framed in alignment with what these stakeholders value (e.g., well-being, resilience, performance). In the authors' experience, contacting medical education leadership and providing tangible evidence of mental skills training effectiveness to maintain trainees' clinical performance in stressful situations (as opposed to reducing burnout) is the most effective approach to garner departmental interest.

Designing an Effective Mental Training Program

Once buy-in has been accomplished, it is time to design and implement an effective mental training program (Chow et al., 2020). Recognizing that healthcare professionals have limited time for mental skills training and highly value evidence-based tools, intervention strategies must be creative and content selection thoughtful. We have utilized a wide variety of intervention strategies and modalities each with its own inherent trade-offs.

Group workshops foster collaboration, hands-on learning, and peer discussion to elevate an individual's understanding and application of the mental skills. Hybrid didactics are another approach for practitioners to consider. For example, we created a series of videos each on a particular mental competency for participants to watch on their own time. Each video contained relevant education, background, and research on a mental skill along with workbook exercises to practice applying the material. We then followed each video module with a group session to reinforce the content, personalize the skills, and answer any questions. Hybrid didactics offer the flexibility to enable self-paced learning while also providing the opportunity to apply the content in a group environment. Finally, both authors have found great success with individual coaching, however, this modality lacks the efficiency of group and hybrid approaches.

As a reminder, healthcare practitioners highly value evidence-based practice and prefer scientifically supported interventions, so be prepared to back up any claims with a deep understanding of the research. In our work with healthcare practitioners, some topics resonate more than others. Given that practitioners often have limited time and work in a dynamic environment, we found they were less receptive to long pre-performance routines (PPRs), unless they were integrated seamlessly into their established clinical routines (e.g., emotional regulation and grounding during pre-op handwashing). However, we found them to be quite receptive to mental rehearsal, and goal-setting to develop action plans for performance. Additionally, given the high-pressure nature of their work, acute stress (centering with rapid relaxation, cognitive reframing) and chronic stress management techniques (mindfulness and boundary setting) were highly effective and well-received.

Working with the healthcare population can be incredibly rewarding because these practitioners are dedicated to helping people in some of the most dire and stressful situations. Developing a keen contextual intelligence of their goals, challenges, needs, and performance factors is critical to develop impactful interventions. They value the science-to-practice model and recognize that when they are working to optimize their well-being and mental performance, they perform and care for patients at a high level.

APPLIED SPORT PSYCHOLOGY IN THE TRAINING OF HEALTHCARE PROFESSIONALS

Helen R Church, John Sandars, Emma Huntley, & James Tomlinson

Healthcare professionals (e.g., surgeons, anesthetists, and paramedics) are expected to consistently maintain their performance in the clinical workplace despite experiencing a variety of challenging situations. For example, surgeons might have to operate on complex high-risk patients whilst encountering numerous environmental distractions, such as the sounds of pagers and equipment. These situations often provoke a range of physical and mental stress reactions which can impair several aspects of their surgical performance, including procedural skills, decision-making, and communication with other members of the operating team.

There has been increasing interest in the application of sport psychology to inform the training of a variety of healthcare professionals so that they can more effectively regulate their reactions to and maintain optimum performance during challenging clinical situations (Church et al., 2017a). In this chapter we outline the ways in which the training of healthcare professionals has gained insights from sport psychology and how these have been translated into practice to improve clinical training.

Pre-Performance Routines

One application of applied sport psychology in the training of healthcare professionals has been in the use of PPRs. These routines have been effective when employed immediately before high anxiety provoking situations, such as having to complete a surgical procedure in a challenging environment. Cotterill (2015) has highlighted that the psychological reactions of healthcare professionals and their approaches to coping are similar to athletes, and this has led to the increasing use of PPRs for healthcare professionals. A recent systematic review of training healthcare professionals in the use of PPRs identified 20 relevant studies, with the majority from the United States and in trainee surgeons (Sandars et al., 2022). The main findings from the review are summarized below:

Content

The majority of studies included training in the use of imagery immediately before performing a specific task, especially related to envisioning a successfully completed task, and most included training in muscular relaxation, positive self-talk, and goal-setting immediately before performing the task. Some training interventions were in only one PPR but most were in a combination of several PPRs.

Delivery

Face-to-face training occurred in all studies and the majority were group-based, with most trainers from a sport psychology background but some were experienced clinicians trained by a sport psychologist. The mean number of sessions was five. The opportunity to practice the use of PPRs in a simulated clinical scenario was only offered in two studies and only one provided an opportunity to transfer the training to the clinical workplace, with the use of a structured reflective diary. Personalized training was absent in most training.

Effectiveness

Overall, the review found that training in the use of PPRs had significant positive outcomes for the development of the PPR used in the intervention or the specific clinical skills. However, it was not feasible to produce an overall effect size since there was wide heterogeneity in the use of different outcome measures, methods of analysis (within or between groups), and presentation of effect size.

The review highlighted the potential value of training healthcare professionals in the use of PPRs but the evidence was limited to their use at an early stage of the acquisition of competence in the performance of specific procedural clinical skills, such as suturing or manipulation of endoscopic instruments. No training was conducted in real-life clinical environments or in challenging situations. Despite these limitations in the available evidence, the authors of the studies were enthusiastic about applying their interventions to clinical practice. Church et al. (2017b) discussed the need to provide personalized training for healthcare professionals so that an individual can dynamically adapt a variety of PPRs during a range of different clinical challenging situations, such as the management of a cardiac arrest or managing an acutely ill patient. The management of these clinical challenging situations requires a dynamic response for using PPRs since several clinical procedural skills are often required within the course of managing a clinical challenging situation.

Dynamic adaptation of PPRs requires metacognitive processes and Church et al. (2017b) proposed an instructional metacognitive processes skills development model, as described by Efklides (2008). This model was implemented in a proof-of-concept study named PERFORM (Performance Enhancing Routines For Optimization of Readiness using Metacognition; Church et al., 2021). In this study, a small cohort of newly qualified UK doctors were delivered a face-to-face training session on using PPRs and this was followed over the next three months by a self-reflective learning approach in which the doctors applied and personalized the model in real clinical situations involving acutely unwell patients, including those with acute heart failure, sepsis, vascular hemorrhage, and diabetic emergencies. Participants' application of the PERFORM model was also extended to other non-acute scenarios, such as managing heavy workloads, conducting difficult conversations with patients and their relatives, and completing unfamiliar and time-critical administrative tasks. The conclusion of the study involved a final in-situ simulated scenario in which the participant was called to attend to an acutely unwell patient (high-fidelity mannikin). The scenario was conducted in a clinical ward environment involving a multidisciplinary team, and the participant did not have prior warning of the scenario. This final data collection point demonstrated a significantly improved ability to manage negative emotions and also to enhance their clinical skills, interpersonal relationships, and personal attributes.

Since this initial study, PERFORM has gained international and cross-specialty interest. Its most notable application to date has been in orthopedic higher level resident training, where a recently completed study assessed surgeon cognitive load, physiological markers of stress, and technical skill in a simulated environment following PERFORM coaching (Howie et al., 2025).

Experience of a Sport & Exercise Scientist (Psychology Support) Working with Healthcare Professionals

With nearly 20 years in sport psychology, primarily educating sport science students, one of the chapter's authors, Dr. Emma Huntley, has recently broadened her scope to support health professionals' education by creating training materials grounded in sport psychology principles. Drawing from her experience with athletes in high-performance environments, she has explored how sports psychology strategies can be adapted to healthcare settings and shares her findings below.

Curiosity

Throughout these research-driven discussions and collaborations, it has become evident that healthcare professionals, particularly in high-pressure roles such as surgery, are keen to learn from sport psychology and recognize that the mental strategies enabling elite athletic performance could offer valuable insights for optimizing their own clinical performance.

Drive for Excellence

This curiosity within the medical profession reflects a shared drive for excellence in high-stakes environments. Though my experience has mainly been with athletes, my research has developed healthcare training models that incorporate PPRs, including mental skills such as goal-setting and cognitive reframing, that originated in sport. This work highlights the importance and relative lack of mental preparation strategies for clinicians during stressful situations.

Potential for Enhancing Performance and Resilience

The opportunity for collaboration has highlighted the potential for psychological techniques to enhance both clinical performance and emotional resilience, reinforcing the value healthcare professionals place on performing at their best.

Conclusion

In this contribution, we have shared our knowledge and personal experiences regarding the application of sport psychology—particularly PPRs—to help healthcare professionals manage stress and optimize clinical performance in high-stakes situations. Notably, well-established techniques from sport, such as imagery, relaxation, and self-talk, show promising results; however, the evidence-base remains in its early stages, with growing interest in the field. We introduced the PERFORM model as an example of personalized, metacognitive training for newly qualified doctors. Following a successful proof-of-concept study, it has now been adopted into higher surgical training and shown to enhance emotional regulation and clinical performance. The future success of such interventions relies on developing firm collaborations between sport and healthcare training with widespread dissemination.

PRESENTING THE HIGH-PERFORMANCE PHYSICIAN PROGRAM

Aman Hussain & Andrew P. Friesen

Each year, physicians must take part in numerous professional development sessions to maintain their qualifications. Typically, this often involves attending conferences, workshops/

seminars, and medical grand rounds. Friesen (2009) had examined the effects of an intervention designed to improve medical resident simulation performance by targeting residents' emotional preparation, resilience, perspective, teamwork, and recovery; and the results of the study were presented at a grand round. Following that presentation, a group of senior emergency medicine residents approached a renowned Canadian sport psychology consultant with whom the first author had worked closely with and who had been a mentor, to request that this program be implemented for their resident cohort. This became known as the High-Performance Physician (HPP) program. There is increased interest in drawing from the field of sport and exercise psychology in this performance domain (e.g., Gray et al., 2020). Applied sport and exercise practitioners have much to offer for performance and well-being in health care settings. Often, there is an underappreciation of how these programs are developed and delivered. With this in mind, we present the HPP program here.

Needs Assessment

When we first began meeting with these resident physicians, we quickly realized that we would need to increase our empathy for the psychological effects in their performance context—the hospital emergency room. To that end, each HPP instructor was paired with an attending physician and observed at least one typical shift in a hospital emergency room (if there is such a thing as a "typical" emergency room shift). These shifts lasted approximately 10–12 hours. Following these observations, we summarized some of the key psychological effects of this performance environment that would become the subsequent framework of the HPP program content:

- Physicians are burdened with enormous pressures, responsibilities, and expectations from the public to perform; and in an environment where the stakes are literally life and death. Our challenge was to help physicians sustain the appraisal that their career is also a privilege to help balance what are often unrealistic expectations.
- It goes without saying that it is unrealistic for physicians to know everything; especially when the rapid evolution of new data and best practices is considered. There is a fine line between being thorough and over-analysis, the latter often costing the physicians their perceptual skills.
- Sport is very familiar with the "favorite versus underdog" mentality; because of their "savior status" within society, physicians identify with being the "favorite" and are therefore more prone to fears of failure. Our challenge was to help them adopt an appraisal more aligned with approaching success rather than avoiding mistakes.
- Emotional management is a crucial skill set for physicians. An emergency physician can expect to feel every emotion in a typical shift, each to its full intensity. In the interest of energy management, team cohesion, and performance, physicians need a full toolbox of emotion regulation strategies that are efficient and effective.
- There is no prototypical physician. A key intervention goal will be to engage in self-awareness activities that help physicians see and appreciate their idiosyncratic strengths and prepare for their weaknesses.
- There is limited capacity to change what Lupien and colleagues (2013) described as NUTS environments (i.e., Novelty, Unpredictability, Threat to ego, and little Sense of control). The default mentality in medicine is to pour on the adversity and only the strongest will survive. Progressively developed coping skills are a critical component to help develop maturity in the field.
- Recovery must be a prioritized skillset in the face of 30-hour shifts. This should include learning how to conduct quality debriefing sessions and incorporating outlet activities into physicians' schedules.

- Teamwork is an essential skill, though difficult to accomplish given the constant rotation of team members. Physicians need to fast-track the team development process to ensure open communication (especially in this environment where any one person's perceptual skills are neutralized).
- The capacity for improvement is high because physicians are high-performance individuals. Many physicians are bright, talented, and fast learners. Any new coping skills that physicians deem useful will be implemented without many miscues.

The High-Performance Physician Program

The HPP program curriculum included the following components:

- The Test of Attentional and Interpersonal Style (TAIS; Nideffer, 1976) and individual feedback on one's results. The TAIS was used to assess interpersonal strengths, tendencies, and attentional profile of participants. Each participant completed the TAIS and engaged in a one-on-one feedback session with an HPP instructor to highlight natural performance strengths, sources of personal stress, and to help identify personalized strategies that may be effective in managing themselves, others, and the environment.
- Participants engaged in four 3-hour group sessions (total of 12 hours). Each session was grouped together under four "first principles" (see Table 11.1). These sessions consisted of a combination of didactic, lecture-style delivery by an HPP instructor and facilitated group discussion(s).
- Individual and small group email discussions also occurred and often prompted targeted topics for discussion and follow-up emails. Follow-up email discussions were always initiated by the participants. These topics focused on reviewing previous content or exchanging additional resources.

Table 11.1 HPP Content

First Principle	*Educational Topics*	*Session Goals*
Mindset	Positive psychology; stress and anxiety	History of HPP and overview of current research on issues pertaining to physician learning, performance, and health/wellness Lessons from high-pressure performance settings Creating and sustaining optimal perspective Overload and perceptiveness Managing stress, recovery, and sustainability
State	Time management; managing distractions	Translating preparation into performance Performance efficiencies Emotional preparation, inoculation, and processing Understanding emotion and decision-making Personal space, sanctuary, and recovery
Perspective	Managing conflict; communication; leadership	Discussing a personal framework for dealing with setbacks, failure, and/or conflict Honoring difficult experiences Identifying and establishing boundaries Creating optimal energy, focus, and feel
Action	Rest/recovery; sleep; wrap-up	Optimizing communication Decision fatigue Leadership and being a value-add teammate Positive rivalries Review recovery strategies for holistic well-being

Practitioner Reflections and Lessons Learned

One of the similarities to providing performance psychology training with athletes that we experienced was the importance of getting buy-in from the senior leadership group. Sport psychology consultants working with sport teams understand how valuable it is to have the captain(s) and leadership group advocate for mental training to establish buy-in from the whole team (Poczwardowski et al., 2020). Similarly, we have delivered different iterations of the HPP program with, and without, an advocating senior resident group. When attending physicians are advocating for the program, there is an opportunity for actual culture change within the area because there is an increased sense of ownership of, and thus commitment to, their own professional (and personal) development. The discussion can then shift from coping with the environment to changing the environment.

A final but important aspect of managing the environment was the concept of sanctuary. We have observed that the crucial element to allow for sanctuary involved senior residents acting as role models to lead by example. This manifested most frequently as senior residents sharing examples or stories first, often disclosing cases that involved a heavy emotional toll, but with a specific takeaway or lesson(s) learned to share with their cohort. By speaking first, they set the tone and worked toward establishing a psychologically safe environment or sanctuary (Edmondson, 2003). When there is high uncertainty and high interdependence, psychological safety or sanctuary is a must. We as practitioners would do well to develop relationships with senior resident leaders and supervisors. By doing so, we enhance trust and can share the importance of sanctuary for junior residents.

In conclusion, the HPP program represents a meaningful collaboration between sport psychology and medicine. Our experiences highlight the vital role of leadership buy-in and psychological safety in fostering a culture of growth and support. As interest grows in applying performance psychology principles in medicine, programs like HPP offer a valuable model for enhancing physician well-being and performance.

We would like to acknowledge Anthony Rossi, Steven Rynne, Jason Brooks, and Cal Botterill for their contributions to this program.

EDITORS' TAKEAWAYS

With some experience in this performance context, I (Andrew) relate to Bean and Anton's point about demonstrating intervention efficacy with empirical evidence. In my experience, however, publishing in sport and exercise psychology journals is not enough—healthcare professionals prefer research conducted with their populations and in outlets they trust. While some SEPPPs have published studies with healthcare participants, greater impact comes from targeting healthcare journals to reach the intended audience. Church and colleagues' discussion of PPRs also resonates with healthcare providers, whose environments are rarely routine. PPRs not only enhance performance but offer a tangible "controllable" amid the chaos of healthcare settings. A memorable challenge during the HPP implementation Aman and I described in our section was gaining buy-in from administrative stakeholders. The default culture often emphasizes enduring adversity, and framing interventions solely as improving doctor well-being was seen as insufficient. Only when we highlighted performance-based metrics—like patient mortality and readmission rates—did decision-makers approve the program. SEPPPs in healthcare must be ready to sell their interventions persuasively and strategically to both decision-makers and the recipients of the services.

RECOMMENDED EXERCISES

1 Consider what comes to mind when you think of hospitals, clinics, or emergency settings.

   a What emotions do you associate with these environments?
   b How do your personal experiences with healthcare (as a patient, visitor, or worker) shape your views?
   c What assumptions might you carry—positive or negative—about healthcare professionals?

2 What similarities exist between athletes' and healthcare professionals' mental pressures?
3 A program director of an emergency medicine training program contacts you to meet with an individual resident who is experiencing performance anxiety. How could you expand your services in this department? Who would you contact? How would you frame your services? What training modalities would you suggest?
4 A surgeon wants to learn about mental imagery after hearing about its use in youth sports. How would you explain its relevance and effectiveness in medicine?
5 You are presenting a 60-minute Grand Rounds within an academic hospital setting.

   a Knowing this setting includes multiple specialties and a wide variety of providers (e.g., not just surgeons), how would you frame your presentation to meet their needs?
   b How would your approach to this presentation for this healthcare audience be similar or different from how you would approach it for other healthcare audiences?
   c How would your approach to this presentation for this audience (i.e., healthcare) be similar or different from how you would approach it for sport audiences?

6 Ask to observe and shadow a "typical" shift in the emergency room with a physician. During your observation: take descriptive notes on the following and prepare to discuss with your physician. Avoid interpretation initially—focus on what is happening, not why.

   a Work rhythms and transitions (e.g., handovers, codes, lulls).
   b Decision-making processes under time pressure.
   c Communication patterns (with patients, nurses, other physicians).
   d Signs of stress, fatigue, or emotional regulation challenges.
   e Cultural norms and informal rules guiding behavior in the ER.

7 Some administrators resist performance psychology programs, particularly for residents often favoring a "toughen through exposure" approach. Craft an elevator pitch demonstrating the benefits and justifying the program's integration despite residents' core responsibilities.
8 Healthcare is not a single culture—it's a collection of distinct professions, each with its own pressures, identities, values, and communication styles. This exercise invites you to explore that diversity and begin mapping out how you might adapt your psychological support across different groups.

   a Research and choose three healthcare roles or disciplines (e.g., surgeon, nurse practitioner, primary care physician, dermatologist, radiologist, and pharmacist).
   b For each: What pressures do they face daily (e.g., emotional, physical, ethical, organizational)? What aspects of their work might cause strain, burnout, or moral distress? What values and motivations do you think typically drive someone in this role? What barriers might they experience in accessing or engaging with psychological support?

c Reflect on them as a whole: What surprised you? Which group do you feel you understand best? Why? Which group feels most unfamiliar or intimidating? What assumptions—positive or negative—might you be bringing to these reflections? How might these assumptions affect your communication, empathy, or approach?

d How would you approach working with these different healthcare audiences: What would be similar or different? What communication style might each group respond best to? How directive, reflective, or collaborative would you be? What practical constraints (shift work, emotional fatigue, pace of work) should shape your intervention style? What topics and mental skills might be most relevant, and why?

e Reflecting on this exercise, what do you need to learn about or develop competency in to be prepared to deliver sport psychology services to healthcare clients?

REFERENCES

Anton, N. E., & Bean, E. (2019). Performance optimization. In D. Stefanidis (Ed.), *Comprehensive healthcare simulation: Surgery and surgical subspecialties* (pp. 107–119). Springer.

Brown, C. H., Gould, D., & Foster, S. (2005). A framework for developing contextual intelligence (CI). *The Sport Psychologist, 19*(1), 51–62. https://doi.org/10.1123/tsp.19.1.51

Chow, G., Bean, E., & Taylor, J. (2020). Creating effective mental training programs. In J. Taylor (Ed.), *Comprehensive applied sport psychology* (pp. 137–144). Routledge.

Church, H. R., Murdoch-Eaton, D., & Sandars, J. (2021). Using insights from sports psychology to improve recently qualified doctors' self-efficacy while managing acutely unwell patients. *Academic Medicine, 96*(5), 695–700. https://doi.org/10.1097/ACM.0000000000003995

Church, H. R., Rumbold, J. L., & Sandars, J. (2017a). What can medical educators learn from the Rio 2016 Olympic Games? *Medical Teacher, 39*(6), 665–666. https://doi.org/10.1080/0142159X.2016.1270440

Church, H. R., Rumbold, J. L., & Sandars, J. (2017b). Applying sport psychology to improve clinical performance. *Medical Teacher, 39*(12), 1205–1213. https://doi.org/10.1080/0142159X.2017.1372564

Cotterill, S. (2015). Preparing for performance: Strategies adopted across performance domains. *The Sport Psychologist, 29*(2), 158–170. https://doi.org/10.1123/tsp.2014-0035

Edmondson, A. (2003). Speaking up in the operating room: How team leaders promote learning in interdisciplinary action teams. *Journal of Management Studies, 40*(6), 1419–1452. https://doi.org/10.1111/1467-6486.00386

Efklides, A. (2008). Metacognition: Defining its facets and levels of functioning in relation to self-regulation and co-regulation. *European Psychologist, 13*(4), 277–287. https://doi.org/10.1027/1016-9040.13.4.277

Friesen, E. K. (2009). *An educational intervention in performance enhancement: What works and why?* [Unpublished master's thesis]. University of Manitoba.

Gray, S. H., Lauria, M. J., & Hicks, C. (2020). The mindset of the resuscitationist. *Emergency Medicine Clinics of North America, 38*(4), 739–753. https://doi.org/10.1016/j.emc.2020.06.002

Howie, E. E., Murray, J., Clarke, R., Totton, N., Peckham-Cooper, A., Church, H. R., Yule, S., Tomlinson, J., & SUPER collaborative group. (2026). Applying elite sports coaching routines to enhance cognitive load management and skill development in trainee surgeons: A pilot study. *Journal of Surgical Education*, 103943. https://doi.org/10.1016/j.jsurg.2026.103943

Kent, J., Thornton, M., Fong, A., Hall, E., Fitzgibbons, S., & Sava, J. (2020). Acute provider stress in high-stakes medical care: Implications for trauma surgeons. *Journal of Trauma and Acute Care Surgery, 88*(3), 440–445. https://doi.org/10.1097/TA.0000000000002531

Lupien, S. J., Ouellet-Morin, I., Trepanier, L., Juster, R. P., Marin, M. F., Francois, N., … Schramek, T. (2013). The DeStress for Success program: Effects of a stress education program on cortisol levels and depressive symptomatology in adolescents making the transition to high school. *Neuroscience, 249,* 74–87. https://doi.org/10.1016/j.neuroscience.2013.01.057

Nideffer, R. M. (1976). Test of attentional and interpersonal style. *Journal of Personality and Social Psychology, 34*(3), 394–404. https://doi.org/10.1037/0022-3514.34.3.394

Poczwardowski, A., Aoyagi, M., Fritze, T., & Laird, M. (2020). Revisiting "gaining entry": Roundtable discussion 25 years later. *The Sport Psychologist, 34*(2), 153–161. https://doi.org/10.1123/tsp.2018-0189

Pololi, L. H., Evans, A. T., Civian, J. T., Gibbs, B. K., Coplit, L. D., Gillum, L. H., & Brennan, R. T. (2015). Faculty vitality—Surviving the challenges facing academic health centers: A national survey of medical faculty. *Academic Medicine, 90*(7), 930–936. https://doi.org/10.1097/ACM.0000000000000730

Rotenstein, L. S., Cohen, D. J., Marino, M., Bates, D. W., & Edwards, S. T. (2023). Association of clinician practice ownership with ability of primary care practices to improve quality without increasing burnout. *JAMA Health Forum, 4*(3), e230299. https://doi.org/10.1001/jamahealthforum.2023.0299

Sandars, J., Jenkins, L., Church, H., Patel, R., Rumbold, J., Maden, M., … Brown, J. (2022). Applying sport psychology in health professions education: A systematic review of performance mental skills training. *Medical Teacher, 44*(1), 71–78. https://doi.org/10.1080/0142159X.2021.1966403

Schneider, S. M., Hamilton, G. C., Moyer, P., & Stapczynski, J. S. (1998). Definition of emergency medicine. *Academic Emergency Medicine, 5*(4), 348–351. https://doi.org/10.1111/j.1553-2712.1998.tb02716.x

Stoll, B. J., & Taegtmeyer, H. (2018). Challenges for today's pediatric physician-scientists. *JAMA Pediatrics, 172*(3), 220–221. https://doi.org/10.1001/jamapediatrics.2017.4954

Tonelli, M., Wiebe, N., Manns, B. J., Klarenbach, S. W., James, M. T., Ravani, P., … Hemmelgarn, B. R. (2018). Comparison of the complexity of patients seen by different medical subspecialists in a universal health care system. *JAMA Network Open, 1*(7), e184852. https://doi.org/10.1001/jamanetworkopen.2018.4852

For Product Safety Concerns and Information please contact our
EU representative GPSR@taylorandfrancis.com Taylor & Francis
Verlag GmbH, Kaufingerstraße 24, 80331 München, Germany